HOUSES OF THE
WEALD AND DOWNLAND

Houses of the Weald and Downland

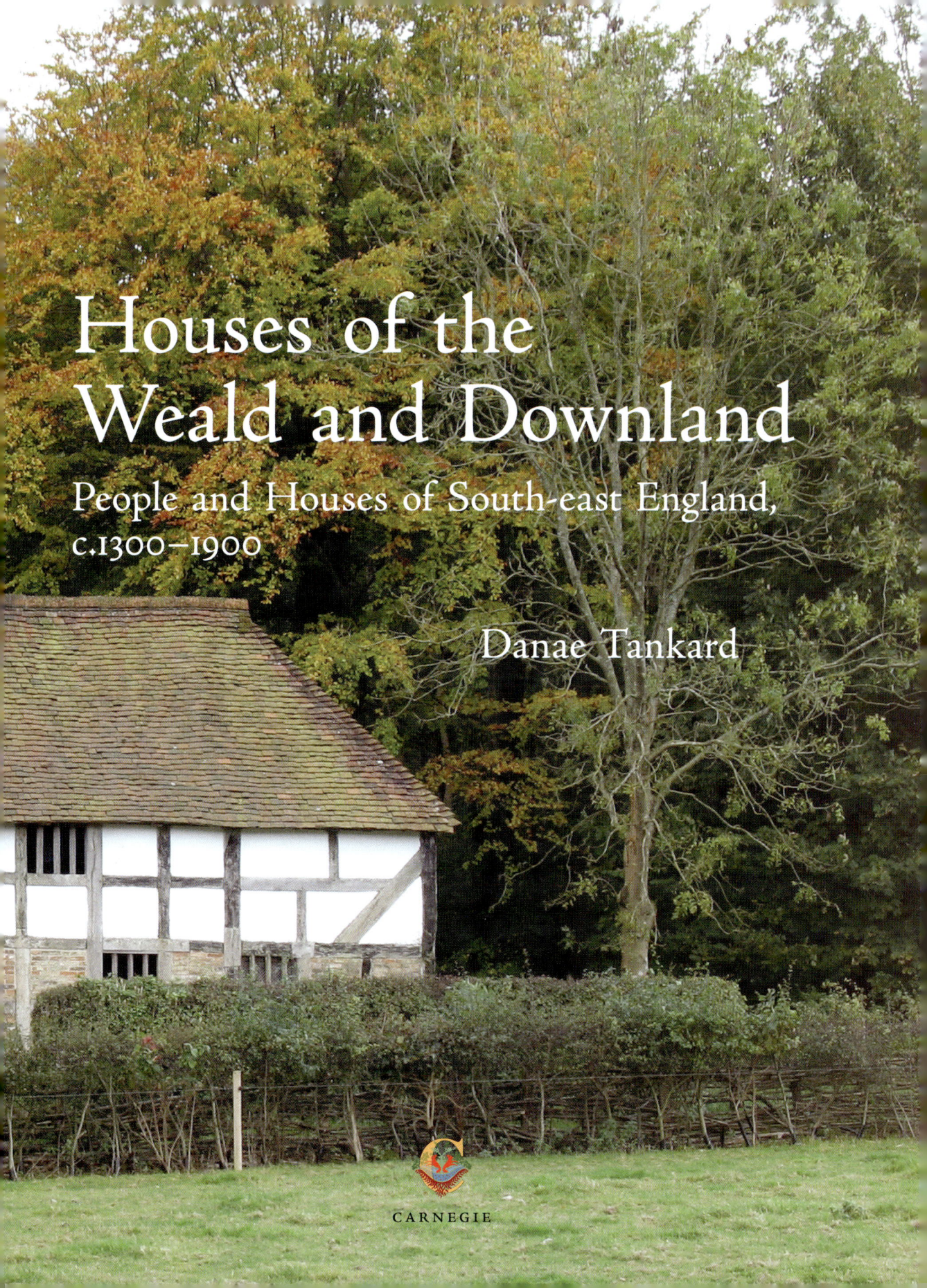

People and Houses of South-east England, c.1300–1900

Danae Tankard

CARNEGIE

Title page: Pendean

Copyright © Danae Tankard

First published in 2012 by
Carnegie Publishing Ltd
Chatsworth Road,
Lancaster LA1 4SL
www.carnegiepublishing.com

All rights reserved
Unauthorised duplication contravenes existing laws

British Library Cataloguing-in-Publication data
A catalogue record for this book is available from the British Library

ISBN 978-1-85936-200-6

Designed, typeset and originated by Carnegie Publishing
Printed and bound in the UK by Page Bros Ltd, Norwich

Contents

Preface	vii
Acknowledgements	ix
Introduction	1

CHAPTER ONE
Hangleton: a thirteenth-century peasant house from Hangleton, East Sussex — 11

CHAPTER TWO
Boarhunt: a fourteenth-century hall house from Boarhunt, Hampshire — 33

CHAPTER THREE
Bayleaf: a Wealden hall house from Chiddingstone, Kent — 55

CHAPTER FOUR
Pendean: a yeoman's house from West Lavington, West Sussex — 79

CHAPTER FIVE
Poplar Cottage: a wasteland cottage from Washington, West Sussex — 101

CHAPTER SIX
Tindalls Cottage: a husbandman's cottage from Ticehurst, East Sussex — 123

CHAPTER SEVEN
Gonville Cottage: an estate cottage from Singleton, West Sussex — 145

CHAPTER EIGHT
Whittaker's Cottages: railway cottages from Ashtead, Surrey — 167

Conclusion	191
Notes and references	194
Bibliography	205
Index	212

For my mother, Lee

Preface

This book is based on research undertaken between October 2005 and April 2008 whilst I was an associate on a Knowledge Transfer Partnership between the University of Reading and the Weald & Downland Open Air Museum. A Knowledge Transfer Partnership (KTP) is a part government-funded programme to encourage collaboration between business and universities in the United Kingdom. Each KTP involves three 'partners': a company (the Museum), a knowledge base (the University of Reading) and an associate (me). I would like to thank the staff at the University of Reading's Knowledge Transfer Centre for their support over the duration of the project.

The remit of the KTP project was to research and write the economic and social histories of ten of the Museum's most important exhibit houses. The question that underpinned the research was 'what was life like for the people who lived in these houses?' In reworking the material for this book I decided to exclude two of the houses – Walderton and the Beeding Toll House – because their histories, both architectural and documentary, were too fragmentary to be able to tell a satisfactory story.

Acknowledgements

I would like to acknowledge the previous research undertaken on seven out of the eight houses which provided a starting point for my own research: for Hangleton, the work of Eric Holden and John and Gillian Hurst; for Boarhunt the work of Edward Roberts; for Bayleaf the work of Cynthia Bacon and Gwendoline Jones; for Pendean the work of Elizabeth Doff; for Poplar the work of David and Barbara Martin and Richard Harris; for Tindalls the work of David and Barbara Martin and Christopher Whittick and for Whittaker's Cottages the work of Richard Harris and Robert Rodrigues.

Many people helped me with my research over the period of the KTP project and whilst preparing the work for publication. I would especially like to thank Roger Champion, Derek Coe, Mark Gardiner, Gwendoline Jones, David and Barbara Martin, Gillian Northcott, Richard Pailthorpe, Edward Roberts, Jonathan Roberts, Christopher Whittick and Diana Zeuner. I would also like to thank the staff at the Surrey History Centre, the Hampshire Record Office, the Centre for Kentish Studies, the East Sussex Record Office and the West Sussex Record Office.

I would like to thank Alan Crosby for his editorial work on the manuscript.

I would like to thank my KTP supervisors, Dr Margaret Yates, senior lecturer in history at the University of Reading, and Richard Harris, Director of the Weald & Downland Open Air Museum from 2001 to 2010.

I would additionally like to thank Richard Harris for all his help with the illustrations for this book. He took a number of photographs of the individual buildings specifically for the book, 'improved' a range of photographs and illustrations from the Museum's archive and elsewhere and very kindly allowed me to use many of his architectural drawings.

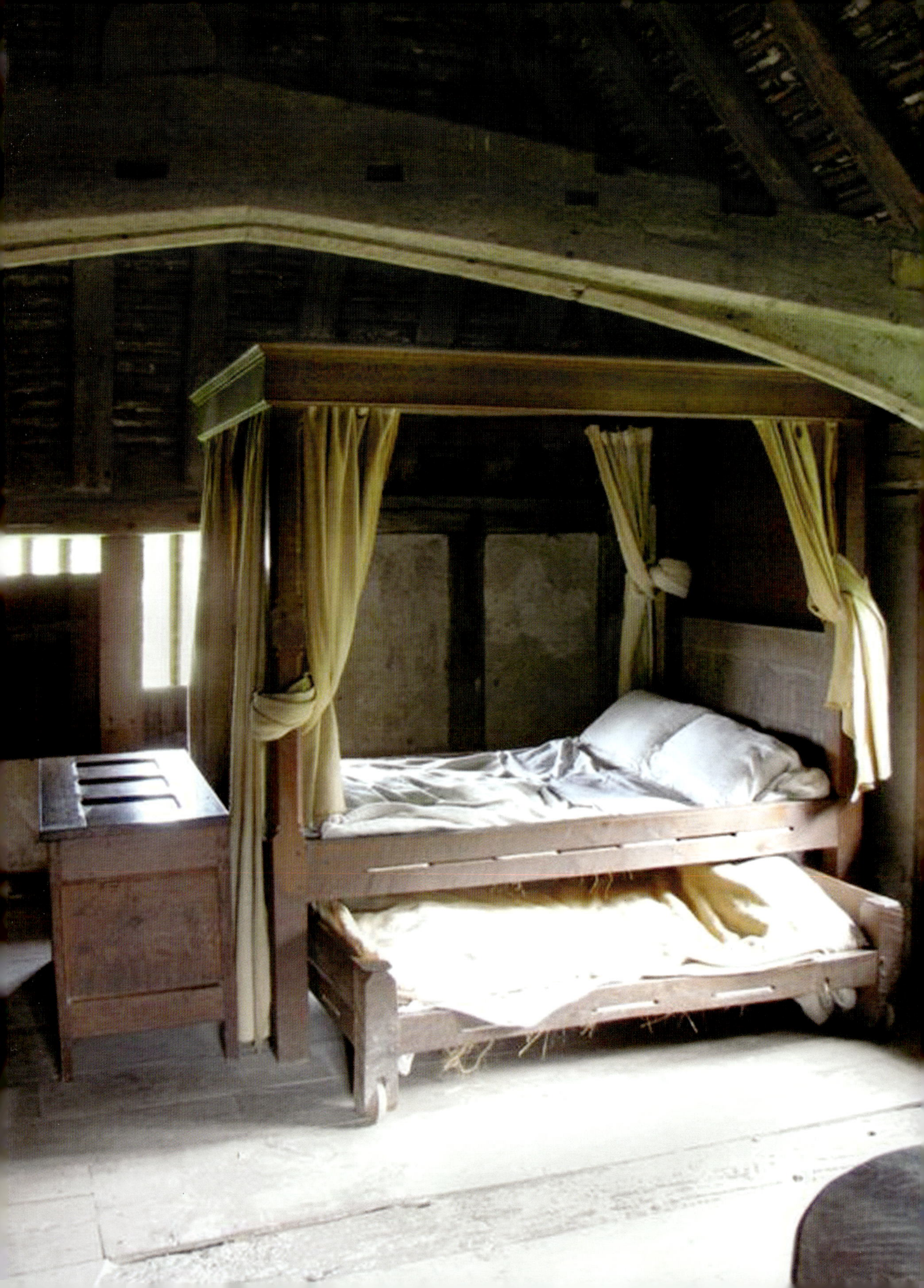

Introduction

Vernacular *n. & adj.* 1 the language or dialect of a particular country   2 the language of a particular clan or group   3 homely speech *adj.* 1 (of language) of one's native country; not of foreign origin or of learned formation 2 (of architecture) concerned with ordinary rather than monumental buildings. (*Oxford English Dictionary*)

In 1610 a petition was submitted to Thomas Pelham, lord of the Rape of Hastings, by the inhabitants of the parish of Warbleton in East Sussex on behalf of a shingler by the name of Thomas Blatcher. It asked Pelham to allow Blatcher to build himself a cottage on a piece of waste ground which Pelham had allegedly granted him. According to the petition, Blatcher had 'prepared all things needful for the said building', and was ready to 'set it up', but Pelham's steward refused to allow him to do so. In consequence, Blatcher, a 'poor man', and his family were 'destitute of a dwelling' and obliged to live in 'an old rotten barn which will not keep out wind or rain'. A subsequent petition records that 'the case of the poor man and his wife and four children does pity us all for they have lain in an end of a barn this month and more where they can make no fire by reason of hay and straw that lies there'. The inhabitants were afraid that Blatcher's wife, 'the poor woman', 'would have gone out of her wits' (which she had done once before) after one of Pelham's officials threatened to cut down the timber frame if they went ahead and erected it. Elizabeth Pelham,

Bayleaf: Bedchamber at upper end of house. The truckle or trundle bed would have been used for the householder's children or his female servants.
RICHARD HARRIS.

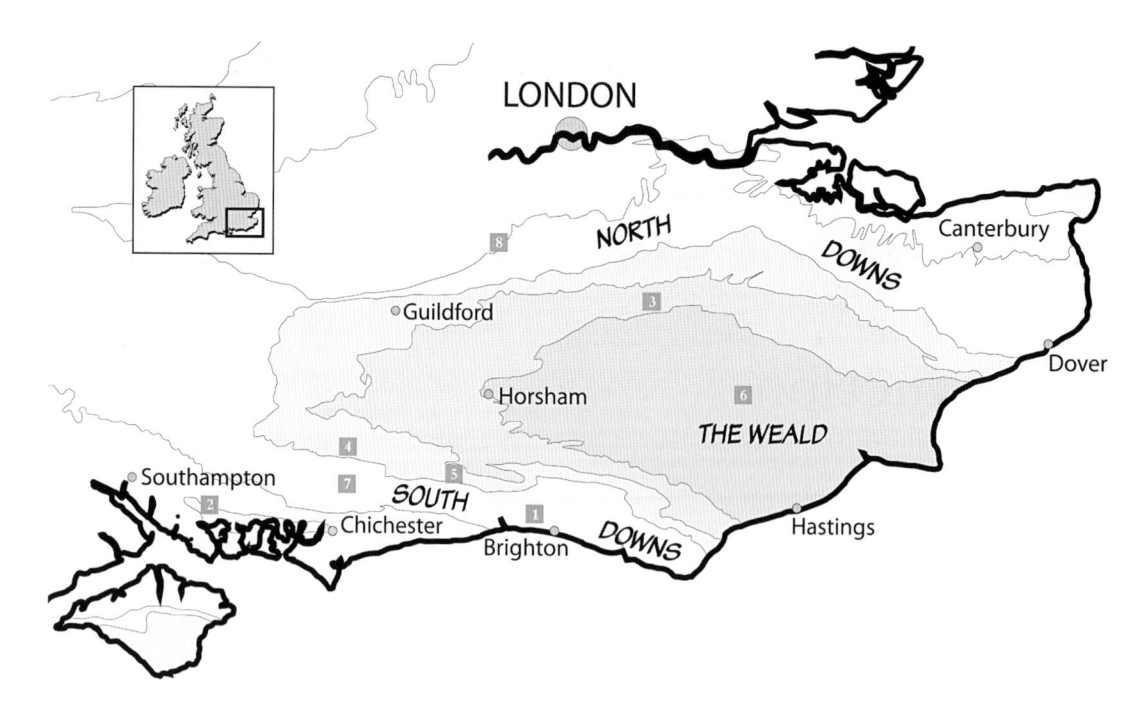

Map of the Weald and Downland Region, showing original location of the eight houses.

Thomas Pelham's cousin, also petitioned on Blatcher's behalf, informing him that 'the poor man ... was destitute of comfort'.[1]

Thomas Blatcher's case is not especially significant in itself. Countless petitions similar to this survive in seventeenth-century records. However, the description of his difficulties highlights the enduring importance of the 'house' as both a physical structure and a place that we can call 'home'. As such, it is a useful introduction to a book about rural houses and the people who lived in them.

This book is about the histories of eight different houses, ranging in date from c.1250 to c.1865, which form part of the historic building collection of the Weald and Downland Open Air Museum in Singleton, West Sussex. Six of the houses – Boarhunt, Bayleaf, Pendean, Poplar, Tindalls and Whittaker's – were moved to the Museum in order to save them from destruction; one – Hangleton – is an archaeological reconstruction; another – Gonville – is an *in situ* cottage lying within the area of the West Dean estate upon which the Museum was established in 1969. Each of these buildings comes from a different area of the Weald and Downland region of south-east England, which comprises parts of the counties of Surrey, Kent, East and West Sussex and Hampshire. They have no shared history, other than that created by their relocation to the Museum, and this book does not try to give them one. What the book *does* provide is a detailed study of the social and economic context of each of the eight buildings, focusing on the domestic, economic and material lives of their earliest inhabitants and offering a detailed account of the communities in which each house was originally located. The book seeks to answer the question, 'what was life like for the people who lived in these houses?'

From its inception in 1967 the principal aim of the Museum has been to establish a representative collection of buildings illustrating the structural development of vernacular buildings in the Weald and Downland region. It now has nearly 50 exhibit buildings – domestic, agricultural and industrial – dating from the thirteenth to the early twentieth century, plus several more which are in store awaiting re-erection. Each of the eight houses considered in this book therefore has a *structural* significance, as an example of vernacular architecture, within the Museum's collections. However, their original structural function – as buildings for human habitation, offering shelter, warmth and a place to sleep – has gone, since no one lives in them any more. In this respect, they continue to be 'houses', but they have ceased to be 'homes'.

The dual function of a domestic building as both a 'house' and a 'home' – the former referring to its physical function, the latter referring to a more nebulous set of ideas and feelings – is reflected in the account of the travails of Thomas Blatcher and his wife. The barn in which they had been forced to take up residence was neither a house nor a home. It was 'old' and 'rotten', providing inadequate protection from the elements; they were unable to light a fire to keep them warm and to cook over; but perhaps, more significantly, it was not theirs. The psychological trauma of not having an adequate and secure place of residence threatened to send Blatcher's wife 'out of her wits'. The description of Thomas Blatcher as 'destitute of comfort' evokes both his physical and emotional deprivation.

The Nuisances Removal Act of 1855, which contained the phrase 'unfit for human habitation', was the first piece of public health legislation to give statutory weight to the idea that some housing was wholly unsuitable for humans to live in. While the Act belongs to the last of the six centuries covered by this book, the idea that underpinned it is clearly apparent in the petitioners' emotive descriptions of the plight of the Blatchers: Thomas Blatcher and his family were living in a building that was simply inadequate for their needs. We can make qualitative judgements about pre-modern houses based on current assumptions about what constitutes an acceptable standard of living, but it is important to remember that pre-modern people made their own judgements based on criteria that were not, in their bare essentials, dissimilar to our own.

Pendean: The kitchen fireplace. The brickwork had been colour-washed using a technique called 'ruddling and pencilling'.
RICHARD HARRIS.

Other assumptions are made on the basis of the number and type of houses that have survived, allied to judgements about the motivations, resources and technical skills of those who built and lived in them. For example, the low survival rate for medieval housing has led many historians to dismiss it as 'flimsy' and 'impermanent', intended to last only for a single generation. The same observation has been made about the cottages built in the sixteenth and seventeenth centuries: they were 'flimsy' and little more than 'huts or hovels'. Today's historians are more likely to view a building's *adaptability* as the key to its survival: many medieval houses and small early modern cottages were simply not capable of adaptation to suit the needs of later occupants and were therefore pulled down.

Moreover, it is important not to apply anachronistic vocabulary to pre-modern house-types. In the seventeenth century, a cottage was neither a 'hut' nor a 'hovel'. Whereas cottages are described as being 'built', 'erected' or 'set up', huts or 'cotes' were 'pitched', suggesting different construction methods, as well as assumptions about permanence. Significantly, until the eighteenth century the word 'hovel' was used to describe an open-sided agricultural or industrial building, not an inferior human habitation.

The word 'cottage' is perhaps the most misused and poorly understood pre-modern house-type. It is also the most culturally loaded term, since today it instantly evokes an image of rustic charm – thatched, rose-covered and *picturesque*. A 'cottage' was distinct from a 'house' because it was smaller in size and generally had little or no land attached to it. Cottage inhabitants comprised the rural working class, as well as the rural poor, dependent upon the parish for financial assistance. However, over the course of the nineteenth century the idea of the 'cottage' underwent a profound cultural shift. Simultaneously with the work of organisations such as the Cottage Improvement Society, which sought to raise the standard of accommodation for rural labourers, the country cottage – suitably improved or, better still, newly built – became the abode of the middle classes, offering them a rustic retreat from the excesses of urban expansion and industrialisation. The country cottage became an increasingly popular subject in nineteenth-century British art, much of it destined to hang on the walls of wealthy industrialists who wanted to be reminded of the bucolic charm of the countryside. In many respects the 'cottage' continues to embody a view of the countryside as *Arcadia*, a pastoral paradise to which many of us secretly long to gain access.[2]

* * *

The collecting policy of the Museum, and therefore the history of each of the eight houses, is defined by its region – the distinctive landscapes of the *Weald* and the *Downland*.

Downland refers to the area of the South East containing the North Downs and the South Downs, two great ridges of grass-covered chalk hills. As well as open downland, the landscape of the Downs includes wooded estate downland, chalk river valleys, major floodplains, clay vale and greensand hills. The North Downs stretch for 120 miles from Farnham in Surrey to the White Cliffs of Dover in Kent; the South Downs, which are about 30 miles to the south, extend for about 70 miles from Winchester to

Pendean: the 'little chamber' over the milk house.
RICHARD HARRIS.

Eastbourne. The North and South Downs, which come together at the Wessex Downs just inside the Hampshire border, enclose the *Weald*, comprising the High Weald, the Low Weald and the Greensand Ridge. The High Weald, which at its highest point reaches 732 feet above sea level, contains the highest proportion of ancient woodlands in the country, as well as open heathland. The Low Weald, which encircles it, lies on a band of impermeable Gault and Weald Clays, which are waterlogged for most of the winter and early spring. These soils are difficult to cultivate and were traditionally kept in woodland or as grasslands, although underdraining from the nineteenth century led to much of the woodland being removed for agriculture. The Museum's collecting region also encompasses the coastal plain, a fertile narrow belt that extends from the Hampshire border to Brighton. Historically, this belt supported the wealthiest and most populous rural communities in the South East; today its coastline is one of the most highly developed in Britain.[3]

The geological regions of the South East have distinctive socio-economic characteristics, which are reflected in the histories of each of the eight houses discussed in this book. Historically, agriculture, driven largely by the proximity of London, has been the predominant form of economic activity.

With its dense woodland and heavy clay soil, the Weald was better suited to cattle ranching than to arable farming. Parishes in the Weald were typically large (up to 23 square miles) and densely populated, and settlements tended to be scattered. Manorial organisation was weak, with little control over immigration. Farm sizes were small, made up of small, enclosed fields, and there was little common land. The Weald is the location of two great forests, St Leonard's and Ashdown, both of which had a reputation for lawlessness. Communications were hampered by the appalling state of the roads, often impassable in winter, and livestock was transported on the hoof. The most significant Wealden industry was iron manufacture, providing seasonal employment for iron-workers and charcoal makers. Glass manufacture took place in Kirdford and Wisborough Green, and other opportunities for employment were provided by the timber industry, leather tanning and cloth production.

The downland and coastal plain area was primarily a corn-growing region, with sheepwalks on the Downs. Water transport links were good, with navigable rivers such as the Ouse and the Adur, and significant coastal ports such as Chichester. Rural industries were small in scale and local in their markets. Downland parishes were small in both acreage and population; manorial organisation was strong, and farm sizes were large. In some areas common land had been enclosed by the seventeenth century, usually with the consent of the tenants; in others, it remained unenclosed until the nineteenth century. Settlements were typically nuclear, with stable populations and little inward migration.[4]

The South East today has been described as 'post agricultural' and in danger of becoming a 'giant theme park' – a place where people choose to spend their leisure time, but where employment opportunities are limited. Whereas in 1841 40 per cent of the population of Sussex were employed in agriculture, the figure currently stands at less than 2 per cent. But this reflects national trends. In 1901 1.3 million men were employed in agriculture; by 1950 this had fallen to 865,000, and by 1991 there were fewer than 200,000 workers of all kinds employed in agriculture. There has been a concurrent rise in the number of leisure trips to the countryside: between 1993 and 2000 alone the numbers of such trips increased by 50 per cent. Our love affair with rural England is also reflected in a desire to relocate to it: a survey undertaken in 1995 showed that 48 per cent of the urban population of England would like to move to the country.[5]

* * *

In many ways the history of the Weald and Downland Open Air Museum reflects broader changes in the second half of the twentieth century which saw the South East under threat from rapid post-war development, with inadequate legislative protection for both the countryside and its historic buildings, and a growth in rural tourism. Shortly after the end of the Second World War Roy Armstrong, who founded the Museum, began teaching an extra-mural studies course on vernacular buildings in what was then the village of Crawley. In 1946 Crawley was designated one of six new towns under the New Towns Act – part of the post-war redevelopment of the London region. With the help of his students, Armstrong carried out a survey of pre-nineteenth-century buildings scheduled for demolition. One of the buildings the group examined contained the remains of a fourteenth-century medieval hall, and they succeeded in getting the Ministry of Works to place a preservation order on it and on its adjoining seventeenth-century barn. However, six months later the Ministry reversed the order and the buildings were demolished. Armstrong and his students watched as most of the timbers were burned on site. Over the next three years, in spite of comprehensive listing of buildings of architectural or historic importance under the Town and Country Planning Act 1947, one building after another – often of unique interest – was destroyed.[6]

Armstrong's determination to rescue these unwanted buildings led to the formation of an open air museum promotion committee in 1965. This was followed by the legal constitution of the Museum in 1969. The Museum, with seven exhibit buildings, opened for the first time on 5 September 1970.

To Armstrong, the Weald and Downland region was particularly well suited to the establishment of an open air museum. Writing in 1967 he observed that:

Hangleton: the outer room showing staked-leg furniture.
RICHARD HARRIS

This is perhaps the most perfect area in England for a Regional Museum of this kind. It has a cultural and geographic unity unequalled by any other area of similar size in the country. It also contains a larger variety of village, farm and small town buildings of timber frame construction dating from the thirteenth century onwards, than any other equivalent area of Europe. This heritage is rapidly diminishing. Every year since the war a large number of such buildings have been destroyed, including several in the last two years which have not only contained some unique features but have been in excellent condition; a fact which makes dismantling and re-erecting a relatively simple matter.[7]

These threatened vernacular buildings, together with rural trades and crafts, represented a 'heritage' that was 'rapidly diminishing'.

'Heritage' is a difficult word to define. The *Oxford English Dictionary* offers three meanings: (1) that which has been or may be inherited; any property, and especially land, which devolves by right of inheritance (2) that which comes from the circumstances of birth; an inherited lot or portion; the condition or state transmitted from ancestors (3) characterised or pertaining to the preservation or exploitation of local and national features of historical, cultural or scenic interest, especially tourist attractions. However, as the cultural historian Raphael Samuel has noted, 'Lexically, "heritage" is a term capacious enough to accommodate wildly discrepant meanings'. From its inception the 'heritage' that the Museum was preserving was more than the physical form of the buildings and smaller artefacts; it was preserving a complex set of *ideas* about the rural past, for which the Museum site and its buildings were merely the outward manifestation. These ideas reflect the ideology of the Museum's founders and subsequent managers; but the Museum also embodies ideas about the rural past held by the six million visitors that have passed through its gates since it first opened in 1970.[8]

Like any open air museum, this one reconstructs the past on a number of levels, including the physical alteration of the site, the reconstruction and internal presentation of the buildings, and the use of costumed interpreters. It is testimony to the Museum's success that these levels blend together so seamlessly. The site does not feel artificial; on the contrary, it has an organic unity that suggests authenticity and longevity. The ambiguity over what is 'real' and what is 'reconstructed' has been present throughout the Museum's history and is neatly expressed in an article about the proposed Museum which appeared in *Worthing Gazette* in March 1967:

> A complete village with houses, cottages, farm buildings, inns and shops may be 'created' in the south of England. And industries such as glass blowing, pottery and ironworking may operate in the village. The strange thing about the little community is that it would be a museum.[9]

The visitor to the Museum is presented with a reconstructed – and therefore interpreted – past to which they add their own preconceptions about what that past must have been like. These are inevitably filtered through our tendency to romanticise the rural past and to imbue it with qualities which, in an age of high modernity, we regard as lost to us. A qualitative survey of visitor perceptions of the rural past as it is represented at the Museum was undertaken by the author in the summer of 2008. The results suggested that to a large extent the Museum reinforced preconceived notions of the rural past as a static entity in which not much happened and an essentially classless population lived in harmony both with each other and with nature. Life was perceived to be simpler and less materialistic; people lived closer to the earth; families and neighbours looked after each other; communities were stable and homogenous. Although visitors acknowledged the negative aspects of the past, they thought that these were counterbalanced by the positive aspects. So, life was harder and people had fewer choices, but since they did not know any different they were happier.

With its rolling hills, hedgerows and picturesque villages the South East is a landscape that lacks visual conflict and where many of the villages seem impervious to the passage of time. It is within this landscape that the Weald and Downland Open Air Museum has been located, the quintessential village of our imagination, at once peaceable and immutable because it lacks the essential ingredient for change and conflict: a resident population. But the landscape is not immutable. It has shaped the lives of its inhabitants over millennia and they, in turn, have shaped the landscape as they sought to wrest a living from it and to raise and nurture their families. This book seeks to return the inhabitants to their long-vacated houses and to give some sense of what it meant to call a house a home.[10]

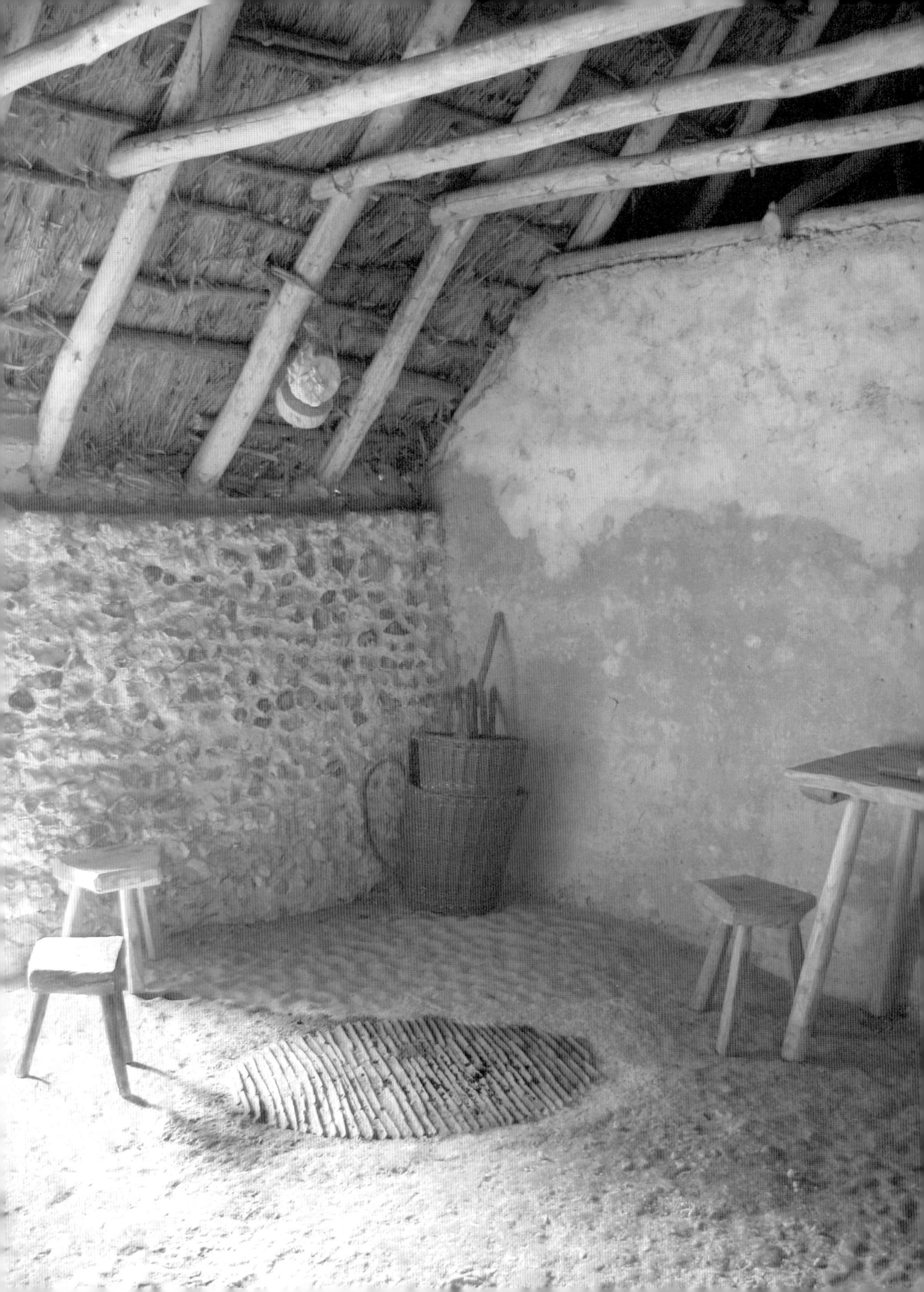

CHAPTER ONE

Hangleton: a thirteenth-century peasant house from Hangleton, East Sussex

A peasant house

This small building is a reconstructed peasant house from the deserted medieval downland village of Hangleton, situated just above Hove, about two miles from the sea. The village of Hangleton was excavated between 1952 and 1954 by Eric Holden and John and Gillian Hurst when plans for additional housing – overspill from Hove – threatened to remove all traces of the village for good, as indeed eventually happened. In total the remains of twelve building groups (with twenty individual structures) were excavated, covering a period from the thirteenth to the fifteenth century. The Museum's building is in fact an amalgam of two of those buildings (numbered 3 and 11 on the original archaeological plan). This was necessary because none of the buildings was sufficiently well preserved to allow for reconstruction purely on its own evidence. Pottery shards found during excavation suggest that these two buildings were in use between c.1250 and c.1325. Both contained two rooms, an inner one with a domed oven and an outer one with a hearth cut into the chalk floor. There has always been some debate about the function of the buildings:

Hangleton: the outer room with a hearth cut into the chalk floor.
RICHARD HARRIS

although they have been interpreted as dwellings, there is the possibility that they were free-standing kitchens or bakehouses.

The building from Hangleton was originally one of three archaeological reconstructions intended to illustrate the early development and antecedents of later vernacular buildings. The reconstructions were supervised by the Museum's Archaeological Committee, which met for the first time in February 1970. Its members included Eric Holden and John Hurst, as well as Roy Armstrong, the Museum's founder; John Lowe, the Museum's director, and principal of West Dean College; Betty Murray, principal of Bishop Otter College; Marjorie Hallam, one of the Museum's founding trustees; and George Newell, Museum trustee and surveyor. The subjects discussed at the first meeting were the proposed reconstruction of a Saxon weaver's hut and of a small house and another building from Hangleton.

The Saxon weaver's sunken hut was reconstructed, complete with a loom, in time for the Museum's opening on 5 September 1970. It was an important feature of the Museum, which at that time had only four other completed exhibits – the tollhouse, Winkhurst (now the Tudor kitchen), Littlehampton granary, and the charcoal burner's hut and kiln. The reconstruction was based on two excavated huts, one at Bishopstone near Seaford and the other at Old Erringham Farm near Shoreham, both in East Sussex. Regular weaving demonstrations were given, and the 1971 Museum guidebook reported that 'many visitors find the loom of greater interest than the hut'. After four years the first hut had decayed; it was removed and a new hut built in a slightly different location.

At the second meeting of the Archaeological Committee in November 1970 it was decided not to proceed with the reconstruction of the second Hangleton building, partly because of the cost of labour and materials, and partly because it was considered that too great an emphasis on archaeological reconstructions, for which many elements were conjectural, would undermine the Museum's efforts to establish its collection of 'real' buildings. However, the reconstruction of the small house from Hangleton proceeded. It was completed between July and August 1971 under the direction of Eric Holden using a labour force of mainly student volunteers.

A note about the reconstruction in the Museum archive records that the builders were careful not to apply any modern methods, and so used no plumb-rules or squares and worked with as little instruction as possible. Volunteers found it difficult to keep the walls plumb, so that walls four and a half feet high started 18 inches wide at the bottom but had shrunk to 12 inches wide at the top. Two or three courses a day was the maximum rate of progress, since otherwise the flints 'floated', that is, their position shifted within the mortar. Long nodules of flint were built across the wall to act as headers. When finished and fully dried out the walls were

Hangleton, as reconstructed at the Museum.
DANAE TANKARD

found to be very sturdy, since flint walls hold together more like reinforced concrete than as individual units, such as bricks held together by cement. Lime mortar was used instead of the more traditional chalk mortar. The reconstruction used some 13 tons of flints, 12 tons of grit and sand mixed, 17 quarters of lime (a quarter is 28 lb) and six bags of cement. The roof, of a hipped construction, is supported by timber beams, or wall plates, running along the top of the walls. The roof timbers were made of sweet chestnut cut from coppice growth of about 15 years, and the battens were made out of hazel rods.

The third experiment in reconstruction was a large Saxon hall, based on evidence from a Saxon village, deserted in the ninth century, on the Downs above Chalton in

Hangleton during reconstruction, 1971. Completed mainly by student volunteers, this reconstruction used no modern building methods.
J.R. ARMSTRONG/WDOAM ARCHIVE

East Hampshire. This was tackled in a different way, with the evidence reproduced to the exact scale on the ground, by marking with short timbers the position of post-holes, and by gravel marking the trenches revealed by the excavations, but without any attempt at reconstructing the superstructure.

The Archaeological Committee met once or twice a year, with the agenda growing to encompass a wide range of projects, including medieval iron-smelting, a replica glass furnace, the medieval clay and pottery group, a tilt hammer and the new project at Butser Hill to re-create an Iron Age farm run by Peter Reynolds. Its work was part of a Europe-wide movement in experimental archaeology, which encompassed Avoncroft Museum's Iron Age huts; the Butser experiment; the reconstructed Saxon village at West Stow, Suffolk; Iron Age reconstructions at Moesgard, Denmark; the Trelleborg Viking village, Asparn, Austria; and Biskupin, Poland. However, in 1983 the Saxon weaver's hut and Saxon hall were removed. There had been on-going maintenance issues with the hut, and it was also felt that the archaeological reconstructions were not at that time being underpinned by active archaeological involvement.[1]

Nevertheless, the house from Hangleton remains an important exhibit for many reasons, not least because it was the first time such a reconstruction had been attempted. A huge amount of archaeological and documentary research has been undertaken since the 1950s, but the Hangleton excavations continue to be widely cited and discussed in any publication on medieval peasant houses.

The appearance of the reconstructed peasant house is conjectural. The archaeological evidence indicated the size of the building; the location of the internal partition; and the position of the hearth, internal oven and doorway. The height of the walls was calculated from the amount of flint rubble that was discovered. However, the position and size of the two windows and, more importantly, the roof type and its covering had to be guessed. Moreover, when Holden excavated the site he found the remains of timber post-holes below the flint walls in building 3. He concluded from this that an early thirteenth-century timber-framed building had been rebuilt with flint around 1250, retaining some of the timber posts. It is possible, however, that the timber frame was not completely replaced but partly underpinned with a flint footing when the post-holes rotted, producing a 'new' house that was part flint-built and part timber-framed.[2]

The village of Hangleton

Hangleton was close to the River Adur, whose estuary in the medieval period extended as far north as Upper Beeding. The nearest towns were Shoreham and Lewes, both of which had weekly markets. The manor of Hangleton formed part of the Fishersgate Half Hundred, together with the neighbouring manors of Aldrington and Portslade, situated within the Rape of Lewes. The lords of the manor from 1291 to 1446 were the de Poynings, a Sussex gentry family who had lands in Kent, Suffolk and Norfolk, as well as extensive estates in Sussex. In the early fourteenth century the population of Hangleton is likely to have been in the region of 200.[3]

All that remains of medieval Hangleton today is the eleventh-century church of St Helen and parts of the medieval manor house, a long, low building to the west of Hangleton Manor House (which is the 'new' manor house, mainly sixteenth-century in date). The medieval village uncovered during the excavations of the 1950s was spread out in a linear development away from the church along two tracks: track 1, which corresponds to what is now Hangleton Way; and track 2, which has disappeared. It was not possible to excavate the whole of the medieval village since much of the land to the west of track 2 had been disturbed by the railway line that opened in 1887 and subsequently by an embanked golf green, obscuring the medieval remains.[4]

The remains of two 'longhouses' were found (buildings 1 and 12A), measuring approximately 40 feet by 20 feet, each divided internally into three rooms. The central portion of building 1 contained two hearths which, together with the remains of domestic pottery, indicate that it was used as a dwelling. Building 12A appears to have been similar, but lack of time meant that it could not be excavated properly. The other buildings identified as dwellings were smaller, at between 18 and 30 feet

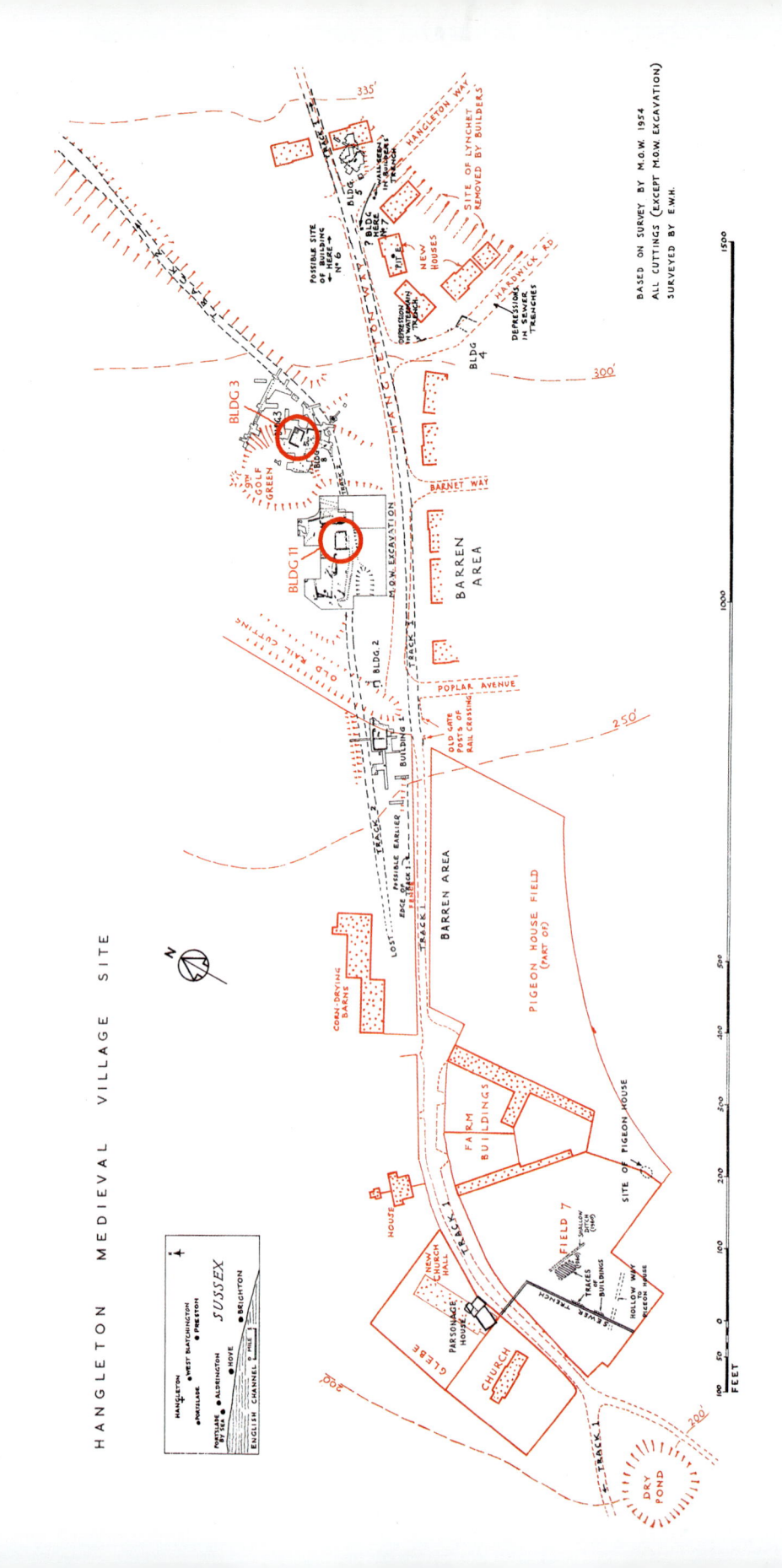

long and 12–16 feet wide. Some of these were divided internally into two rooms; others (such as building 10A) had only one. The remains of six ovens were found, two within what otherwise appear to be dwellings, three in separate 'outshuts' (two in one outshut and one in another), and one within a free-standing kitchen. Evidence from building 4 suggests that it originally functioned as a human habitation but may subsequently have been used to house animals. A large shallow depression to the south of track 2 might have been a pond to supply the village with fresh water.[5] The pattern of building, combined with the dating of pottery shards, suggested that the period of the greatest density of occupation was from c.1250 to c.1325, but that the population of Hangleton contracted substantially soon after that. This, as we will see, is consistent with what we know from the documentary evidence.

Medieval Hangleton was a nucleated settlement of a type seen widely across south-east England. A typical medieval nucleated village plan consisted of a street with peasant holdings or 'tofts' (also described as messuages or tenements) arranged on either side. However, marked variations in plan-types can be identified. The regularity of some medieval settlements, in which each house occupied a similar-sized piece of land along a street or a green, suggests that they were the result of deliberate planning or replanning by the lord. Other settlements were polyfocal; that is, there were small groupings of holdings in close proximity to each other, representing a more organic development. The plan of Hangleton uncovered during excavation, although it is incomplete, indicates that the village was in the latter category.[6]

The archaeological excavations are the main source of evidence for medieval Hangleton, since there are few documentary sources for this period. There are no manorial records, but we do have a small number of other sources such as such as tax returns (the 1327 and 1332 lay subsidies, and the 1379 poll tax), the *Inquisitiones nonarum* (Inquisitions of the Ninths, also referred to as the Nonae Rolls) of 1341, and an *inquisition post mortem* taken on the death of Thomas de Poynings in 1339.[7]

Hangleton's peasant community

Historians use the word 'peasant' to describe small-scale rural cultivators, farming 50 acres or less, and occupying a relatively lowly social position. Within peasant communities, however, there were distinctive social gradations. The most important of these was the division of the population into free and unfree tenants (also known as *villeins* or *serfs*), the principal distinction being that the former were protected by

Hangleton excavation plan. Buildings 3 & 11 are circled in red (3 to right, 11 to left).
ERIC HOLDEN AND SUSSEX ARCHAEOLOGICAL COLLECTIONS, 1963, REDRAWN BY RICHARD HARRIS

common law and the latter were not. 'Unfree' refers both to personal status and to the tenure by which they held land. Unfree status was inherited through the male line, and unfree tenants were (in law, at least) effectively chattels of their lord: they could be bought or sold along with his other property and evicted from their land at will. In return for holding land, unfree tenants were required to provide labour services, which were meticulously set out in manorial custumals or surveys. Unfree tenants were liable for a variety of fines such as *chevage* (a fine for the right to leave the manor), *merchet* (the right to marry), *heriot* (giving the best beast to the lord, in return for the right to succeed to property), and *leyrwite* and *childwite* (compensation for illicit sexual unions and their product). In practice, by the thirteenth century many of the requirements of unfree tenure were protected by manorial custom: unfree tenants were unlikely to be evicted unless they failed to maintain their holdings; they had the right to sell or alienate their holdings; and their heirs could expect to inherit their land. Unfree tenants were able to buy more land and their children could leave the manor without much interference from the lord. Their annual rents and services were defined, sometimes in writing, and it was difficult for the lord to increase them.[8]

While unfree status was viewed as inferior, there was in reality no direct correlation between wealth and land tenure: unfree tenants could hold more land, and thus be wealthier, than their free neighbours. That meant that within the peasant community there was also a social division based on wealth rather than legal status. The relative wealth of the Hangleton villagers can be assessed from their tax assessments, but it is also reflected in the archaeological evidence. The traditional view of the role of a longhouse in such communities is that it housed animals as well as people, but the two longhouses at Hangleton – the largest buildings excavated – were more likely to have belonged to substantial peasants.

Hangleton during reconstruction, 1971. Flint walls were topped with a hipped roof, made from sweet chestnut timbers and hazel rods.
J.R. ARMSTRONG/WDOAM ARCHIVE

Saxon weaver's hut and Saxon hall, *c*.1974. Evidence was reproduced to the exact scale on the ground, with short timbers marking the positions of post-holes.
J.R. ARMSTRONG/WDOAM ARCHIVE

Excavation site, 1953 (building 3 is in the left foreground).
ERIC HOLDEN ARCHIVE, BARBICAN HOUSE MUSEUM

Building 3: view looking east, with Eric Holden measuring oven, 1953.
ERIC HOLDEN ARCHIVE, BARBICAN HOUSE MUSEUM

A summary of the rents and services that the unfree peasants of Hangleton owed to the lord is contained in the *inquisition post mortem* taken on the death of Thomas de Poynings in 1339. The tenants owed:

Rents of assize £8 11s. 9d., payable at the feast of St Thomas Apostle £4 9s. 0d. and at Pentecost £4 2s. 9d.; of rent called Eggyngselver 10s 8d. payable at Michaelmas [29 September]; of rent at Michaelmas called Ocsegheld and Saltgheld 4s. 1½d., of rent at the same feast 19s. 0¾d. called aid of the vill [and their works] from Michaelmas to feast of Annunciation of the Blessed Mary [25 March] are worth 5s. and from then until 1 August 52s. 8d.; Autumn works worth 24s. 10d.; works of carrying wood 30 works between [?] St John Baptist [24 June] and St Peter ad Vincula [1 August] 5s., price of the work 2d.; of rent of eggs at Easter 360 [?] yearly price per 100 3d.[9]

This is the only description of the obligations of the tenants. It lacks the detail that one would expect to find in a custumal, such as those surviving for the bishop of Chichester's manors or for the manor of West Boarhunt in Hampshire, discussed in the next chapter. The reference to 'rents of assize' suggests that by 1339 some of the labour services owed by the tenants had already been commuted to cash payments, a trend that was increasingly common from the late thirteenth century onwards. The cash rents called *eggyngselver*, *ocsegheld* and *saltgheld* were probably customary payments that had originated in the pre-Conquest period as payments in kind. All three words are Old English (that is, Anglo-Saxon): *selver* and *gheld* (silver and geld, or tax levy) refer to the payment element while *eggyng* (eggs), *ocse* (oxen) and salt refer to the goods to be rendered. However, a possible alternative explanation is that *saltgheld* refers to the carriage of salt from the salt works in the Adur valley to the manor house.[10]

Status within the village would also have been acquired through holding office in the community. Thus, the lay subsidy of 1327 lists a man named Gilbert le Reve who may indeed have been the village reeve, a manorial official answerable to the lord for the management of the demesne (the area of land within the manor set aside for the exclusive use of the lord). This was a responsible position that accorded the office-holder various privileges, including, on some manors, rent-free accommodation. The office could be held for a year, a term of years, or for life; on some manors it seems to have been inheritable. On the Sussex manor of Laughton in 1292 the reeve, who was selected by the lord from among his unfree tenants, received an annual salary of five shillings. In addition, he was released from all his labour services, stabled and fed his horse at the lord's expense, ate with the lord's household when the lord was in residence and received a corn allowance during harvest. In return, he would collect rents and all moneys, account for receipts and expenses, and have some general supervision over the cultivation of the demesne arable. He might also keep the farming grange and granary and account for all produce going in or out of them. In Chaucer's *The Canterbury Tales* the reeve is depicted as a hard-nosed business man who had amassed considerable wealth through creative accounting, to the extent that he was able to offer loans to his lord of what were essentially the lord's own goods. Outward signs of his wealth and status were his house, which was 'ful faire upon an heeth; With grene trees yshadwed' (on a heath, shaded by green trees) and his horse, 'a ful good stot, That was al pomely grey and highe Scot' (a stallion that was all dapple-grey and called Scot).[11]

Another official on the manor of Laughton was the beadle, who guarded the lord's corn during harvest, sowed the lord's land with the lord's cornseed, and harrowed the whole of the lord's land by himself and his man. He also had to guard all the demesne land, corn, meadow, and pasture outside the park, and issue summons and distraints to the manorial court. His privileges included being quit of 2s. rent and of works valued at 28d. a year; pasture for three beasts with the lord's beasts over summer, valued at 2s.; and herbage (pasture) for his horse for the whole summer, worth sixpence. On other manors this official was called the hayward or *messor*. Laughton also had four unfree tenants who acted as oxherds for the year, tending the demesne ploughs as long as ploughing continued. If rain or other impediment prevented ploughing, the reeve would assign them other work. Their privileges included being quit of all rents and works for the year, receiving at Christmas 1½ bushels of barley, one bushel of oats and a flitch (or quarter) of bacon, and pasturing two beasts on the lord's pasture for the whole summer.[12]

Farming and the peasant economy

In 1339 the demesne of Hangleton – the lord's own land, exclusively his – comprised 'a capital messuage [the manor house together with the garden] worth yearly clear 6d., a dovecote worth yearly 12d. and not more because old and ruinous; 120 acres of arable land worth yearly 35s., price the acre 3d. [and] a pasture called Shepelese worth yearly 8s. 4d.' In the absence of manorial records there is little specific information about how land was organised and farmed in Hangleton in the late thirteenth and

Tending sheep.
LUTTRELL PSALTER, BRITISH LIBRARY, ADD MS 42130, C.1325–1335

fourteenth centuries. On some manors elsewhere in the country we know that the land of the peasants was intermingled with the arable demesne, but in Sussex it seems to have been more common for demesnes to be cultivated separately, with the arable land of the peasants scattered in narrow strips in common fields. The chalk downland above Hangleton is covered with a mantle of clay-with-flints, a 'soil' which is heavy, sticky and very difficult to cultivate for arable, so it is likely that this upper area was used as sheep pasture and that the crops were grown on the light chalk soils south of the village. This seems to be confirmed by the excavations carried out on the higher downland in 1989 and 1990, in advance of the construction of the A27 Brighton bypass. No evidence of medieval cultivation was found.[13]

At the start of the fourteenth century the area of coastal Sussex in which Hangleton was situated was one of the wealthiest regions in England. The primary crops were wheat and barley, but this part of Sussex was also the country's leading producer of legumes, the peas and beans grown both as animal feed and as part of the staple diet of the peasants themselves. More intensive agriculture, made possible by the elimination of a fallow period on the best arable fields, meant that sowing rates were higher than elsewhere in England. A system of sheep-corn husbandry allowed sheep-farming to coexist with the extensive cultivation of grains. The sheep were penned in folds on arable land overnight, so that their dung and urine would *tathe* (manure) the ground. They were then returned to the sheepwalks during the day. As a food animal sheep were kept more for their milk than for meat, but their real value was their wool. The majority of Sussex wool and wool-fells (fleeces) were exported through Shoreham, Chichester and Seaford, with the eastern ports such as Pevensey and Winchelsea playing a lesser role. The Hangleton flock may have been relatively small in comparison with other coastal Sussex manors, possibly about 400 animals. In contrast, we know that in 1340 the neighbouring communities of West Blatchington and Patcham were pasturing 1,000 and 2,000 sheep respectively.[14]

A fairly crude estimate of the average size of peasant arable holdings in Hangleton can be made on the basis of the number of peasant-owned plough teams recorded in the Domesday Survey of 1086. There were five teams, which would plough an average of 100 acres each a year; by this reckoning the manor had about 500 acres of arable land. On this basis each householder held approximately 11 to 12 acres, a figure that correlates almost exactly with the amount of land (10–12 acres), which historians estimate was needed to feed a peasant family of five. In practice, of course, the size of individual peasant arable holdings would have varied widely depending on wealth. Where specific information about landholding is available for individual manors, the general trend in the late thirteenth and early fourteenth centuries was for holdings to become smaller, as they were subdivided in response to rapid population growth.[15]

Peasants usually grew much the same crops on their arable strips as lords grew on their demesnes. Historians previously thought that peasant crop yields were lower because they had fewer animals to produce manure and to provide draught power, and because they might have had less adequate farming equipment. However, recent research has indicated that peasant cropping regimes were similar to, and sometimes more intensive than, those on the manorial demesne. Production of crops on the small area of land adjoining the house, though inevitably on a small scale, could also be profitable. Some information about the farming activities of Hangleton's peasants is provided by the *Inquistiones Nonarum* return of 1341, a parish-by-parish assessment undertaken for a proposed new tax (which was never levied) that would have collected a ninth of the value of agricultural produce. In addition to larger livestock such as cows and sheep, Hangleton villagers kept chickens, geese, pigs and bees. We know that they grew flax (used in the manufacture of linen cloth) and the hemp from which was made canvas, coarse cloth and cordage. Based on what is known about crop production in peasant gardens elsewhere, it is probable that they also grew onions, leeks, peas, beans, vetches and fruit such as apples and pears. While most of this would have been for household and livestock consumption, any excess would have been available for sale on the markets, thereby boosting the cash income of at least some peasant families.[16]

Most crafts and industries did not provide full-time employment, but were supplementary to agricultural work. Before 1350 the main evidence for by-employment in Hangleton is the existence of ovens, which may have been used for baking bread for sale both inside and outside the village. It is also likely that the villagers were brewing ale. If we were to reinterpret the Museum's building as a detached kitchen, the outer room with open hearth might have been a service area used for drying malt, possibly on blankets or wooden racks suspended from the roof, while the inner room with the dome-shaped oven was used for baking. In the late thirteenth and fourteenth century ale production was largely a domestic activity, undertaken by women to supplement the household income.[17]

The reference to the payment of a rent called *saltgheld* suggests that the villagers may also have been involved in salt-making in the numerous saltworks (salterns) operating in the Adur valley, many of which were owned by religious houses. Salt was made by washing salt-impregnated sand with water to produce brine, which was then boiled to produce a wet salt that could be dried in blocks. The production of salt created sand mounds or spoil heaps along the estuary, some of which survived until 1960 when they were removed for farming purposes. Cottages or 'cotes' were built on top of the spoil heaps, and it was in these that the brine was boiled and dried. However, salt-making in the Adur valley virtually ceased after 1350, for reasons that will be discussed below.[18]

Reaping & binding.
LUTTRELL PSALTER, BRITISH LIBRARY, ADD MS 42130, C.1325–1335

We also have some occupational data from the 1379 poll tax return for the Fishersgate Half Hundred. In Hangleton there were three carpenters, in Aldrington two carpenters and a thatcher, and in Portslade a thatcher, two masons and a tailor of woollen cloth. Other crafts or trades, although not recorded, are likely to have been pursued in one or all of the three villages that made up the Half Hundred. There would almost certainly have been a blacksmith, shoeing horses and oxen and making domestic and agricultural ironwork. At Portslade and in the neighbouring manor of Hangleton-Benfields there were windmills (the Portslade example from at least 1280), which would have employed millers.[19] Peasants were only partly self-sufficient. Goods that they were unable to produce themselves, such as ironwork, pottery and textiles, had to be bought. In addition they needed money to pay rent and taxes or for the services of specialist craftsmen, such as the thatchers, carpenters, masons and tailor who appear in the 1379 poll tax returns.[20]

Peasant houses, *c.*1250–1350

Very few thirteenth- and early fourteenth-century peasant houses survive in Britain, something which historians and archaeologists previously interpreted as evidence of their flimsy construction. Peasants, it was argued, lacked both the inclination and the ability to build themselves robust houses and were content to make do with less durable dwellings. This view has been revised substantially over the last thirty years following careful re-examination of the available evidence, while new research has identified important changes in construction methods.

Given the almost complete absence of standing buildings, evidence for peasant housing comes either from archaeological remains, as in the case of Hangleton, or from documentary sources such as manorial court records, which preserve building agreements between tenants and lords. However, both of these sources present problems. In the archaeological record, rebuilding and changes in function make dating and interpretation of excavated remains difficult, while it has been argued that building agreements give an unrealistic idea of peasant houses since they refer to proposed rather than to actual buildings.[21]

In south-east England, people and animals were usually accommodated in separate buildings. The typical peasant holding (or toft) would include a separate living house, a building for animals (such as a byre or sheepcote) and a barn or granary for storing crops, all grouped around a yard. In Hangleton only two of the thirteenth-century dwellings have been identified as having associated agricultural structures – 9B (9A, tentatively identified as a yard) and 3 (8, possibly a barn) – and in neither case is the function of the associated building entirely clear. Moreover, the function of a building might change over time so that, for example, a dwelling might be converted into an agricultural building or vice versa. That would explain why some of the sites at Hangleton which were thought to have been in agricultural use contained shards of domestic pottery and domestic waste.

In Hangleton the majority of dwellings had only one or two rooms. In a two-roomed house, the outer room with the open hearth is likely to have been used as the hall, the main social space in a house, serving numerous functions including eating and sleeping. The inner room, or chamber, would have been used primarily for sleeping, but might also be used for storage (including storage of valuables). Only two buildings, the longhouses (buildings 1 and 12A), were divided into three rooms, probably comprising a service end (used for storage or food preparation), a partially screened cross-entry, a hall with hearth, and a chamber. This layout is characteristic of the medieval tripartite domestic plan that we will see more fully developed in the hall house from Boarhunt, discussed in the next chapter.

The number of people accommodated within these small buildings can only be guessed: the average peasant family size was approximately five, but actual family size would have varied enormously, depending on wealth (wealthier families tended to have a larger number of children), survival, and position within the life-cycle (that is, whether the householder was young or old). The poor widow in Chaucer's 'Nun's Priest's Tale' lived in her 'narwe' (small) two-roomed cottage with her two daughters. Kitchens were usually free-standing buildings, although in some cases they may have occupied the end bay of a dwelling house or an outshut, as was the case in Hangleton. Free-standing bakehouses may also have been used for brewing.[22]

Tofts were sometimes separated from the street, and from their neighbours, by a ditch. There might also – or alternatively – be a bank with a hedge, wooden fence

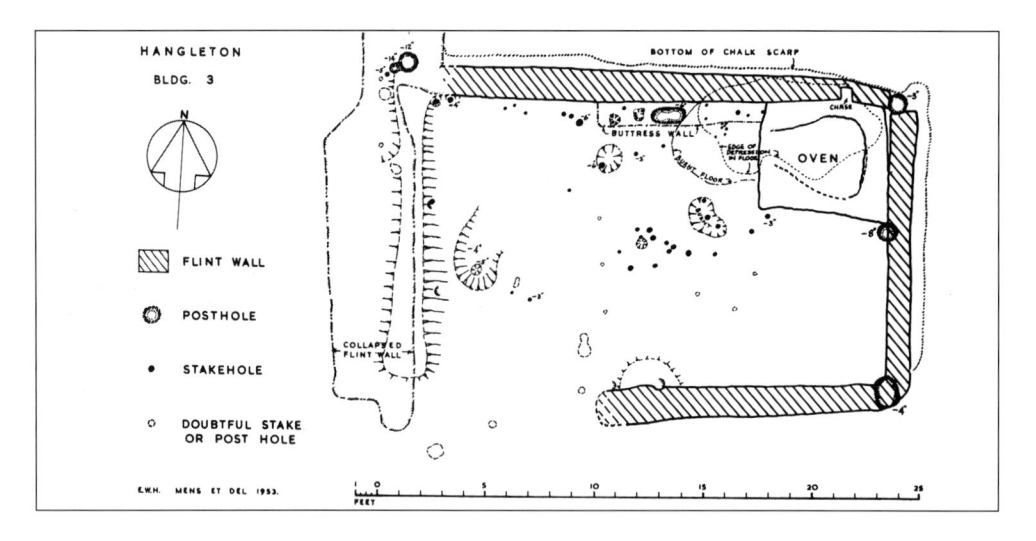

Hangleton, building 3.
ERIC HOLDEN ARCHIVE, BARBICAN HOUSE MUSEUM

or palisade on top. At Hangleton there was no sign of ditches, but there is evidence of wooden palisades around some of the buildings, notably numbers 3 and 8. The reason for these barriers is unclear. They may have served to keep animals out – or to keep animals in. Alternatively, or additionally, they may have been intended to deter intruders or to define the family holding. The need (or desire) for security is attested by the quantity of locks, keys and chest fittings that have been discovered at various sites. A key was found inside the remains of building 1 at Hangleton, although it is not clear whether it was for a door or a chest.[23]

It has been suggested that manorial lords built only a minority, perhaps as few as one in a hundred, of tenant buildings, and that the costs and practicalities of building were therefore normally borne by the peasant landholders. However, on his manor of Preston near Hangleton the bishop of Chichester was responsible not only for repairing existing cottages but also for building new ones. Where tenants were responsible for building their own houses, we now know that they were employing specialist craftsmen to do so. Evidence from other parts of the country shows that carpenters were routinely employed by peasants on their buildings; the services of other specialists such as masons and thatchers were also bought in. The 1379 poll tax return for Hangleton records the presence of three carpenters in the village, a sizeable number considering that the total adult population recorded at that time was only eighteen. The presence of thatchers in each of the neighbouring villages of Aldrington and Portslade has already been noted; Aldrington also had two carpenters and Portslade two masons. Although the buildings at Hangleton were constructed from the materials most immediately to hand – especially flint – other materials such as timber and ironwork would have been

Hangleton, building 11.
J G HURST, SUSSEX ARCHAEOLOGICAL COLLECTIONS, 1964

purchased. In the West Midlands, during a slightly later period (1350–1500) a peasant would have paid between £2 to £4 for the construction of a house and barn, which gives at least a rough impression of the likely cost of a building such as that from Hangleton.[24]

The most significant change to be identified in thirteenth-century peasant houses is the use of different forms of foundation instead of the earth-fast poles that had been used in rural buildings since prehistoric times. In some cases stone walls might have been built to sufficient height to carry the rafters, but historians now associate the use of stone foundations with the development of timber-framing, in particular the use of the cruck – pairs of long curved timbers that rise from ground level to support the roof timbers. A few examples of cruck-framed peasant houses survive from the period around 1300. The replacement of earth-fast poles with flint in building 3 has already been noted, but there is no way of knowing whether this continued to roof height or served as a foundation for a timber superstructure.[25]

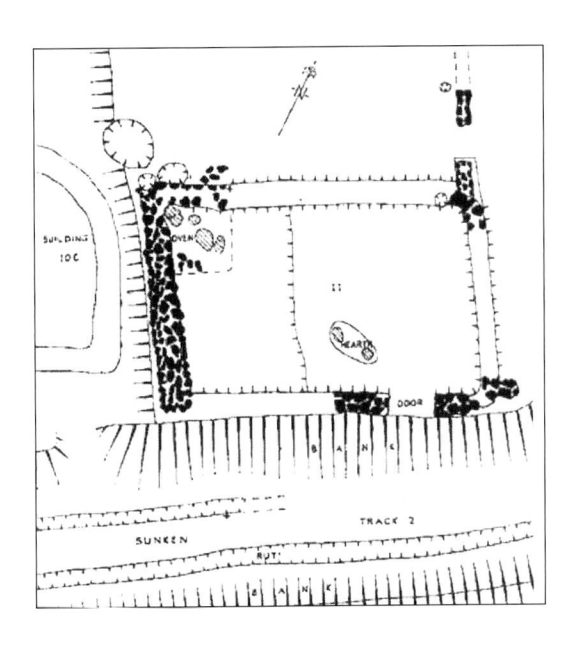

In the light of revised interpretations of the quality of thirteenth- and early fourteenth-century peasant houses, different explanations for their low survival rate can be suggested, rather than the wholly negative one that they just fell down because they were so poorly built. For reasons that will be explored in more detail in the next chapter, many of these houses were probably pulled down or rebuilt in the period after the Black Death, either because they were surplus to requirements or because they no longer fulfilled the social and economic needs of their peasant occupants.

Standards of living and material culture

Trying to reconstruct the material culture of the peasant home in the thirteenth and fourteenth centuries is difficult, simply because of the limited amount of evidence available. Although the archaeological record is informative on some aspects of domestic life – for example, the materials from which cooking and storage vessels were made – it is silent on other aspects. We have almost no information about how houses like those from Hangleton were furnished. Limited documentary evidence for peasant furnishings, much of it from the period after the Black Death, suggests that their houses were furnished with a table, one or two stools and one or two storage chests. There is little evidence for ownership of beds, leaving us to speculate about what the occupants slept on. Given the lack of space, they might have had woven straw palliasses which could be removed to the side of the room or stored above the open rafters during the day. There is also the question of storage for foodstuffs and agricultural produce. Were the rafters partially boarded over, to provide additional storage and to keep the floor space clear? These small houses would certainly have been crowded with goods and furnishings connected with the domestic and economic lives of the inhabitants.[26]

The excavated finds from Hangleton included a substantial amount of broken pottery, among which cooking pots, bowls and storage jars predominate. This was 'coarse ware', with the fabric containing fragments of flint and shell, as well as sand and grit. The colours ranged from grey to brown, buff and red. Most of this pottery was wheel-thrown, but some larger vessels were hand-made and subsequently trimmed on a slow wheel. There was little decoration, other than a few incised lines round the necks of the jars and pots or applied to the strapping. Some of the pottery was partially glazed, either internally or, in the case of jugs, externally. The external glaze colours varied from olive-brown green to deep green, suggesting that although copper was the principal constituent, some lead and some iron oxide had also been used. During the excavation the only cooking vessel recovered that was *not* made of pottery was the remains of a bronze cauldron, found inside building 1 (one of the two longhouses). This had sooty residue both inside and out; material removed from the inside was thought to be the residue of animal fat. It is significant that this, the only higher-status object found during the course of excavation, was located within one of the most substantial dwellings. A few broken stone vessels were found, mostly rotary querns (used to grind grain). A broken diamond-shaped trough that was recovered might have been used as a mortar, although the fact that it was made of sandstone would have limited its utility for pounding, except with a wooden pestle.[27]

The archaeological evidence also provided clues about the meat consumption of the peasant inhabitants of Hangleton. The bones of oxen, sheep and pigs were found. Where they could be assessed for age it was evident that they were from mature animals, suggesting that they were killed only after they had performed other useful roles. This is consistent with evidence found at other medieval settlements and reinforces the point that sheep were kept primarily for their wool and their milk, rather than their meat. Despite the references to eggs that have already been noted, no chicken bones were discovered, and neither were there any rabbit bones, but this is likely to be because of their small size and fragility.[28]

In the thirteenth century the main elements of the peasant diet in Sussex were bread (normally made of barley or wheat), cheese, some meat (usually bacon), preserved fish such as salt cod or herring, and pottage made from oatmeal, peas and beans. The peasants drank ale, milk or water. Everyone in medieval England, no matter what their status, was required to abstain from eating meat on Fridays and fast days, and to eat fish instead. We know a lot about the diets of harvest workers because many manorial lords provided them with food in exchange for their labour, and these food payments are recorded in manorial records such as accounts or custumals. The harvest workers on the manor of Laughton, and also their households, received two meals a day. At *prandium* (lunch, but probably not eaten until 3 p.m.) they had a wheaten loaf, ale and the flesh of an ox. After *prandium* they drank ale in the field. At *cena* (supper) they had one 'wastrell' loaf, one herring and ale. On the Sussex manor of Goring the workers received just one meal, comprising barley bread, pottage, two herrings, cheese and water, or wheaten bread, pottage, meat, cheese and ale. Other foodstuffs were consumed that would have reduced the monotony of this staple diet and increased its vitamin content: vegetables (such as onions, leeks and cabbages), fruit (apples, pears and cherries) and dairy produce such as curd and cream. Flavour could be enhanced by the addition of garlic or salt. Other 'spices' that might have been available were pepper, peony seed and fennel seed (the latter for fish). The quality, quantity and variety of food would have depended on wealth, seasonality and proximity to food sources (such as the sea or rivers). The large number of oyster and other marine mollusc shells found during excavation at Hangleton is unsurprising, given the village's proximity to the Adur estuary and the sea.[29]

The disappearance of the medieval village

In 1300 Hangleton appears to have been a thriving community of approximately 200 people, making a living predominantly from agriculture. By 1340, though, the village was in trouble. In that year the villagers of Hangleton told the tax assessors of the Inquisitions of the Ninths that many lands in the parish were barren and uncultivated, and that they were unable to live by their lands and tenements alone (the implication being that they were obliged to seek some kind of supplementary employment in order to make ends meet). Even allowing for an element of exaggeration, intended to reduce their tax burden, the complaints of the villagers do suggest some kind of economic crisis. What had happened? There are two interrelated explanations. First, the period from about 1275 to 1315 was characterised by rapid population growth, which put increasing pressure on land. During this period peasant holdings tended to become smaller, as land was subdivided to accommodate adult children. The effect of this was to create a large class of impoverished smallholders, with insufficient land (perhaps as little as one acre) to support their households.

The second explanation is environmental change, which led to increased storminess at the end of the thirteenth century, possibly accompanied by a slight rise in sea level. Along the coast of Sussex flooding became a regular event: the 'great flood' at Appledram in 1274–75 was followed by the great storm of 1287, which destroyed Old Winchelsea and caused severe flooding in the Pevensey Levels and along the coast of Kent. Severe flooding along the whole length of Sussex and Kent in 1331–32, combined with repeated floods during the 1330s and 1340s, ruined much low-lying arable land, as recorded in the Nonae Rolls of 1341. Hove lost 150 acres, Portslade 60 acres and Aldrington 40 acres. This flooding might well explain the apparent collapse of salt-making in the Adur valley during the fourteenth century. Nationally, the period 1315 to 1322 saw a prolonged agricultural crisis, with a succession of poor harvests caused by wet weather, accompanied by disease among sheep and cattle. It is estimated that in some parts of the South East crop yields fell during these years by as much as half. The resultant famine may have increased mortality by between ten and fifteen per cent. Food prices soared, and opportunities for casual employment decreased as producers (both large and small) tried to cut costs. The combination of these factors may have spelled disaster for Hangleton: the holdings of the villagers were too small to support their families, and they were unable to afford the additional food that was needed.[30]

But this was disaster on a small scale in comparison with what was about to befall them. In the summer of 1348 the Black Death arrived in southern England, reaching London in the autumn and northern England the following year, and killing an estimated forty to seventy per cent of the population. A contemporary chronicler described the arrival of the plague:

> In 1348, at about the feast of the Translation of St Thomas the martyr [7 July], the cruel pestilence, hateful to all future ages, arrived from countries across the sea on the south coast of England at the port called Melcombe [part of modern day Weymouth] in Dorset. Travelling all over the south country it wretchedly killed innumerable people in Dorset, Devon and Somerset. It was, moreover, believed to have been just as cruel among pagans as Christians. Next it came to Bristol, where very few were left alive, and then travelled northwards, leaving not a city, a town, a village, or even, except rarely, a house, without killing most or all of the people there, so that over England as a whole a fifth of the men, women and children were carried to burial. As a result, there was such a shortage of people that there were hardly enough living to look after the sick and bury the dead.[31]

Evidence from the 1379 poll tax return suggests that the population of Hangleton may have fallen by 60 per cent in the wake of the Black Death and subsequent outbreaks of plague. The tax of 1379 replaced the flat rate of fourpence per head that had been used in 1377 with an elaborate sliding scale. All adults over the age of 16 were assessed (as opposed to those over 14 in 1377) and only the truly indigent were exempt. Husbands and wives were assessed together. In Hangleton there were nine married men and five single men and women, each assessed at fourpence. Four of the single men and women shared the same surname (Philp') and may therefore have formed one (presumably childless) household. There were also three craftsmen, each of whom was assessed at the higher rate of sixpence. We can assume that they were married and had their own households. Using the figure for average family size of 4.5 or 5, we can thereby calculate the total population of Hangleton in 1379 as being between 65 and 80.[32]

Conclusion

One immediate consequence of the reduced peasant population was that there was more land available for the survivors. Unfortunately, there is insufficient evidence, either archaeological or documentary, to see how the reduction in population affected the pattern of habitation and landholding in Hangleton. Two fourteenth-century buildings, possibly barns (buildings 9C and 9D), were replaced at a later date (perhaps the later fourteenth century) with a farm complex, comprising a living house and free-standing kitchen, both with tiled roofs, and a barn (buildings 9E, 10C, 10D). This farm complex might hold the key to understanding changes in the size and social composition of the village. Whereas in the early fourteenth century there was a sizeable community of more than 200 peasants, most of whom were small landholders, and each holding had approximately eleven to twelve acres of land, by the late fourteenth and early fifteenth century the village was more sparsely settled, with larger and wealthier peasant landholdings, whose social status was reflected in the increased sophistication of their buildings. This explanation, though only partially supported by the evidence, is consistent with the general trend in landholding observed elsewhere in the country after the Black Death. The population continued to decline and by 1428, when there were just two householders, the medieval village had in effect ceased to exist.[33]

The story of Hangleton must be told through the archaeological record, supplemented by the small amount of surviving documentary evidence and the substantial body of secondary literature on peasant culture produced by historians and archaeologists over the last fifty years. For those who encounter it, it is a story defined by its ending – the cataclysmic events of 1348 to 1351. As in so many other places, these events profoundly and irrevocably altered the medieval community of Hangleton.

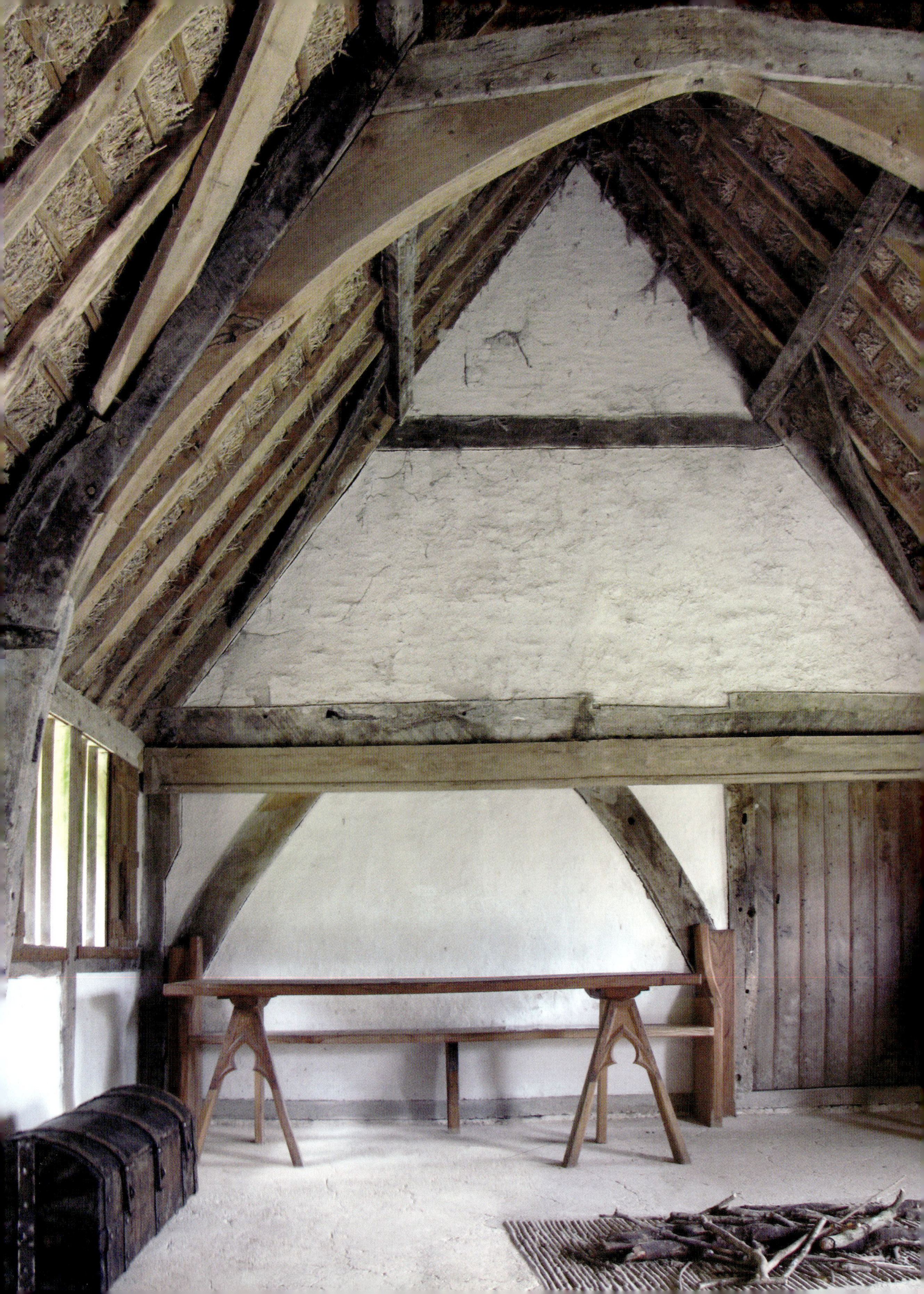

CHAPTER TWO

Boarhunt: a fourteenth-century hall house from Boarhunt, Hampshire

A medieval hall house

The Boarhunt hall house is a good example of the late medieval tripartite domestic plan, which we saw at an earlier stage of development in the Hangleton 'longhouses'. It has recently been dated by dendrochronology (tree-ring dating); this confirmed that two of the timbers (both from the same tree) were felled some time around c.1355–90. That is consistent with the approximate date previously assigned to the house on the basis of structural evidence (in particular, the distinctive 'seesaw' marks that appear on some of the timbers).

When the house was rescued in 1971 it was in an advanced state of decay. At that time it was a timber-framed structure containing two rooms: a two-bay base-cruck hall (so-called because the crucks do not continue to the apex of the roof), and a room – possibly a service room – under the hipped end. It had brick walls, of several different dates, and a thatched roof, and was attached to a small brick cottage of late nineteenth-century date. At some point an upper floor had been inserted over the

Boarhunt: the hall, looking towards the upper end
RICHARD HARRIS

hall and a large brick chimney, serving two ground-floor hearths and a bake oven, had been built in the lower end of the hall. The service room was still open to the roof, and the rafters and thatch battens were heavily sooted from the original open fire. Much of its thatch was missing, and there was considerable rot to the lower timbers, including one of the base crucks. In all, only about 30 per cent of the original timbers survived. However, a reconstruction was considered worthwhile since the surviving timbers were well distributed throughout the frame, allowing for the position of those that were missing to be established with reasonable confidence. Nevertheless, the reconstruction presented a number of problems, not least the fact that the room at the upper end of the hall (the chamber) had been removed entirely to make way for the 'modern' extension. The dimensions of this room in the reconstructed house are therefore conjectural. The disintegration of the wall plate (the horizontal beam forming the top of the walls) also meant that the location of the doors and the windows had to be postulated from other features.

The process of reconstructing the hall house at the Museum was a long and complicated one, owing to the fragmentary state of the surviving building. Repairs to the timbers began in 1976, but progress was delayed by difficulties in finding suitable timbers for the roof and for the base-cruck blade and by the departure of the original carpenter in 1979. It was officially opened to the public by the Duke of Gloucester in May 1981.[1]

We do not know who lived in the hall house in the medieval period. However, it is most likely that they were moderately prosperous peasants who had benefited from the increased availability of land and the weakening of the manorial system in the period after the Black Death.

Boarhunt prior to dismantling, 1969.
J.R. ARMSTRONG/WDOAM ARCHIVE

Medieval Boarhunt

Boarhunt lies on the northern slope of Portsdown, approximately four miles north of Portchester in Hampshire. There are now two settlements, North and South Boarhunt, separated by the Wallington river. North Boarhunt, running northwards along Trampers Lane, is the more populous part, while South Boarhunt consists of a few scattered farms, the church of St Nicholas and the former manor house (now Manor Farm). During the medieval period, though, Boarhunt was divided into at least three manors – West Boarhunt, Boarhunt Herberd and Boarhunt Herbelyn – with a possible fourth manor of East Boarhunt. The principal manor was West Boarhunt, which appears to have been roughly coterminous with the parish of the same name (now known as South Boarhunt). In about 1190 this manor was given to Southwick Priory, a house of Augustinian canons approximately two miles distant, and in 1369 the priory also acquired the neighbouring manors of Boarhunt Herberd and Herbelyn. The hall house, which is now in the Museum, was situated a short distance from the church of St Nicholas and the manor house of West Boarhunt.[2]

The area around Boarhunt is classic 'woodland' or 'wood pasture' landscape – meaning an area of land characterised by a mixture of pasture, woods, arable and heaths, with some hedged fields. This was therefore a landscape with trees, in contrast to 'forest', which in the medieval period referred to any territory subject to forest law. Such forests were reserved to the crown or its lessees and were used for deer ranching, hunting and timber.[3] An excellent example is the Forest of Bere, which stretched for several miles from the Meon Valley to the Sussex border, just north of Boarhunt.

Because of the distance between the main settlement (North Boarhunt) and the medieval church and manor house, Boarhunt has been identified as a deserted medieval village (DMV). This would imply that it had characteristics in common with Hangleton. However, closer analysis shows that in the case of Boarhunt the population seems to have recovered quite rapidly after the Black Death, although it declined over the fifteenth century. At no point was the settlement deserted. The designation of Boarhunt as a DMV is based on an assumption that the medieval settlement would have been nucleated, as is common in other parts of south-east England. But in fact the area of Hampshire in which Boarhunt is situated was always characterised by dispersed settlements, typical of woodland or wood pasture landscapes. The evidence from the medieval records of Boarhunt shows that the late medieval population was scattered throughout the parish, with much of the settlement spreading northwards from Boarhunt Mill, past Staple Cross, Shoot

Hill and up as far as Hipley. In this sense it was not a 'village' at all, but should be described as a settlement or community.[4] It clearly was not a DMV.

In the early fourteenth century the peasant population of West Boarhunt is likely to have been about 180. In the immediate aftermath of the Black Death this shrank to between 120 and 135, but recovered relatively quickly to reach about 170 by the end of the fourteenth century. By 1470 it had again declined, to about 120, possibly as a result of the serious plague of the 1460s.[5]

Boarhunt's peasant community

Like the villagers of Hangleton, the majority of peasants holding land in West Boarhunt in the fourteenth century were unfree tenants, 'unfree' referring both to personal status and to tenure. However, whereas Hangleton is poorly documented, the survival of a custumal or survey for the manor of West Boarhunt, dated 1353, provides a detailed account of each unfree tenant's labour services. This is the entry for Stephen *Bercarius*, or shepherd:

> Stephen the Shepherd holds six acres of land which were Luke the Miller's paying for it 2s. 6d. per annum equally at the four principal terms [i.e. feast days] and he must reap daily in Autumn with one man and ... he will hold the lord's plough and tend the lord's sheep and he must plough seven and a half acres equally through three terms and if he will plough he will have lunch as a harvester and come after lunch to reap, but if he tends the lord's sheep he does not come to reap after lunch. And he owes churchscot of one cock and three hens and pannage for his pigs. And if he tends the sheep he can fold them on his land for twelve nights and have the 'belflus' [best fleece] and 'mirkynglamb' and ewes' milk on St John the Baptist's day. And if he will not plough nor tend the lord's sheep he must hoe for two days and carry fodder for the two said days and he will harrow by day as much as can be harrowed with one man and one horse.[6]

The distinction between unfree *status* and unfree *tenure* is important because, as we will see, by the early fifteenth century the majority of Boarhunt tenants were personally free, even if they held villein land. Two free tenants are listed in the 1353 custumal: John, son of W(illiam) atte Hale, and (illegible) atte Houke. John atte Hale was holding one virgate of land (about thirty acres) and another piece of land called 'le Coliare', for which he paid 2s. rent per annum, and owed suit of court and a *heriot* (or death duty) of a saddle and bridle. Houke held a tenement for which he paid 6s. 8d. per annum, and owed suit of court and a heriot. He also held two tenements for 4s. per annum.[7]

Boarhunt, as reconstructed at the Museum.
DANAE TANKARD

Here, as at Hangleton and any other medieval community, status could be acquired through office-holding. The manorial jury or *homage* usually comprised about a dozen men, chosen from the more substantial tenants of the manor. Besides their other duties they were responsible for the annual election of manorial officials, such as the reeve and the hayward. As we saw in the previous chapter, the reeve was responsible for the day-to-day running of the manor; the hayward or *messor* oversaw the mowing and the harvest. In Boarhunt there was also a woodward, a manorial official responsible for woodland and hedges, reflecting their importance in the local economy. Above the reeve was a bailiff, who was a salaried, and therefore professional, official, responsible for the management of two or three manors.[8]

Social and economic changes after the Black Death

At least a quarter of the population of Boarhunt died in the Black Death. As a result, Southwick Priory was faced with the immediate problem of a reduction in its income, because there were far fewer people to pay rents. It is not surprising, therefore, that in 1353 it chose to survey its manor of West Boarhunt, specifying the land held by each tenant, and the terms and conditions of their tenure. At the time of this survey, or custumal, peasant holdings were uniform in size: a virgate (usually about thirty acres but in Boarhunt probably closer to twenty), a half-virgate (about ten acres), a farthingland (that is, a 'fourthing' or a quarter-virgate), or four acres. The majority of peasant holdings consisted of five acres of land or less and were held in villeinage. The largest villein holding was the virgate of land held by Robert Kynch, for which

Boarhunt during dismantling, 1969.
J.R. ARMSTRONG/WDOAM ARCHIVE

he paid 2s. 6d. *per annum* and was required to provide labour services. At the other end of the scale, Philip atte Hale and William Couke each held a piece of purpresture land (an illegal encroachment, usually onto common land), for which Philip paid 6d. *per annum* and William Couke, two capons *per annum*. Three tenants, Henry Brese, William (surname illegible) and Hawysia Borgh, were effectively landless, each having just a cottage (presumably with its curtilage), for which they paid a penny *per annum*. Although 36 tenants and their holdings are listed in the custumal, seven of them were already dead, and their lands were then in the lord's hands because they had no surviving heirs. The lands of a further two tenants had also reverted to the lord, although whether this was because they had died or had left the manor is unclear. This evidence suggests that in 1353, five years after the outbreak of the Black Death, almost a quarter of tenant holdings were still vacant because the priory had been unable to find new tenants.[9]

The century and a half following the Black Death was a difficult time for landlords. Faced with a shortage of tenants, increased tenant mobility, and agricultural depression, they were forced to make customary tenancies more attractive, by 'improving' holdings (for example, by adding more land), lowering entry fines, and reducing or removing labour services (which were often associated with the direct cultivation of the demesne being abandoned). This period witnessed the gradual decline and ultimate disappearance of villeinage, both as a form of unfree tenure and as unfree personal status. In its place two, more advantageous, forms of tenure emerged: leasehold and copyhold. The most common form of leasehold involved holding land for a fixed term (normally for years, but sometimes for a life or lives) and for an agreed annual rent. The tenant paid rent levels at the market rate, which was generally higher than the rents attached to villein tenures, but was subject to no other obligations – and the tenancy was secure for the length of the lease. Copyhold emerged from tenancy-at-will, which meant that tenants held their land 'at the will of the lord' or 'according to manorial custom' but, unlike villein tenure, their obligations extended only to the payment of an annual cash rent, suit of court, an entry fine and a *heriot*. By the end of the fifteenth century tenants were receiving a written copy of the court roll entry recording the terms and conditions of their tenure, and hence they were said to hold 'by copy'. The security of copyhold tenure was increased further when it was recognised by the Court of Chancery at the end of the fifteenth century.[10]

By that date, therefore, the division of the peasantry into 'free' and 'unfree' had become irrelevant. Instead, there was a new social stratification, based on economic condition: there was now an upper rank of yeomen who might hold around 80 acres or more; a middle category of husbandmen; and at the bottom the labourers who held insufficient land to support themselves and were therefore obliged to work for others in return for wages.[11]

The shortage of tenants after the mid-fourteenth century meant that many peasants were able to acquire larger holdings, as well as gaining personal freedom, improving their tenure, and benefiting from higher wages. The standard peasant holdings of the period before the Black Death disappeared, as the land was reorganised and redistributed into larger and more efficient units, among a reduced tenant population. This was also a more mobile population, despite attempts by manorial lords to use their courts to prevent migration.[12]

Some of these changes can be identified in the manorial records of Boarhunt. A rental of 1396 shows that the traditional 'villein' labour services had been commuted to cash rents. By then only two tenants, John atte Shete and Philip atte Hale, were still performing labour services, although these were light in comparison with those listed in the 1353 survey: they each performed unspecified 'autumn' works, to the value of three shillings. By 1413 – the date of the earliest surviving court roll – unfree tenants were a small minority. In that year, of eight tenants fined for default (failing to come to court) only one, John Hay, is described as *nativus* (serf). The fact that the status of the remaining seven was unrecorded suggests that villein status was the exception rather than the norm.

On the other hand, the court rolls show that in the early fifteenth century villein tenure remained widespread, and the priory used the manor court to enforce custom. In 1418 the court recorded that, despite a previous order to Richard Leche that he and his family must occupy his villein messuage, they had continued to reside elsewhere. As a result the lord had taken it back into his possession. The seizure of a customary holding by the manorial lord was very much a recourse of last resort, particularly when replacement tenants were in short supply.[13]

These court rolls also reveal on-going problems with the enforcement of manorial custom. Tenants were abandoning their holdings or allowing their tenements to fall into ruin, their land being described as lying uncultivated, unoccupied or vacant. In 1416 John atte Brigge surrendered (gave up) his messuage and eight acres of 'uncultivated and unoccupied' land into the lord's hands. The priory was able to re-let this the following year to John atte Oldemulle, who paid an entry fine of five shillings. In 1418 Richard Russell 'refused' to hold a cottage, which therefore remained in the lord's hands, and William Waterman surrendered his cottage, described as 'completely decayed' as a result of 'waste and destruction'. The same year the priory began an inquiry into 'waste' on tenants' holdings. It is interesting that Richard Russell was already holding land in free tenure (discussed below), so his refusal to take up what was presumably a customary cottage might have been based on a reluctance to hold property by a less favourable form of tenure.[14]

To illustrate the problems that the priory was facing, we can look at the activities of John and Simon Roche, a father and son, as they are recorded in successive court rolls from 1413 to 1420. John Roche or his father may have been a relatively recent migrant to Boarhunt, since the surname does not appear in the 1353 custumal. They were possibly among those in the post-plague generation who were keen to take advantage of the changed economic circumstances. John Roche was holding a mixture of customary and free land in different parts of the manor. In the 1396 rental he is described as holding three (customary) cottages, for which he paid 2s. 3d. every quarter year. At the time of his death in 1416 he was also holding a messuage and three acres of villein (or customary) land from the priory, and a tenement (a complete peasant holding, with house, land and any outbuildings) in free tenure from Richard Russell. That might have been the property on which he lived.

In 1413 it was recorded in the manor court that John Roche had allowed his 'tenement' to fall into ruin, and he was ordered to repair it before the next court. It is likely that in this and subsequent entries the 'tenement' referred to was the messuage with its three acres. The fact that he was failing to maintain it suggests that he was

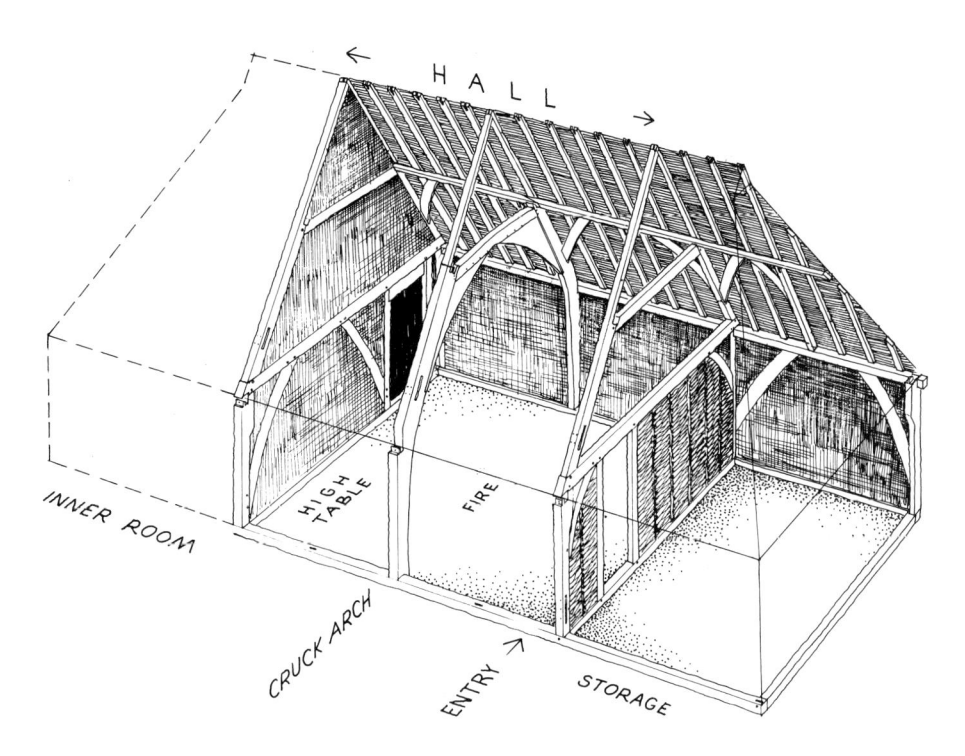

Cutaway plan of hall house, showing the cruck arch over the middle of the open hall.
RICHARD HARRIS

really interested in the land attached to the holding, rather than the house itself, which was surplus to his requirements. In 1414 he was fined threepence for allowing the ditch in front of his tenement to overflow onto the road, and again ordered to repair his tenement (described as ruined and decayed) before the next court.[15]

When he died in 1416 John Roche owed the court sixpence for allowing his 'tenement' to fall into ruin and threepence for removing manure and crops from the freehold tenement he held from Richard Russell, both debts for which his son, Simon, became liable. In 1417 the court recorded that no *heriot* was due on the death of John Roche, because he held his messuage and three acres of customary land in joint tenancy with Simon, who came into court to do fealty. In 1418 Simon was fined threepence for failing to repair his tenement, and ordered to do so on pain of a 20s. fine. The same court roll records that he surrendered a cottage with five acres of customary land, lying barren or uncultivated, into the hands of the lord, who re-let it to William Skryveyn for a fine of two capons. In 1420 and 1421 Simon Roche was again fined for failing to repair his tenement. After this the court roll series ends, and he disappears from view. It is possible, though, that he had no surviving sons because the name Roche does not appear in the 1470 rental.[16]

Boarhunt during dismantling, 1969.
J.R. ARMSTRONG/WDOAM ARCHIVE

This pattern of piecemeal accumulation of often quite small parcels of land continued into the fifteenth century. By the time of the 1470 rental there was no such thing as a 'standard' peasant holding. For example Thomas Blakeman held a messuage with a garden and sixteen acres of land that had previously belonged to John Aleward, and a toft, messuage and eight acres of land called 'Brigges', for which he paid 14s. *per annum*.[17] In contrast, John Forster held a messuage with a garden and four acres of land for 5s. *per annum*. In 1418 this land had been forfeited by Richard Leche, for failing to live on it. Both these holdings survived intact into the sixteenth century, when they are listed (with the same rental value) in an incomplete rental compiled some time between 1514 and 1521. By the 1520s the court rolls were distinguishing tenants as either 'free' or 'customary', and customary tenancies were being given 'according to the custom of the manor'. Customary tenants were still paying entry fines and *heriots* and doing suit of court. The court rolls for these years do not refer specifically to tenants holding their land 'by copy of court roll' but evidently some did: when the manor was sold in 1545 the indenture of sale between Thomas Wriothesley and Ralph Henslowe described a 'customary tenement or copyhold' called Collyns Close 'lately in the tenure of Thomas Henslowe'.[18]

Boarhunt being re-erected, 1980; a problematic reconstruction.
J.R. ARMSTRONG/WDOAM ARCHIVE

Another change in England after the Black Death was that manorial lords increasingly withdrew from direct cultivation of their demesnes and began to lease them to farmers for a fixed annual rent, along with other assets such as mills. Although this trend had already begun by 1348, falling grain prices and rising labour costs in the 1370s meant that the practice became widespread in the 1380s and 1390s. Farmers first appear as a distinct social group in the second poll tax of 1379, when they were placed in the same economic bracket as lesser merchants, franklins and innkeepers. The significance of this transition from direct management of demesnes to leasing is that the decision-making about land management on manors across the country passed out of the hands of the aristocracy and landed gentry and into the hands of a new breed of entrepreneurs, many of whom (in the late fourteenth and early fifteenth centuries) had their origins in the peasantry. In West Boarhunt the demesne was not leased out until about 1448, suggesting that the priory might have hung on to it for as long as possible in the hope that more favourable economic conditions would return.

As we have seen, however, the first half of the fifteenth century was a difficult time for the priory, with tenants surrendering their holdings, allowing their houses

Boarhunt rental, 1353.
HAMPSHIRE RECORD OFFICE, 5M50/82

to fall into ruin, and leaving their lands uncultivated. The cumulative effect of these years may have left the priory with no choice but to abandon direct cultivation of its demesne, with its attendant labour problems, and instead opt for the security of a fixed rent. The first farmer of the demesne (that is, the person who leased it) was John Knyght, who had previously been the manorial bailiff. Knyght was almost certainly a peasant, and possibly held lands in a neighbouring manor rather than in West Boarhunt itself. It is no coincidence that at about this date the manorial accounts record the cost of repairing the manor house, described as being in a state of great decay, and building a new kitchen. Landlords repaired manorial buildings in advance of leasing out the demesne in order to maximise their rental income and attract lessees of quality.[19]

Farming and the peasant economy

At the end of the fourteenth century the manorial demesne of Boarhunt comprised approximately 230 acres. In 1381 some 111 acres of land were being used for arable and 110 acres for pasture, with a further ten acres of meadow (to grow hay) and an unquantified amount of land described as 'underwood with pasture'. By 1398 the balance between arable and pasture had shifted: 90 acres were being used for arable (60 acres under plough and 30 acres lying fallow and 'in common'), and there were 131 acres of common pasture for 'large animals and sheep', with nine acres of 'rushy meadow'. This shift from arable to pasture was part of a general trend, reflecting the changed economic conditions after the plague. A reduced workforce of labourers, and rising wages, meant that animal husbandry became more profitable than the more labour-intensive arable farming. The description of 30 acres of arable lying fallow as 'in common' suggests that tenants had the right to graze their animals on demesne arable land when it was not under crops. This was a mutually beneficial arrangement, since the dung from the livestock manured the ground. The priory and the tenants of West Boarhunt and Boarhunt Herberd had rights of common for all kinds of animals on Walton Heath and Stroud Heath.[20]

No. 49 Southwick, likely to have been built around the same time as, or possibly slightly later than, the Boarhunt hall house.
DANAE TANKARD

Shepherds.
LUTTRELL PSALTER, BRITISH LIBRARY, ADD MS 42130, C.1325-1335

The arable field system in West Boarhunt consisted of a combination of open common fields and closes – enclosed parcels of land bounded by ditches and hedges. Each tenant probably held a mixture of land, some interspersed with the parcels held by other tenants in the common fields, and some enclosed. The crops on the demesne lands were wheat, barley and oats, grown in a three-course rotation: that is, the arable was divided into three courses or broad strips, with each being used in turn, first for winter grains, then for spring grains, and then let fallow. On the demesne of the neighbouring manor of Boarhunt Herberd beans, peas and vetches were also grown. The crops the tenants grew were much the same as those grown on the demesne: sixteenth-century probate inventories for the parish of West Boarhunt record wheat, barley and oats, rye and peas.[21]

The lord's sheep flocks were pastured with the sheep belonging to the tenants, on the downland on the north side of Portsdown. In 1421 John Borewell was presented in the manor court for killing a sheep worth 14*d*. with his cart on 'Portesdon'. In the mid- fifteenth century the priory maintained a flock of approximately 300–350 sheep in West Boarhunt, a small number in comparison with the flocks on the manors of the bishop of Winchester, which could number up to 2,000 animals. In 1450–51 the priory also had twelve oxen, twelve cows and twelve bullocks. The number of oxen suggests they were used for ploughing, and possibly for hauling as well. The cows were probably kept for milk, which was used to make cheese and butter. The tenants would have kept a variety of livestock, depending on their wealth and the size of their holdings. They paid pannage for the right to let their pigs forage in the woodland, the amount determined by the age of the pig: from 2*d*. for a one-year-old pig to ½*d*. for a weaned piglet.[22]

In a woodland community such as Boarhunt the wood itself was a valuable asset. The *woodward*, the manorial official responsible for its management, had the duty to 'present', that is report, to the manor court anyone who had infringed manorial custom – in this case, by illegally removing wood. For example, in 1476 John Maundevyle was presented for cutting down a *pepeler* (poplar) in front of his house, while in 1527 the woodward presented John Roper for cutting wood called 'hasylls' in Hamercley and the servant of Richard Snodden for cutting wood without licence. What this wood was being used for, and whether it was for commercial or domestic use, is a matter of speculation. Poplar had a variety of uses, including the timber framing of houses (although oak and elm were more favoured), and the production of household furniture and domestic implements such as spoons and bowls. Hazel was most commonly used for fencing or for wattling, but could also be used for making baskets.[23]

The labour services of some Boarhunt tenants included the requirement to bake loaves for the harvest workers. In the custumal of *c.*1220 five of the thirty-one tenants had to 'take turns to bake bread, using the lord's wheat and wood, for the boonworks'. In that of 1353 John Dummory, a villein tenant holding half a virgate of land, was required to take six bushels of grain (probably barley) to the mill, and then to use his own oven or bakehouse to bake sixty loaves of bread for the harvest workers. This would have been about a day's work, since it takes approximately two hours to bake twelve loaves. Four other unfree tenants (three holding half a virgate and one a farthingland) were described as owing the same services as John Dummory, so presumably were required to bake bread too.

Regular presentments in the manor court reveal that both brewing and baking took place on a commercial basis, with ale and bread being offered for sale within the community or the immediate vicinity. The assize of bread and ale was intended to ensure that the products sold by bakers or brewers within the manor met required standards of quality and quantity. In practice, presentments were not made for genuine breaches of the assize as such, but instead represented a form of licensing, whereby brewing or baking could be conducted without risk of further presentment if any breach were to take place. The bread that the priory gave its harvest workers was made of barley, but some of that consumed by the peasants was probably made with rye. We know that the tenants grew rye, and indeed one of the bakers fined in the manor court for breaking the assize was called William Riebred. In the early sixteenth century the bakers presented for breaking the assize of bread are described as 'common bakers of human bread', presumably in order to distinguish them from 'common bakers' of horse-bread, which was made of bran and peas or beans and fed to livestock.[24]

Like brewing and baking, cheese-making may have been carried on by many of the Boarhunt tenants to supplement their income from farming. Cheese production probably took place on a small scale within individual households, in the rooms identified in the sixteenth-century probate inventories as kitchens (which were integral to the houses rather than being free-standing bakehouses). For example, the 1557 probate inventory of Nicholas Gonwyn, an affluent husbandman, records that in the loft over the chamber he had 33 cheeses, valued at 16*s.*, and two shelves to put cheeses on, worth 6*d.*, and a further seven cheeses, worth 20*d.*, and a cheese press, worth 6*d.*, in the chamber over the hall. The probate inventory of Richard Lukes, made in 1559, records that he had six cheese 'mottes' (moulds), a butter churn and a cheese press worth 3*s.* 4*d.* in his kitchen.[25]

A large amount of fragmented pottery found in the 1970s in a small coppice known as Jack-O-Tooles Row is thought to have been a dump associated with a medieval kiln, the location of which has not been identified. The pottery, manufactured from clay, has been dated to the late thirteenth and early fourteenth centuries, giving at least some indication of when the kiln was operational. Pottery from this kiln has been found at Wickham, Portsmouth and probably at Portchester, and it is likely that it supplied other medieval settlements in the area, including Boarhunt. Although the pottery was fragmentary, it was possible to identify a range of domestic ceramics, including pitchers and jugs, cooking pots, curfews (fire covers), skillets and roof furniture (including tiles, ridge tiles and chimney pots).[26]

Peasant houses, c.1350–1500

After the Black Death the shortage of labour led to higher wages, which the Statute of Labourers of 1351 and subsequent legislation tried unsuccessfully to pin back. Labour legislation, together with the sumptuary legislation of 1363, which attempted to regulate clothing according to social status, were practical responses to a widespread perception that the Black Death had subverted social order, and that strenuous intervention was needed to keep things as they had always been 'until the world improves'. An anonymous sermon of the late fourteenth century, describing 'the plague of pride', observed that 'there is scarcely a villein today who is satisfied with his lot', and that 'little men are always bustling about to make themselves the equals of their betters – or even, if they can wangle it somehow, to make themselves greater than them'. The increased wealth of the peasantry was reflected in a rising standard of living – a better quality of housing, improved diet and a larger number of material possessions.[27]

Documentary evidence for medieval peasant housing on the manor of West Boarhunt is sparse, and there are no records that refer either to the dimensions of the houses of the tenants, or to their internal layout. The floor area of the hall house (as reconstructed) is c.679 square feet, which can be compared with two box-framed medieval cottages surviving in the neighbouring village of Southwick. The priory was there, and these dwellings almost certainly housed priory tenants. Number 30 Southwick, originally comprising an open hall, service bay and chamber, has a floor area of approximately 756 square feet, while no. 49 Southwick, partially destroyed by a lorry a few years ago, originally had a floor area of approximately 722 square feet. These houses are likely to have been built around the same time as, or possibly slightly later than, the Boarhunt hall house.

The fairly limited evidence for Boarhunt can be compared with what we know about peasant houses elsewhere in the country at this time. On the better-documented manors of Titchfield Abbey, most of which lay within a few miles of Boarhunt, peasant houses were typically of two or three bays, divided internally into a hall, a

Two men sawing a plank.
SMITHFIELD DECRETALS, BRITISH LIBRARY, ROYAL MS 10 EIV

chamber or solar at the upper end and (for three-bay houses) a service room at the lower end. Many dwellings had a barn, usually a detached building, and they might also have a detached bakehouse. We know from the 1353 custumal that some West Boarhunt tenants had their own bakehouses in the mid-fourteenth century. Extensive research on surviving building agreements for tenant housing in the West Midlands has shown that at least 80 per cent were of two or three bays, with floor areas of between 450 and 675 square feet. There was not necessarily a close correlation between the size of buildings and the amount of land tenants held: three-bay houses are found on holdings as small as a quarter yardland (about seven acres), while even larger houses of four or five bays might be built on relatively modest holdings. The weight of evidence strongly suggests that the Boarhunt hall house was fairly typical of peasant dwellings both in Hampshire and elsewhere in England in the period after the Black Death.[28]

Boarhunt probate inventories from the second half of the sixteenth century indicate that even at that date some tenants lived in two- or three-room open hall houses, like the hall house in the Museum. A good example is John Carter, a husbandman who died in 1570. He had a three-roomed house, with a hall, chamber and kitchen. The room described in Carter's inventory as the 'kitchen' was clearly the service room at the lower end of the hall, used for storage and food preparation (including dairying). Cooking and eating took place in the hall. The chamber was where the family (Carter, his wife and two daughters) slept and stored their linen, clothing and valuables (in his case, 20 lb of wool). The probate inventory of Roger Tyler, a husbandman, dated 1557, records two rooms: a chamber, containing a bed, bedding, chest and clothes; and a kitchen, which included pots, pans, a kettle, a 'broche' or spit, gridiron, pot-hanger and pothooks (as well as tools such as whip saws, axes and a shovel), suggesting that this room was being used for cooking as well as food preparation. By the late sixteenth century the Boarhunt hall house and others like it would have been old-fashioned, their low height making them difficult to adapt for two-storey living.[29]

On the manors of Titchfield Abbey the houses of the tenants were built by the abbey, although the tenants were responsible for maintaining them. If Southwick Priory was following the same policy it would explain why the hall house was built to such a high standard. We know that the priory was using specialist sawyers for its manorial buildings. The manorial accounts for *c*.1448 record the payment of 12*d*. to cart timber from 'Westwode' to South Fareham, to be sawn into boards to roof a 'skilling' (in this context, probably a wooden agricultural building), which was to be built within the manorial complex. The sawyer, Henry Jolyfe, was paid 3*s*. 4*d*. for his labour, the amount (for the job rather than per day) reflecting the skill involved. The roofing of the skilling was done by a local man, Henry Maundevyle (probably the father of John Maundevyle, mentioned earlier), for which he was paid 4*d*., the standard daily amount for a labourer at this date. This was for a building within the manor house complex, but a similar arrangement may have operated for the houses of the tenants as well. We can speculate that the hall house might have been among the new houses which the priory built at its own expense after 1350, in order to keep existing tenants from leaving the manor or to attract new ones from elsewhere. In common with the practice on other manors, the tenants of West Boarhunt were required to maintain their houses. As has already been described, the court rolls contain numerous presentments of tenants for failing to do so, and it was typically the same tenants who were presented in successive courts, although the nature of the repairs is rarely specified.[30]

Standards of living and material culture

As with Hangleton, reconstructing the material life of the medieval peasant household is difficult, but not impossible. Evidence from sixteenth-century probate inventories can be used as indicators, bearing in mind that late fourteenth-century and fifteenth-century peasant houses were likely to contain similar, but fewer, domestic items.

However, in comparison with the Kent probate inventories of 1565 discussed in the next chapter, those of Boarhunt contain a limited range of household goods, suggesting both a lower level of wealth and a less well developed consumer market.

The house itself provides some clues about how the hall might have been furnished. There is evidence that the cross beam at the upper end of the hall had a moulded dais rail fixed to it at doorhead height, which was almost certainly used to display some kind of wall-cloth or hanging. The arch braces beneath the cross beam add further visual significance to this part of the building. These elements suggest that when the hall house was built in the second half of the fourteenth century there was already a clear spatial hierarchy between the 'upper' and 'lower' ends, as is so clearly apparent in later buildings such as Bayleaf. John Carter's probate inventory records that at the time of his death in 1570 his hall contained a table, form and hangings, but no other furniture. The late fourteenth-century occupant of the hall house is unlikely to have had much more furniture in his hall – perhaps some stools and a chest. As was noted in the previous chapter, there is little documentary evidence for beds in peasant houses of the late medieval period; however, the fact that the hall house had three rooms instead of two, allowing one to be used as a sleeping room, might suggest that the upper chamber contained at least one bedstead, even if some family members still had to sleep on the floor. In 1570 Carter's chamber contained two bedsteads allowing him, his wife and two daughters to sleep in relative comfort.[31]

Cooking over the open hearth would require a 'broche' or spit, and a range of cooking implements, mostly of metal (iron, or latten, an alloy resembling fine-quality brass) or pottery. The most important was the cauldron, used for boiling food (the traditional method of cooking in the late medieval period). It is unlikely that peasant households would have owned any pewter in the late fourteenth century, although wealthier households might have had one or two pieces a hundred years later. However, ownership of even a small number of brass cooking-vessels (such as a cauldron or pot) would have provided some scope for social display. The hall might also contain eating and serving utensils, such as platters and trenchers, usually of wood; bowls and saucers of wood or pottery; and pitchers and jugs made of leather or pottery. Most food was eaten off communal utensils, such as trenchers, using a knife and spoon. The general rise in living standards that followed the Black Death is reflected in the food that peasants ate; they obtained a greater proportion of their calories from bread rather than pottage; they drank more ale, and they ate more meat.[32]

Detail of table at upper end of hall
RICHARD HARRIS

Detail of roof, showing curved windbraces
RICHARD HARRIS

Conclusion

Southwick Priory was dissolved in 1538, and the priory and the lands given to Thomas Wriothesley, later Earl of Southampton. Wriothesley sold the site and buildings of the priory to John White, who pulled the priory church down and took up residence in the other buildings. In 1545 Wriothesley sold the manor of West Boarhunt to Ralph Henslowe, 'gentleman', for £577, retaining the advowson and patronage of the parish church for himself. Ralph Henslowe, who became MP for Portsmouth in 1555, was the son of a yeoman called Thomas Henslowe, a previous farmer of the demesne and himself the son of a customary tenant. The rise of the Henslowes from peasantry to gentry within three generations is symptomatic of the changes that were taking place in rural society in the 150 years or so after the Black Death. For manorial lords the immediate effect of the mass mortality of 1348–50 was a reduced income from lost rents and a shortage of labour, exacerbated by a newly mobile peasant population. In order to fill vacant holdings and retain their remaining tenants, they were obliged to offer higher wages, to charge lower entry fines and to demand less onerous labour services. Over the course of the late fourteenth and fifteenth centuries villeinage both as a form of personal status and tenure disappeared, being replaced with more favourable leasehold or copyhold tenancies. Peasants benefited not only from the weakening of landlords' economic power, but also from the reduced peasant population, which enabled them to enlarge their holdings by the piecemeal accumulation of land. The wealth they were able to generate in this way is reflected in the greater survival of peasant houses from the late fourteenth century onwards, and in their new social classification as husbandmen and yeomen.[33]

The overall impression of Boarhunt in the late medieval period is of a small, scattered agricultural community, practising mixed farming combined with by-employment such as baking, brewing and dairying, and small-scale industrial activities such as potting. External trade links seem to have been weak, and many Boarhunt tenants may have had only a limited surplus produce for sale. Southwick Priory was a conservative landlord, keeping the manorial demesne in hand for as long as possible. Nevertheless, it was unable to resist the economic pressures of the post-plague years, and by the early fifteenth century the majority of its tenants were effectively free, with their labour services commuted to cash payments. By the sixteenth century its tenants probably held their land 'by copy of court roll', giving them greater security of tenure, and the division of the peasantry into 'free' and the 'unfree' had been replaced by a tripartite system of social and economic classification. The relative poverty of Boarhunt is reflected in the fact that in the second half of the sixteenth century husbandmen such as John Carter were still living in traditional open hall houses, with few material possessions.

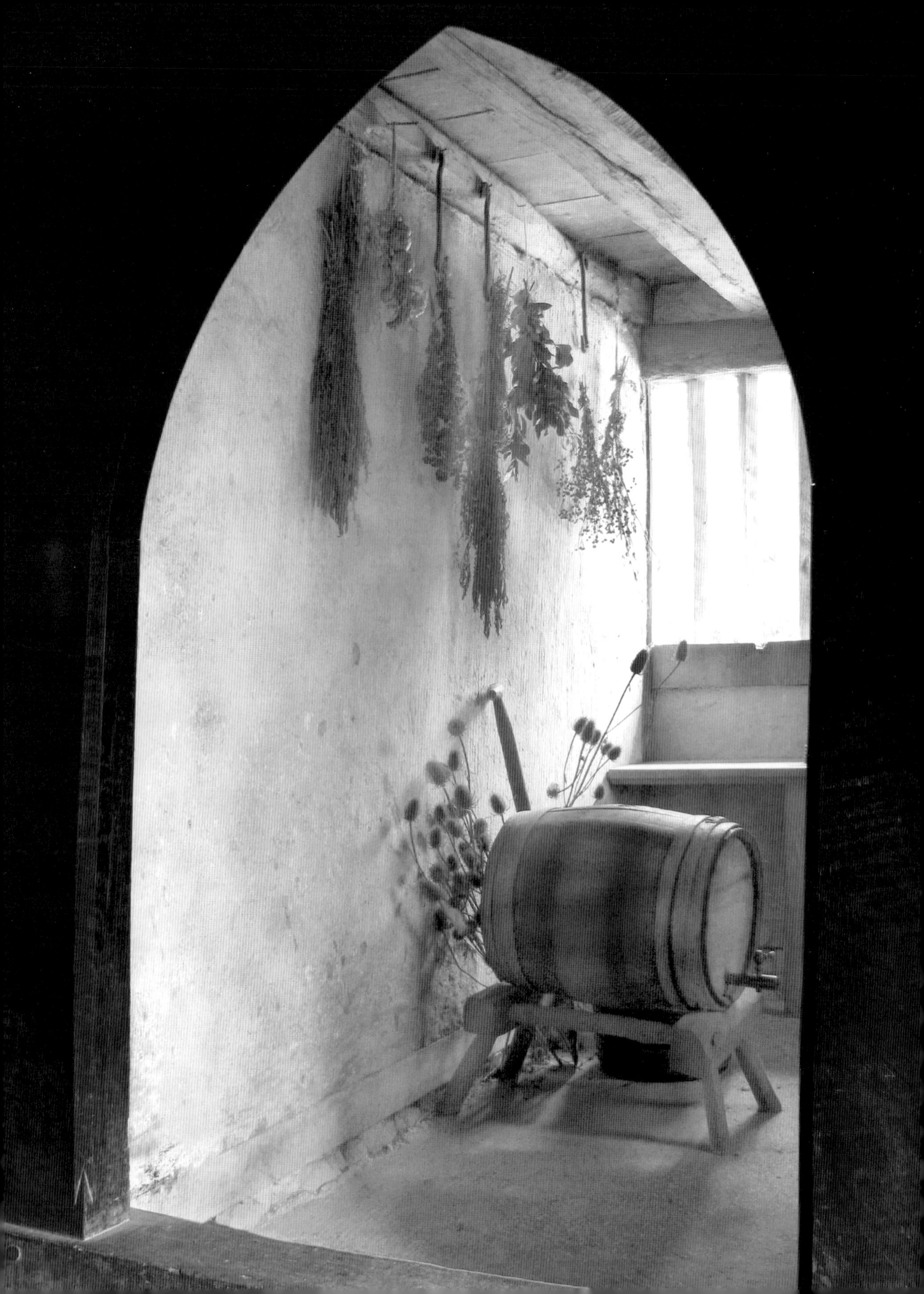

CHAPTER THREE

Bayleaf: a Wealden hall house from Chiddingstone, Kent

Bayleaf is a timber-framed Wealden hall house from Chiddingstone in Kent. It has six rooms, four on the ground floor and two upstairs, and was built in two phases. The earliest part, which has been dated by dendrochronology to 1405–30, consisted of an open hall and service end. This was probably attached to an earlier structure, which stood where the upper end bay now stands. The upper end bay, which gives the building its present form, has been dated by dendrochronology to 1505–10. By 1636 the open hearth had been replaced by a brick chimney stack and the hall had been ceiled over.

A Tudor farmstead has been recreated at the Museum by the addition of buildings that were not originally connected to Bayleaf. Thus, Winkhurst kitchen (c.1492–1537), from the neighbouring parish of Sundridge, is typical of the sort of detached kitchen that a house like Bayleaf would have had, while the barn (of 1536) is from Cowfold in West Sussex. There is also a farmyard, orchard and garden. The house itself has been furnished with replica furniture after a substantial research project coordinated by Richard Harris, the research director at the time.

Bayleaf was one of three buildings presented to the Museum in 1967 and 1968 by the East Surrey Water Company. All three were facing demolition to make way for

Bayleaf: view through doorway into the buttery, one of two service rooms at the lower end of the house.
RICHARD HARRIS

Bayleaf, as reconstructed at the Museum.
DANAE TANKARD

the new Bough Beech Reservoir. The first of the three buildings to be dismantled and placed in the Museum's store was Winkhurst House (now the Tudor kitchen), which comprised a two-bay hall open to the roof at one end and floored over at the other end to provide an upper chamber accessed by an internal staircase. Originally interpreted as a small house of late fourteenth-century date, it was re-erected at the Museum in 1969, set on its own at the top of a slope, becoming the first exhibit building. The second, Little Winkhurst, consisted of a much-altered four-bay open hall house with a kitchen added to the service end in the sixteenth century. This has not been re-erected at the Museum because the open hall part of the building was extremely fragmentary, and many of the timbers had become badly decayed after being stored for a long period in the open.

Bayleaf, the finest of the three buildings, was re-erected at the Museum during the winter of 1971–1972. 'Wealden' houses are particularly associated with the Wealden region of south-east England, but are also found in other parts of the country. Their characteristic features are the recessed front wall of the hall and jettying to the front

Bayleaf prior to dismantling, 1969: note the central brick chimney stack.
WDOAM ARCHIVE

of the upper and lower ends. A jetty consists of an upper wall projecting or jutting beyond the wall below, forming an overhang. The wall of each storey is constructed as a separate frame, the upper one being supported on the ends of the floor joists which rest on, and project beyond, the wall frame of the storey below. The projection of jetties varied from a few inches to two feet or more. The main advantage of jetties in urban houses on constricted sites was that they increased upper floor space by as much as 20 per cent. However, in rural areas they are primarily an architectural symbol of wealth and status and are typically restricted to the front of the house where they would be immediately visible to visitors and passers-by.

The entrance door to Bayleaf opens into a cross-passage, which is divided from the hall by short screens at either side of the wide opening. Structurally the building is of five bays; one for the upper end chambers, two for the open hall, one for the cross-passage, and one for the service end. The lower hall bay has no windows; in contrast, the upper hall bay has double-height windows, emphasising the importance of this part of the house.

The position of the hearth in the open hall is conjectural, but is based on the evidence of hearths discovered by archaeologists in similar houses. The smoke from the fire might have escaped originally through the triangular gablet at the service end of the house – the usual arrangement in other hall houses with hipped roofs – or through apertures formed in the ridge of the roof. In practice, most of the smoke seeps out through the gaps between the roof tiles. There is evidence in the rafters that a louvre had been built on at the service end of the hall. It is therefore possible that there was an intermediate stage of improvement prior to the insertion of a brick chimney stack when the hearth was moved to the lower end of the hall with a wattle and daub canopy to direct the smoke through the new louvre outlet.

When the brick chimney stack was dismantled a number of items were found hidden within it: a pair of worn and muddy shoes, three wooden lasts and some torn doeskin gloves. It is thought that these may have been deposited at the time the chimney was constructed or altered in 1636 as luck-tokens to ward off evil spirits. The practice of concealing clothing and other objects in buildings was common in the pre-modern period. They were usually hidden at entry or exit points, such as fireplaces, or in voids, such as sealed cupboards.[1]

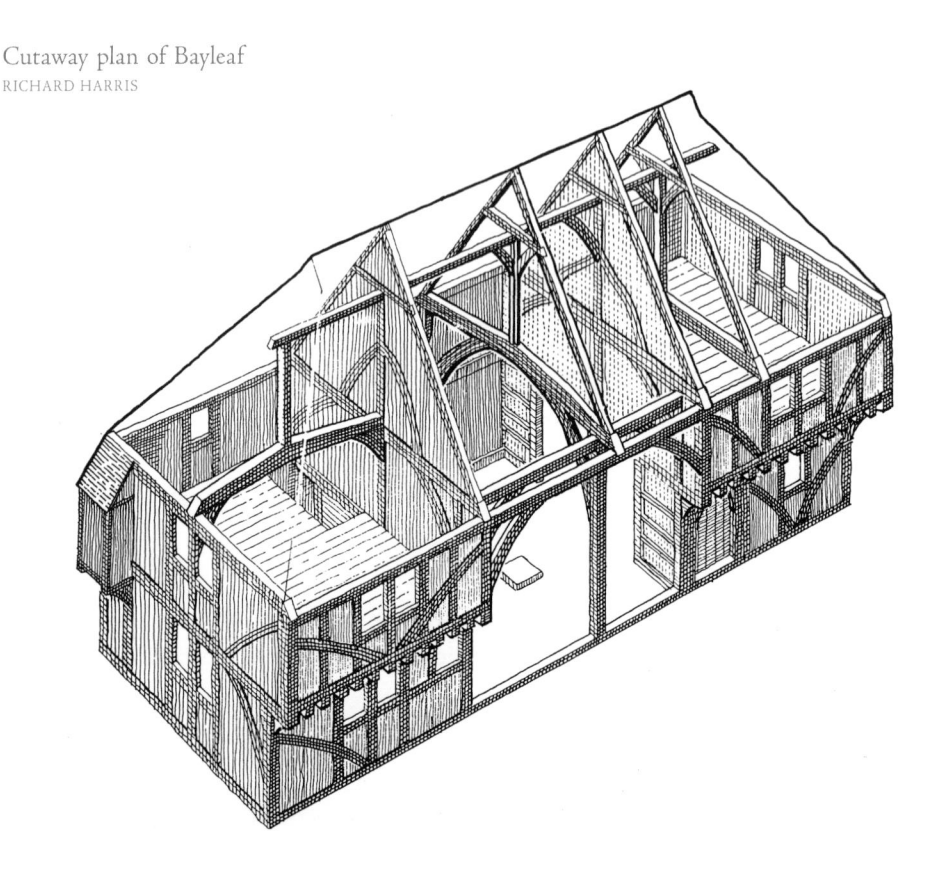

Cutaway plan of Bayleaf
RICHARD HARRIS

Bayleaf being re-erected, 1971
J.R. ARMSTRONG/WDOAM ARCHIVE

The Wells family

The occupants of Bayleaf were tenants of the 'gentry manor' of Bore Place. In the sixteenth century Bayleaf was inhabited by members of the Wells family, who were prosperous yeomen farmers and possibly carpenters. Surviving documentary sources are insufficient to provide exact dates of occupation, but we know that the first Thomas Wells held Bayleaf from roughly 1500 to 1510, and Edward Wells from then to about 1520. Another Thomas Wells was there from at least 1556 to about 1600. In 1520 a man called Richard Scoryar was holding the lease, but it is unclear for how long. He was certainly dead by 1541 when his widow, Katherine, was assessed to pay 10s. in tax.[2]

The only one of these men about whom anything is known is the second Thomas Wells, and he is therefore the focus of much of this chapter. It is unlikely that he was the son of Edward Wells, because this would imply that he was born before 1520. While it is not impossible that this was the case, he does not appear in the records until the 1550s, and the baptism register, which begins in 1566, shows that his wife was having children approximately every eighteen months between 1569 and 1578, suggesting a relatively young couple. He may have been the son of yet another Thomas Wells, who was presented in the Otford manorial court in 1520 (after Richard Scoryar brought an action of debt against him) and again in 1534 for trespass on the lands of Robert Peke. There was only one substantial male householder called Thomas Wells in Chiddingstone between 1565 and 1585, since only one person of that name is recorded in the parish rate book. We can therefore identify him confidently as the occupant of Bayleaf. When he died is unknown. The burial register ends in 1599 and, since his death is not recorded in it, he was presumably still alive at that date. There were other adult males surnamed Wells in Chiddingstone in the late sixteenth century – Ralph, Henry, Samson and John – all of whom had households of their own.[3]

The only probate material surviving for Chiddingstone in the fifteenth and sixteenth centuries is a group of fourteen wills which were proved in the Prerogative Court of Canterbury [PCC] between 1488 and 1600. Nine of these are the wills of yeomen. This was the most senior probate court and only catered for wealthier testators. The wills and probate inventories of the majority of Chiddingstone householders would have been proved in the ecclesiastical court of the deanery of Shoreham,[4] but unfortunately these were destroyed by fire long ago. No probate material at all survives for any of the men named Wells.

Bayleaf re-erected at Museum, prior to daubing, 1972.
WDOAM ARCHIVE

Bayleaf during reconstruction, showing position of crown posts.
WDOAM ARCHIVE

Bayleaf during reconstruction, showing jettying, an architectural symbol of wealth and status.
WDOAM ARCHIVE

Sixteenth-century Chiddingstone

The parish of Chiddingstone, containing about 6,000 acres and with an estimated population of 475 in the 1560s, is on the western side of the Kent Weald, close to the Surrey border. The village of Chiddingstone consists of a single street and the church of St Mary. Most of the settlement was (and still is) dispersed, scattered throughout the parish. Chiddingstone straddles the Low and High Wealds; the original site of Bayleaf lies in the Low Weald. The High and Low Wealds were distinct both demographically and economically, the former being more heavily populated and industrialised. Overall, though, the Weald was the poorest of Kent's agricultural regions, and within that region the western part was poorer, less industrialised and more sparsely populated than the remainder. The contrast with the central Weald, where the woollen textile industry was based, was particularly clear. However, in comparison with other regions within south-east England, such as the downland communities of Hampshire and Sussex, even the poorest parts of

John Fitzherbert, *The book of husbandry* (London, *c*.1530).
BRITISH LIBRARY

the Kent Weald appear affluent. Greater levels of personal wealth are reflected in the size and quality of surviving houses, while the proximity of London and continental trade networks meant that a wide variety of manufactured goods and imported foodstuffs were available to buy.[5]

In the late medieval period all land in the Kent Weald, as everywhere else in England, was either held of a lordship or directly from the Crown. However, manorial control in Wealden areas was weak, and the involvement of tenants with their manor was limited to paying a small annual quitrent or ground rent, doing occasional suit of court and paying a heriot (usually the best beast) for the right to take up land on the death of the previous tenant. A feature of the late fifteenth and sixteenth centuries was the emergence of what are often described as 'gentry manors' or estates in all parts of the Weald, the result either of successful estate-building by local residents, or of purchase by newcomers to the district. These estates frequently included land held of more than one manor. An example of this was the Bore Place 'manor' (more accurately described as an 'estate') which had lands in at least three different manors. The owners of Bore Place, like most other landowners in the Weald during this period, managed their property by leasing out large blocks of it, so that rents formed an important part of their income. Unlike some landowners, though, they retained demesne lands, which in 1518 included approximately 50 acres of arable and 150 acres of pasture, together with meadows, woods and parkland. This functioned as the home farm, supplying the needs of the Bore Place household, and probably the London residences of the owners as well. It also generated additional revenue through sales of livestock.[6]

The Bore Place estate was owned by a succession of eminent London lawyers, all of Lincoln's Inn, one of London's four Inns of Court. On his death in 1489 John Alphegh left Bore Place to his daughter, Margaret, and her husband Robert Rede, who had been ten years his junior at Lincoln's Inn. Rede was made a justice of the King's Bench in Westminster in 1494, was knighted in 1501, and in 1506 was made chief justice of the Court of Common Pleas. He maintained a London residence in the parish of St Sepulchre without Newgate. Three of his daughters married London lawyers, including Bridget, who married Thomas Willoughby, later Sir Thomas Willoughby, also of Lincoln's Inn. Another daughter became a nun at West Malling, eventually becoming abbess. Thomas Willoughby, who inherited Bore Place on Rede's death in 1519, enjoyed a successful career at the bar and in 1537 was appointed one of the judges of the Court of Common Pleas. He was a member of the Willoughby family of Wollaton near Nottingham, one of the richest gentry families in the midland counties: his brother was William, Lord Willoughby. On the death of Sir Thomas, Bore Place passed to his widow, Lady Bridget, who held it until her own death in 1558. It then passed to her grandson, Thomas Willoughby, who was also a member of Lincoln's Inn and maintained a London residence in Lincoln's Inn Fields. He died in 1596.[7]

Bayleaf farm

The origins and development of Bayleaf are unclear. The name 'Bayleaf' is a corruption of the word 'Bailey', and it has usually been assumed that this meant that it had been built to house the Bore Place bailiff. However, it is more likely that Bayleaf took its name from the original occupant, possibly Henry Bailey. We know that at the end of the fourteenth century Henry Bailey was holding about 100 acres of land in the area that later became Bayleaf farm, and that he died around 1430. He may therefore have been responsible for building the original house. The surname 'Bailey' does suggest that an earlier member of the family had been a bailiff, but by the fifteenth century the link between the occupation and the surname had clearly become historic. The earliest reference to Bayleaf ('Bayles') is in the will of John Alphegh, dated 1489, and it thereafter appears regularly in rentals and other documents throughout the sixteenth century as 'Baylys', 'Bailes', 'Bayleaze' and 'Baylies'.[8]

From the early sixteenth century Bayleaf is described as a 'fee farm', and the tenants paid an annual rent of 110*s*. (£5 10*s*.) to the owners of Bore Place. The description of the tenants as 'farmers' (*firmarius*), and the fact that they were paying a fixed rent, indicates that Bayleaf was being held on a long-term lease, for a term of years or for a succession of lives. The latter system involved naming specific people, usually three in number, and the lease lasted until the death of the last survivor. Without a surviving lease, though, the terms on which it was held are unknown. Because the tenants of Bayleaf were leaseholders they were unaffected by the custom of *gavelkind*, which was distinctive to Kent and was characterised by partible inheritance among male heirs (that is, land was split equally among them). When a survey of the Bore Place estate was made towards the end of the sixteenth century, Bayleaf had just over 100 acres of land. The survey indicates that at this time Thomas Wells also held another separate parcel of land of just over 50 acres.[9]

In 1556 Thomas Wells, described as a carpenter and farmer to Lady Bridget Willoughby, entered into a covenant with her to provide Bore Place with wheat and oats for a period of five years and, for a period of twenty years, to bring each year from London 'one sufficient wain load of such victuals and stuff as she or any other to her use shall buy and provide for her house [i.e. to Bore Place]'. The background to this arrangement is unclear; the fact that he was to receive nothing in return suggests that it might have been a condition of his lease. It is significant for a number of reasons: it is the only document in which Thomas Wells is described as a carpenter; it tells us that he was growing wheat and oats on his farm, that he was provisioning Bore Place, and that he had regular contact with London. In 1566 when Thomas Willoughby mortgaged Bayleaf to Richard Waters, with Thomas Wells as tenant, Wells was described as a yeoman.[10]

Probate inventory of William Goldfinch of Rolvenden, Kent, 1566.
CENTRE FOR KENTISH STUDIES, PRC 10/1/46

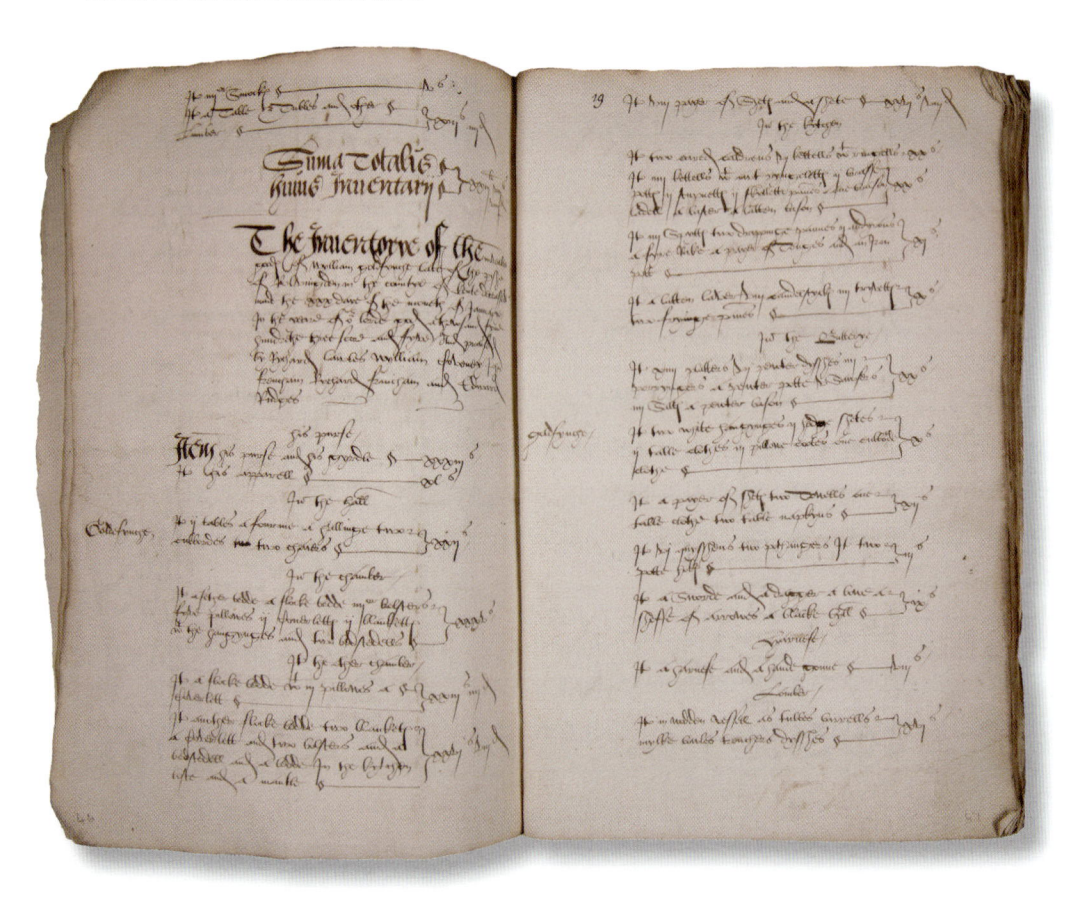

Social status and the Chiddingstone community

We have three occupational or socio-economic descriptions of Thomas Wells: in 1556 he is described as both a farmer and carpenter, and in 1566 as a yeoman. These are not mutually exclusive: 'farmer' simply meant that he was a leaseholder; 'carpenter' meant that he earned his living, at least in part, from carpentry; 'yeoman' described his socio-economic status, related both to his landholding and his wealth.

As we have seen in the previous chapter, by the end of the fifteenth century the large and rather amorphous group that comprised the 'peasantry' had become subdivided into three categories based on economic condition: yeomen, husbandmen and labourers. Historians define yeomen as large-scale farmers, usually farming at least 80 acres, sometimes holding land in more than one parish, and distinguishable from husbandmen by their superior wealth. They produced a large marketable surplus

Probate inventory of William Goldfinch of Rolvenden, Kent, 1566.
CENTRE FOR KENTISH STUDIES, PRC 10/1/47

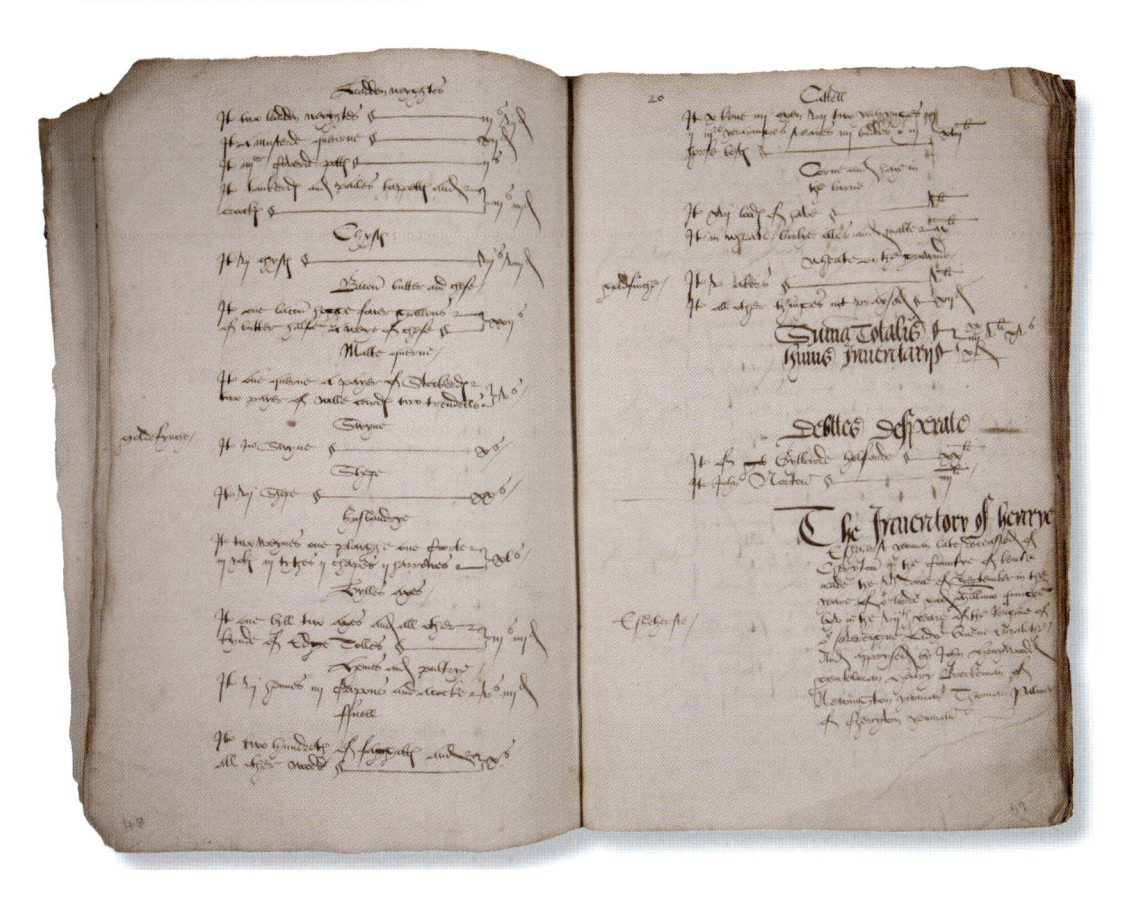

each year, and were regular employers of non-family labour. These men constituted a rural middle 'class', below the ranks of gentry but above the ranks of husbandmen and labourers. For an insight into the more subtle characteristics of this group we can look at the observations of a late sixteenth-century social commentator. William Harrison wrote his *Description of England* in 1577, and in a chapter entitled 'Of degrees of people in the commonwealth of England' he observed that 'we in England divide our people commonly into four sorts, as gentlemen, citizens or burgesses, yeomen, and artificers or labourers'. Yeomen, according to Harrison, were 'those which by our law are called *legales homines*, freemen born English, and may dispend of their own free land in yearly revenue to the sum of 40s. sterling, or £6 as money goes in our times'. 'This sort of people,' he continued, 'have a certain pre-eminence and more estimation than labourers and the common sort of artificers, and these commonly live wealthily, keep good houses, and travail [work] to get riches.' 'The fourth and last sort of people' were 'day labourers, poor husbandmen, and some retailers (which have no free land), copyholders, and all artificers, as tailors, shoemakers, carpenters, brickmakers, masons, etc.' The poor are excluded from Harrison's four 'sorts', and are discussed in a separate chapter in which they are themselves divided into three groups: the impotent poor, those who are poor 'by casualty', and the 'thriftless' poor.[11]

Harrison's observation that yeomen 'travail to get riches' distinguishes them from the gentry, since yeomen typically farmed the land themselves rather than earning rental income from it. In terms of wealth, however, yeomen could be as rich as, if not richer than, the minor gentry, and could enjoy a similar standard of living. As Harrison subsequently describes, yeomen 'often, setting their sons to the schools, to the universities, and to the Inns of Court, or otherwise leaving them sufficient lands whereupon they may live without labour, do make them by those means to become gentlemen'. In other words, yeomen were socially ambitious and were capable of promoting their sons to the ranks of the gentry by educating them at the right places and providing them with enough land. We saw an example of this at the end of the last chapter with Thomas and Ralph Henslowe.[12]

We know nothing at all about Thomas Wells' activities as a carpenter. The wealth levels and social status of rural craftsmen varied considerably: the wealthiest were on a par with yeomen; the less affluent were closer to husbandmen. Most craftsmen held some land, and part of their income would be derived from farming. Evidence from London, where carpenters were organised in a craft guild (the carpenters' company), suggests that the profession was not a very profitable one. However, outside London and the larger provincial towns the activities of carpenters were unregulated, which means that there are few details of how the craft was organised or of the wealth it generated. As a carpenter, Thomas Wells might have been responsible for building entire houses as well as commercial and industrial buildings. The more successful carpenters acted as architect-contractors, arranging for materials and sub-contracting with other craftsmen.[13]

Analysis of tax and poor rate assessments suggests that Wells was a wealthy man within his community – in the top 10 per cent of the Chiddingstone population – which would have made him a substantial and respected figure. This is reflected in his office-holding. In 1562 he was chosen as constable of the hundred of Somerden, an unpaid position that he would have held for two years. A hundred was a unit of administration covering a number of parishes, and as constable he would have overseen the collection of poor rates, the supervision of parochial officers and the maintenance of roads and bridges. Together with petty constables, who served for individual parishes or townships, the constables of the hundred were also responsible for controlling any disturbances within their communities.[14]

Under Harrison's system of social classification Thomas Wells would have belonged to the third 'sort' of people. By the early seventeenth century the use of a 'language of "sorts"' had become widespread, with the populace divided, broadly, into three 'sorts' – an upper sort, comprising those of gentry status and above, a middle sort, comprising yeomen, merchants, more substantial craftsmen and some husbandmen, and a meaner or poorer sort comprising anyone below this level, including labourers, poorer craftsmen and the parish poor.[15]

Poverty and poor relief

Between 1565 and 1566 Thomas Wells also served as one of two collectors of the poor, an office (later called overseers of the poor) that emerged from the developing poor law legislation of the sixteenth century.[16] As such, Thomas would have been responsible for assessing competing claims for parish funds from those unable to support themselves. The growth in population from the 1520s, coupled with rapid price inflation, meant more people were living in poverty, and there was a growing problem of vagrancy. The threat to public order posed by the increase in population was noted by social commentators such as William Harrison, who observed that 'Some ... do grudge at the great increase in people in these days, thinking a necessary brood of cattle far better than a superfluous augmentation of mankind'. The response of government was the promulgation of a succession of laws, beginning in 1536 with the requirement that churchwardens collect and account for weekly voluntary alms within the parish. Over the next decade some towns and cities replaced voluntary collections with compulsory poor rates. Legislation of 1552 moved towards the introduction of a national poor rate by requiring local registers of the needy poor and records of the weekly contributions of parishioners. In 1563 further legislation imposed fines on those refusing to be collectors for the poor and the presentment before justices of the peace of those refusing to contribute to the poor. In 1572 this 'voluntary' system of poor relief finally became compulsory: henceforth parishioners were to be 'taxed and assessed' to provide for the poor, and each parish was to appoint overseers of the poor to ensure its distribution to appropriate recipients.[17]

The poor in sixteenth-century England were not seen as a homogenous group, but were instead divided into two broad categories: those who deserved charitable relief, and those who did not (although, as we have seen, Harrison divided them into three categories). In most rural communities those deemed to be deserving of poor relief were small in number. They were individuals or families who were resident within the community, as opposed to migrants or vagrants from elsewhere. The commonest recipients were widows. Landless labourers might require assistance during the winter months, when they were unable to earn a living from agricultural work. Others might require occasional assistance as a result of sickness or accident. Dependency on poor relief was also linked to the life-cycle, with the very young and very old making up a substantial proportion of recipients. During their year as collectors Thomas Wells and William Bassett spent a total of 25s. 4d. on needy cases, including 6s. for a surgeon 'for healing of Richard Ebsted's leg', 12d. 'to the relief of Delton's wife and his children being sick', 18d. to 'Holland's widow', 18d. to 'father Bugges', and 5s. 6d. to 'Arnold for the relief of his sick wife'. We do not know how many applicants for poor relief Wells and Bassett turned away.[18]

As the sixteenth century progressed the punishment for vagrancy became increasingly harsh. In 1531 an act was passed that required vagrants to be whipped and then returned either to the place where they were born or to where they had last lived for three years. Beggars were to be licensed by the justices of the peace or face prosecution. In 1572 the act which instituted compulsory poor rates also required vagrants to be imprisoned and tried at the quarter sessions or the assizes. The punishment for being convicted of vagrancy was whipping and burning through the ear for a first offence, and hanging for a second offence. These punishments were evidently considered too severe, and whipping was restored in 1598. The Chiddingstone collectors made occasional payments to vagrants – in 1567 they paid fourpence to a 'poor wayfaring woman' – but most of the vagrants who turned up in the parish are only known to us because their deaths are recorded in the burial register: a 'way faring woman whose name could not be known' buried in December 1570, a 'strange man, a beggar' buried in March 1590, and 'a poor maid that went about' who was buried in January 1591. It is no coincidence that they all died during the winter months. The transience of this group is reflected in the fact that their names were usually unknown.[19]

Farming and the rural economy

The Weald was the poorest of Kent's arable regions because the combination of wet and heavy clay and dense woodland meant that natural drainage was poor and the soil relatively unproductive and difficult to work. Unlike other areas of south-east England, where farming was undertaken in communal open fields, Wealden holdings were separate and enclosed, usually in small, irregular fields. Wheat and oats were the most important crops, followed by peas and beans, which were grown mainly for fodder. Rye and barley were grown relatively infrequently and only in small amounts. The bailiff's accounts for Bore Place, covering the period 1513 to 1518, record that the only crops being grown on the demesne were wheat and oats, intended solely for the household's use. Additional grains – wheat, oats, and barley – were bought to supply the household, and, as we have seen, in 1556 Thomas Wells entered into an agreement with Lady Bridget Willoughby to supply the household with wheat and oats. In 1516–17 the bailiff, William Walker, accounted for nineteen quarters of wheat, fourteen of which had been bought. Six quarters of wheat were used as seed (three quarters in 1516 and the same in 1517), and twelve quarters were delivered to Margaret Kere, one of Sir Robert Rede's servants, with which to make bread. Walker also bought 45 quarters of oats and ten quarters of barley, all for the household's use.[20]

Most Wealden farmers had cattle, but fewer than half had sheep, and these were kept for household use, providing meat and wool for domestic spinning. The commercial value of cattle was in their meat and hides, with dairying limited to the needs of individual households. Some of the cattle reared in the Weald, especially by the more substantial farmers, were destined for the London market, and farmers in the area are known to have bought in cattle from the North Country and Wales to fatten before being sold on.

The Bore Place bailiff's accounts provide a detailed insight into how the livestock trade was organised in Chiddingstone in the early sixteenth century. In 1516–17 much of the stock that was raised on the demesne went to feed the lord's household, which probably means both Bore Place and Sir Robert Rede's London residence. Most of the livestock recorded in the accounts would have been transported 'on the hoof', sometimes over considerable distances. Walker sold livestock to individual traders over an approximately 40-mile radius from Chiddingstone. Among these was Stephen Davy of Gravesend, nearly thirty miles from Chiddingstone, who in 1517–18 bought four oxen, three steers (bullocks), one bull, two cows and forty sheep. He also sold seven oxen and six calves to a man called Draks of Southwark, nearly forty miles away, and eight oxen to 'a butcher of London'. The accounts suggest that after

Sir Robert Rede and Sir Thomas Willoughby, William Tideman was the biggest livestock dealer in Chiddingstone. In 1513–14 Walker sold him a mare and a horse, a cow and a calf, and a bay nag, and bought from him three oxen, three steers, ten heifers, and twelve oxen and steers. By 1517–18 Tideman was dead, and Walker dealt instead with his widow. While Walker seems only to have sold to individuals, he bought both from individuals and from fairs, including those held at Dorking (31 miles), Croydon (22 miles), Groombridge (10 miles) and Wrotham (18 miles).[21]

Cloth production was the predominant industry in the northern and central Weald of Kent, but not in the western Weald where Chiddingstone was situated. The most significant industry in that area in the sixteenth century was the manufacture of iron. Iron ore is found in almost every English county, but was particularly abundant – and easily extracted – in the Weald of Kent, Surrey and Sussex. Ironstone was mined in pits a few feet deep, and the ore was then processed at a bloomery, which could be either permanent or temporary. It was washed and roasted, which caused the ore to fracture so that it could be broken up into small pieces, and then smelted in a shaft or a bowl furnace powered by hand-driven bellows. The resulting metallic iron, called a bloom, was extracted with tongs and hammered and heated to remove the remaining impurities. The size of the furnace, and therefore of the bloom, was determined by the capacity of the bellows. Hand-powered bellows gave a very limited capacity, but the introduction of water power for bellows and hammers enabled smiths to increase their output from only a few kilograms to nearly a tonne of iron a day. On the continent waterwheels were used to drive hammers and bellows as early as the twelfth century, but the earliest known example in England, from Chingley in Kent, dated from the first half of the fourteenth century. The first English blast furnace was built at Newbridge in Sussex in 1496, a century after the technology was first used on the continent. The earliest blast furnaces were operated by skilled French and Flemish immigrant workers, but by the later sixteenth century the workforce was predominantly English. By 1550 there were about fifty furnaces and forges in the Weald, around Robertsbridge and Panningridge in East Sussex, and Tonbridge in Kent.[22]

The evidence for iron production in or near Chiddingstone before the 1580s is sparse, but there is sufficient to suggest that it was taking place, though possibly only on a small scale, from at least the early fifteenth century. The first surviving link between Chiddingstone and the iron industry is provided by a rental from 1420–21, which records the rents paid by John Alfey, 'irmonger', who was probably the father of John Alphegh, the owner of Bore Place. The smiths of the Kentish Weald had been supplying London ironmongers with small quantities of iron from as early as the thirteenth century. Ironmongers themselves were not involved with the production of iron or the manufacture of iron products, but they sold the iron, both unworked in rods and as manufactured goods. English iron was used for nails, horseshoes, wedges, spades and pickaxes, while iron from the continent was used to make siege engines and weapons.[23]

In 1542 Sir Thomas Willoughby leased various lands in Penshurst to Thomas Broker, smith, for a period of ninety years including a 'parcel of land that now the working forge of Thomas Broker stands on', for an annual rent of 2s. There was a furnace in Penshurst from at least 1550, on land leased by Ninian Burrell to Sir Nicholas Pelham. In 1589 Thomas Willoughby sold for £1,074 to Thomas Browne, 'forgemaster', 160 acres of land in Chiddingstone and Hever, known as 'Dudendene', Bough Beech, and 'Clinton' lands, together with 'all manner of furnaces, houses, buildings, waters, ponds, bays, woods, underwoods, profits and emoluments', plus 22 acres 9 poles of land called 'Cransted lands and gravel pits' in Chiddingstone and some small parcels of meadow. Like the lease of the working forge, this was clearly being sold as a going concern, indicating an earlier history for the furnaces, although documentary confirmation of this is lacking. There is archaeological evidence for two furnaces in Chiddingstone, both water-powered. All that remains of one is the pond bay and spillway, although a heavy scatter of slag, brick and tile indicates the approximate site of the furnace house. The location of the other furnace is reflected in the place-names Furnace House, Furnace Field, Furnace Bank and Pond Mead, and indicated by the discovery of glassy slag and forge cinder. It is likely that there was at least one forge nearby.[24]

In 1596 Thomas Browne began legal proceedings in the Court of Chancery against Richard Snelling of Lewes, in a dispute about the sale of iron. In his bill of complaint Browne alleged that he was unable to repay Snelling the sum of £200 after failing to deliver fifteen tons of iron, because 'he does daily disburse great sums of money by necessity of his trade for that he keeps always at the least one hundred and fifty men at work'. Even if the figure is exaggerated, this meant that he was among the biggest employers in the area. Iron-making was a seasonal trade, so the men Browne employed were likely to have had other occupations or smallholdings to support themselves when they were not working for him.[25]

Household size and structure

The concept of the 'household' in the late medieval and early modern period meant a group of people (including servants) living under the same roof, under the authority of the household head – who was usually an adult male. In terms of family structure, English households were typically nuclear, consisting of a husband and wife and their children. Complex, or three-generation, families were rare. The average size of sixteenth-century households was between 4.5 and 5 persons, but any such figure disguises wide variations. By and large wealthier households were larger: not only did they have more surviving children, but they were far more likely to have resident servants. In contrast, therefore, poorer households tended to be smaller households. Young couples were expected to establish households when they married, but in the sixteenth century the average age at first marriage was relatively late – about 26 for women and 27–29 for men – although this varied within individual regions and communities and among different socio-economic groups.[26]

We can use details of testamentary bequests in the small number of surviving PCC wills for Chiddingstone yeomen to estimate average household size within this group. For yeomen, the average number of children listed as beneficiaries was 5.5, with the smallest family having three children and the largest two families having eight. This gives a higher than average household size (excluding servants) of 7.5, assuming the survival of both parents and the co-residence of children at least up to adolescence. This is consistent with what we know about the family of Thomas Wells from the parish register covering the period 1565 to 1599. The baptism register records the birth of five of his children within a ten-year period – three boys and two girls. By this date he already had at least one son, Thomas (there is a record of his burial in 1572). The five christenings were those of Percival (12 June 1569), who died in 1571; Anne (7 October 1571); Henry (27 September 1573); Ralph (17 January 1576); and Martha (2 November 1578). A 'snapshot' of the Wells family in December 1578, at home in Bayleaf, would therefore find Thomas and his wife (her name is unknown), Anne (7), Henry (5), Ralph (2) and Martha (1 month). There may also have been one or two older children whose births predate the start of the baptism register and who survived to adulthood.[27] If we allow for this possibility, we can postulate a household of between six and eight people in 1578, excluding servants.

Another characteristic of yeomen which, Harrison felt, distinguished them from the gentry was that they had servants who 'get both their own and part of their master's living', in contrast to the 'idle servants' of gentlemen. What he means is that yeomen's servants were essential to the economic livelihood of their master, rather than merely reinforcing his social status. In the early modern period the majority of adolescents entered some form of service or apprenticeship, from their mid-teens onwards. 'Life cycle' servants such as these would remain in service until they got married, and then establish their own independent households. They usually lived with their employer, and might be engaged in domestic or agricultural work. Evidence from Chiddingstone PCC wills suggests that a yeoman household such as that of Thomas Wells would have had one or two living-in female servants. The fact that such servants are often named as beneficiaries in these wills suggests that their employers valued them, wishing to reward them for their service. When William Woodgate, a wealthy yeoman, died in 1541 he left a cow and a sum of money to each of his former servants, Parnell Granger and Joan Warde, and to each of his current servants, Margaret Warde and Julian Halle. The male equivalent of these young women was the 'servant in husbandry', who worked alongside his master on the farm. None of the surviving wills specifically records this type of servant, so it is unclear how widely they were employed in Chiddingstone households. If we estimate that a 'typical' yeoman household in sixteenth-century Chiddingstone included two female servants, the average household size increases to between eight and ten people.[28]

A large gentry household such as Bore Place included a wider variety of servants, some carrying out more specialised tasks for the duration of their working life. Sir Thomas Willoughby's will of 1545 distinguishes between waiting servants, women servants and husbandry servants, although it does not give either their names

Bayleaf privy.
RICHARD HARRIS

Bayleaf buttery.
RICHARD HARRIS

or numbers. When Lady Bridget, his widow, died in 1558, she made bequests to William Bassett, her rent collector; William Wells, her bailiff; two waiters, and two 'men labourers'; Agnes Heyward, her maidservant; three other maidservants; and Bridget Aware, her former servant. The status of the servants within the household is reflected in the value of the bequests she made to them. William Bassett, who witnessed her will, received a grey gelding; Agnes Heyward received 40s., the two waiters 20s. each, and William Wells, the two labourers and the three maidservants 13s. 4d. each.[29]

The sixteenth-century house

With Bayleaf we are in the last phase of the medieval domestic plan. The sixteenth century was a period of transition. Architectural surveys show that many houses in Kent retained their open halls until the late sixteenth or early seventeenth centuries, and new open hall houses were still being built in the first half of the sixteenth century. However, the conversion of traditional houses by the insertion of a wooden or brick chimney stack, and the ceiling over of the hall, began in the early sixteenth century. Two-storey houses with enclosed fireplaces were being built from the first decade of the sixteenth century onwards. This mixed picture is corroborated by evidence from Kent probate inventories (which survive from 1565 onwards), which show that at that date some houses had ceiled-over halls ('the chamber over the hall'), while in others they were still open. The date at which Bayleaf was converted is unclear. When it was dismantled a brick was found in the chimney inscribed with the date 1636, which might suggest a relatively late date for conversion. However, there may have been an intermediate phase of development prior to this when the hearth was moved to the lower end of the hall with a wattle and daub canopy to direct the smoke through a newly constructed louvre outlet in the roof. This sequence of 'chimney' development is seen in other surviving medieval houses, such as the Museum's house from North Cray, which had a smoke bay built in the location of the open hearth in the sixteenth century, followed by a large brick chimney stack in the seventeenth century.[30]

Bayleaf follows the conventional late medieval plan of a communal open hall, with service rooms at the lower end and a private chamber at the upper end, probably called the parlour. This could have been used both as a private sitting room for the householder and his wife and as an additional bedchamber. Upstairs there are two further chambers, which would have been used for sleeping and storage. Even without the integral privy the chamber at the upper end of the house would have been the principal bedroom. It has been suggested that the chamber at the lower end would have been the servants' room, but this is far from certain. Some of the yeomen's houses described in probate inventories do record separate rooms for servants – for example, John Gorney of Eythorne had a 'servants' chamber' containing four beds in a house that was similar in size to Bayleaf. In other instances, though, the servant or servants seem to have slept in the same room as their master. John Redborowe's house had a 'chamber over the parlour' which contained a 'bedstedle with one other feather bed with the apparels to the same bed', '1 old mattress with the furniture of a servant's bed', and '1 old flock bed for a servant's bed'. It is probably safest to conclude that the sleeping arrangements of the various occupants of Bayleaf depended on the size of the household at any particular time.[31]

After houses and barns, detached kitchens were the most common type of building in south-east England in the fifteenth and sixteenth centuries. Very few have survived, and those that do are typically large, multi-room, two-storey buildings. These might more accurately be described as 'service blocks', with downstairs rooms used for baking and brewing and upstairs rooms providing storage and additional sleeping accommodation. Many kitchens are likely to have been little more than a single-room, single-storey outhouse. Detached kitchens were usually located at the back of the house near the lower end, and were accessed through the rear doorway. In some instances they were connected to the house by a covered passage. By the sixteenth century detached kitchens were going out of use; instead, kitchens came to be integrated within the main range of the house, frequently as an additional bay beyond the service end. Other services previously associated with the detached kitchen, such as brewing and baking, were relocated to outshuts, attached to the exterior of the house.[32]

When the ex-Carthusian monk and medical author Andrew Borde published his *Book of Knowledge* in 1542 he included the following advice on domestic sanitary arrangements:

> Beware of pissing in drafts and permit no common pissing place be about the house or mansion; and let the common house of easement be over some water, or else elongated from the house. And beware of emptying piss pots and pissing in chimneys, so that all evil and contagious airs may be expelled, and clean air kept unputrified.

Borde's advice that the 'house of easement' (or privy) should be set away from the house reflected the prevalent view that 'dirty' activities should be at a distance from the main living areas. It is probably for this reason that integral privies – such as the one that has been reconstructed in Bayleaf – were relatively rare. There are no surviving original examples, but structural evidence shows that such privies projected from the end of the wall, usually at the back of the house. They could be located at the upper or the lower end, and usually there was some kind of structure or chute below to collect the waste.[33]

One of the most famous passages from Harrison's *Description of England* is his account of the domestic changes that had taken place within his lifetime. According to Harrison, 'there are old men yet dwelling in the village where I remain which have noted three things to be marvellously altered within their sound remembrance'. The first was the 'multitude of chimneys lately erected, whereas in their young days there were not above two or three'. The second was 'the great (although not general) amendment of lodging, for (they say) our fathers, yea, and we ourselves also, have lain full oft upon straw pallets, on rough mats covered only with a sheet, under coverlets made of dagswain or hap-harlots (I use their own terms),[34] and a good round log under their heads instead of a bolster or pillow.' Now, he claimed, men expected to lie on a feather or flock bed and at least to have chaff pillows. The third change was 'the exchange of vessel, as of treen [wooden] platters into pewter, and wooden spoons into silver or tin'.[35]

While we might be suspicious of his claim that men had formerly lain their heads on a 'good round log', Harrison's general point – that the standard of domestic 'comfort' had increased over the course of the sixteenth century – is consistent with what we know from other sources. However, the benefits were not universally felt. The village where Harrison lived was in Essex, a county which, like Kent, occupied a relatively privileged position in terms of personal wealth and access to material goods. By the mid-1560s, when Kent probate inventories begin to survive in considerable numbers, many households already contained feather or flock beds, bolsters and pillows and a variety of pewter tableware, although furniture in their halls continued to be sparse – a table with its frame, a form or bench, some chairs and stools and the occasional cupboard. Few houses contained upholstered chairs, but some had cushions and many had painted wall-hangings. More extensive analysis and comparison of probate inventories surviving for Cornwall and Kent during the period 1600 to 1750 shows that in the first half of the seventeenth century Kent households contained a much higher proportion of new types of furniture such as court cupboards, and a greater number and variety of chairs and tables. More of their chairs were upholstered, and they were more likely to have cushions and featherbeds. Kent households also had a greater variety of cooking and hearth equipment, more pewter and more linen.[36]

Conclusion

During Bayleaf's forty-year history at the Museum it has frequently been said that its occupants were the bailiffs for Bore Place. There are two reasons for this: the first is because its name was believed to be a corruption of the word 'bailiff'; the second is the reference to 'William Wells my bailiff' in Bridget Willoughby's will of 1558. The first of these has been addressed: the name is in reality a corruption of 'Bailey' and probably indicates that the house was built by or for Henry Bailey. Regarding the second point, it is reasonable to assume that William Wells was related to Thomas Wells, but he was not living in Bayleaf and may not even have lived in Chiddingstone, since his name does not appear in parish records or taxation lists. Moreover, we know that during the tenancy of Edward Wells at Bayleaf the Bore Place bailiff was a man called William Walker. But though the postulated link between 'Bayleaf' and 'bailiff' may be false, it is clear that the occupants of Bayleaf did have a close relationship with Bore Place. Bayleaf was a substantial farm, geographically close to Bore Place and economically tied to it by the requirement that it provide the gentry household with grain. The 'returns' for the Wells family may have been in social capital rather than hard cash, as their status and reputation were enhanced within the local community.

Chiddingstone stands out from the other medieval and early modern communities considered in this book because of its closer proximity to London, its affluence, and the presence of a substantial rural industry. Bayleaf is the best known of the Museum's houses and – in the words of Richard Harris – has become 'iconic', appearing in photographs and paintings in books and on people's walls throughout the world, as well as on jigsaw puzzles, tapestries, tea-towels and as three-dimensional models. As a house type its significance is even more pronounced, because it represents the last phase of the open hall tradition. As such, it looks both backwards and forwards: backwards, in the continued use of an open hall with a centrally located hearth and clearly distinct upper and lower ends; forwards, because of its upper chambers and the increasingly specialised use of space for food preparation and storage.

The reasons for the decline of the open hall are unclear. The technology of chimney construction was already available, and the cost of adapting traditional houses was not excessive. Historians generally agree that the reasons should be sought in wider social and cultural changes, but proving a causal connection is not easy and is made more complicated by the lengthy process of transition to the fully 'closed' house plan. By the late sixteenth century, however, a new house type was becoming common, finally replacing the medieval house plan that had endured for the best part of four centuries.

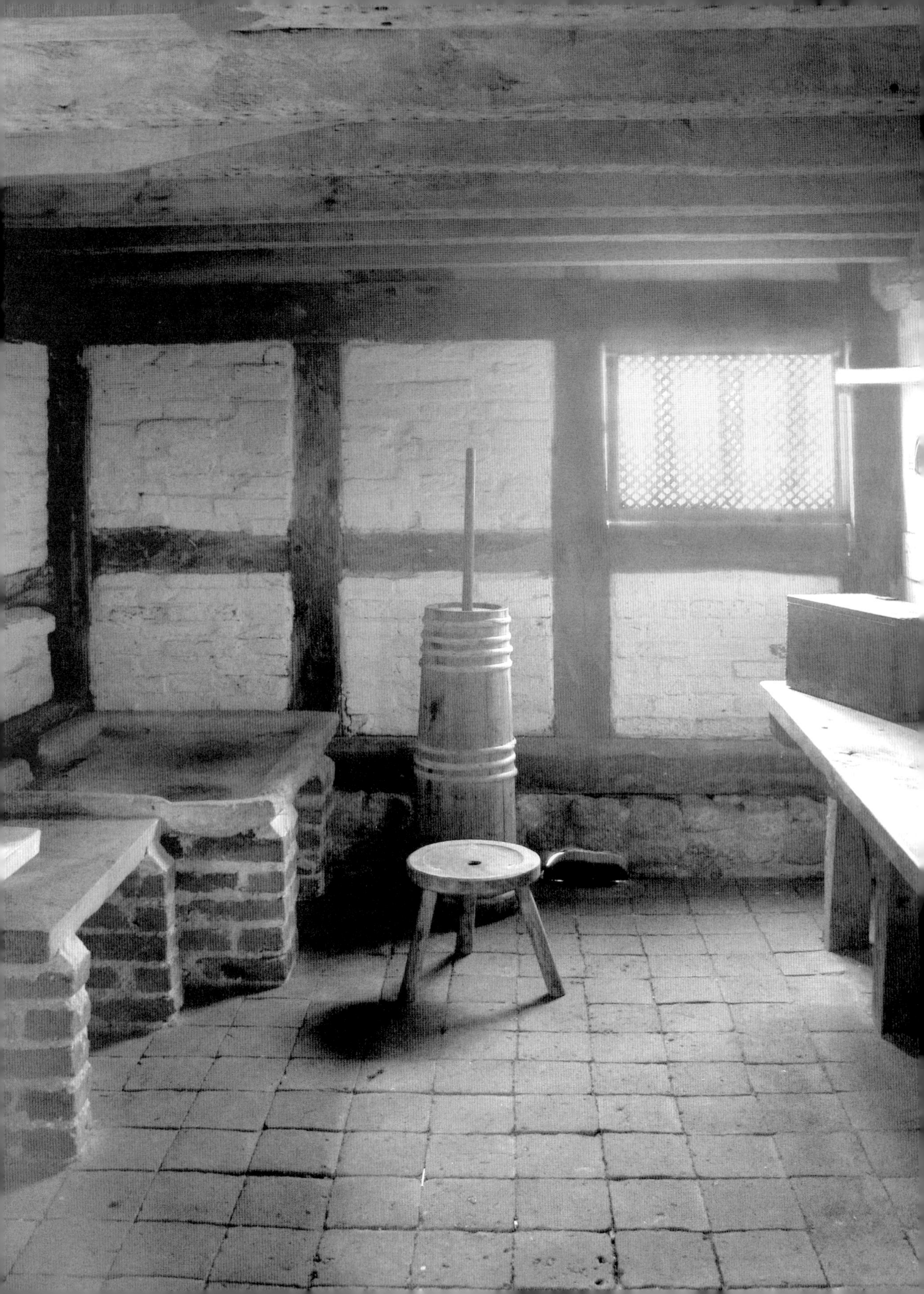

CHAPTER FOUR

Pendean: a yeoman's house from West Lavington, West Sussex

A 'closed' house

In 1953 W. G. Hoskins published an article that had a profound effect on the development of vernacular architecture studies. He argued that the period 1570 to 1640 was marked by 'a revolution in the housing of a considerable part of the population', a phenomenon he characterised as 'the Great Rebuilding'. Existing houses, he said, were adapted by the insertion of chimney stacks, while new fully two-storey houses were built. Hoskins attributed this unprecedented wave of rebuilding to three main causes: rising levels of wealth among the middling classes, a growth in population, and an increasing desire for privacy. Hoskins' idea, and the methods he used to support it, are now generally regarded as untenable, because we have a more sophisticated understanding of vernacular buildings and of the wider social and economic changes during this period. Nevertheless, it is still reasonable to argue that by the late sixteenth century the traditional domestic plan had undergone a 'revolution' in the sense that the open hall, with its well defined upper and lower ends, had gone for ever, and a new domestic plan, of a type that is essentially still familiar to us today, had emerged.[1]

This new domestic plan is clearly visible in Pendean, a timber-framed house of the three-unit lobby entry type, with an internal axial chimney stack and back-to-back fireplaces. Houses like Pendean, which could alternatively be of two units, became

Pendean: the milkhouse or dairy.
RICHARD HARRIS

Pendean, as reconstructed at the Museum.
DANAE TANKARD

common from the late sixteenth century onwards; such houses have been described as 'closed', to distinguish them from their 'open' hall predecessors. Dating of Pendean's timbers revealed that they had been felled in 1609, confirming that the house was built at around that date.[2]

Pendean's chimney is a sophisticated construction with four flues; the two back-to-back fireplaces, a small fireplace in the best bedroom above, and a flue that presumably conducted warm air from the back of the inglenook to circulate in the upper part of the house. In addition, there is a round vent at first-floor level leading into a wooden-sided smoke chamber for curing meat and fish. The changes to the domestic plan were accompanied by external structural changes such as the use of square panel framing and brick-infill, which updated the appearance of the front of the house. Internal structural changes included the use of side purlins in the roof in place of down braces and crown roof post construction seen in earlier houses such as Bayleaf. The house nevertheless retained 'medieval' features, such as unglazed windows with diamond-shaped mullion bars, upper floor rooms still open to the rafters, and wattle and daub used throughout the interior partitions and for the outer wall panels of the upper storey. There was a clear distinction between the quality of the wattle used on the upper panels of the outer walls and that used for the interior partitions, the former being entirely of split oak, while the latter used hazel for the horizontal weave.

Pendean was one of the first buildings acquired by the Museum. It was presented to the Museum in 1968 by Messrs Hall & Co. (who had obtained permission from the Ministry of Housing and Local Government to demolish it) and was dismantled in the winter of 1968–69 with the help of a £400 grant from West Sussex County Council. Although protected under the 1947 Town and Country Planning Act, demolition was permitted to allow the digging of industrial sand-working pits.

In comparison with some of the other buildings at the Museum, Pendean had been altered little since its original construction. In the later seventeenth century two additional outshuts were added to the east and north-east sides, and the location of the oven and staircase had changed; it was converted into two cottages in the late eighteenth or early nineteenth century, and had returned to being a small-scale farm in the twentieth century. This meant that to rebuild it as it was first designed presented fewer problems than was the case with Bayleaf. Its reconstruction involved little more than the omission of the two outshuts, the second flight of stairs and the partitions that had been added when it was divided, and the restoration of the original windows (mortices for which remained in place), instead of the varied assortment of casements, wood and metal windows inserted from the seventeenth to the twentieth centuries. The house opened as an exhibit in 1976.[3]

In 2000 and 2001 the Museum undertook a substantial re-interpretation project for Pendean with the help of a grant from the Government's Designation Challenge Fund. A number of structural changes were made to the house, including the rebuilding of the chimney stacks and the replacement of a 'ladder' staircase with a typical early seventeenth-century stair with winders at the bottom, which was easier for visitors to climb. The interior brickwork of the chimney was colour-washed using a technique known as 'ruddling and pencilling' to make it appear more uniform

Pendean prior to dismantling, showing position of north-east outshuts, 1968.
J.R. ARMSTRONG/WDOAM ARCHIVE

Pendean prior to dismantling, showing position of north-east and south outshuts, c.1940.
WDOAM ARCHIVE

and of higher status than it actually was, and the interior of the brick infill panels was lime-washed. Although there was no direct evidence for internal paintwork in Pendean, we know that this form of decoration was extremely common in the seventeenth century. The house was furnished with replica oak furniture, domestic utensils and soft furnishings. Finally, a timber-framed pigsty with an integral human privy was built to the rear of the house.[4]

Seventeenth-century Woolavington

The farm called Pendean was originally situated about one mile south of Midhurst, in a detached portion of the parish of Woolavington (now West Lavington) and within the manor of Woolavington. Its immediate neighbours were two larger farms, Hurstlands to the south comprising 100 acres, and Balls Farm to the north comprising 140 acres. There was also a watermill called Costers Mill north of Pendean, on a tributary of the river Rother.[5]

The manor and parish of Woolavington, with a population of about 150 in the seventeenth century, were split into two parts: one lay east of Graffham (and is now called East Lavington) and the other south of Midhurst (now West Lavington). The two halves of the parish were almost four miles apart and, because the church of Woolavington was in the eastern part, residents of the detached western portion were baptised, married and buried in Midhurst parish church and presumably attended services there too. A church was finally built in the detached portion in 1851, and it became a separate parish.[6]

The manor of Woolavington, with the adjoining manors of Wonworth and Graffham (or Wonworth in Graffham) and East Dean, were owned by the Fitzalan family (the earls of Arundel) until 1578, when all three were sold by Henry Fitzalan, the twelfth earl, and his son-in-law John Lumley, to Giles and Francis Garton for £4,000. Shortly after this purchase Giles Garton, a London citizen and ironmonger, rebuilt the manor house (which was in the present East Lavington) in a more fashionable style, complete with crenellated turrets. He died in 1592, and the manors descended to his son, Peter Garton, and then successively to Peter's three sons. On the death of William Garton in 1675 the three manors were inherited by Robert Orme, who had married William's sister. The manor house built by Giles Garton survived until 1794, when it was pulled down and replaced with the building now occupied by Seaford College.[7]

The court books for the manor of Woolavington begin in 1489, providing details of the landholdings of the tenants and some information about manorial customs. In addition, a map of the manors of Woolavington (excluding the detached portion), Wonworth and Graffham, and East Dean was made in about 1597, showing the

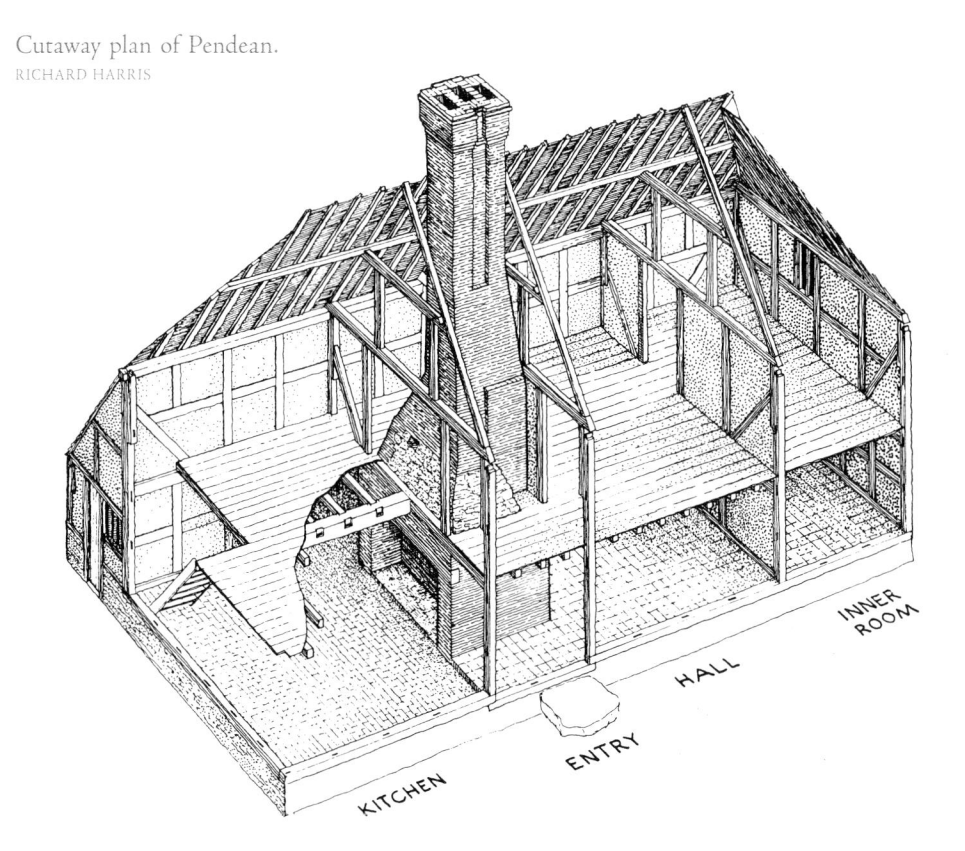

Cutaway plan of Pendean.
RICHARD HARRIS

Pendean being re-erected at the Museum, 1974.
J.R. ARMSTRONG/WDOAM ARCHIVE

distribution and type of landholding in each manor, including areas of common land. A survey of the manor of Woolavington made in about 1489 and included in the earliest court book, records that at that date it comprised 300 acres of arable, 300 acres of pasture and 14 acres of meadow. The map of c.1597 depicts Old Lavington Common (now Lavington Common) in East Lavington, about 260 acres in extent. We know from a later map that Woolavington Common in West Lavington covered some 140 acres, with Pendean's land abutting its south side. Tenants had rights of herbage (or pasture) on the common for their cattle, sheep and pigs, but could be fined for overburdening it. The number of animals that individual tenants could pasture depended on the amount of land they held. The court book does not record how this operated on the manor of Woolavington, but in neighbouring East Dean the tenants were allowed to common sixty sheep and fifteen pigs for every yardland (about sixteen acres) that they held.[8]

Woolavington tenants were allowed to cut turf, bushes and underwood on the commons, and to take sand, but were fined for taking fern, chalk or marl. They had no right to timber either on the commons or on their copyhold lands; if they needed timber to repair their buildings they had to obtain the lord's permission to remove it. This is in contrast to the custom in East Dean, where tenants had the right to take rough timber for the 'necessary reparations' of 'houses, barns, stables, stalls and other buildings'. Woolavington tenants were obliged to take their grain to the lord's mill to be ground, unless prevented from doing so by poor winter weather, and were not allowed to fish in the river 'called the brook' without the lord's licence. Tenants of Woolavington, as in the adjoining manors, held their land in enclosed fields, bounded by hedges and ditches. The map of c.1597 shows one common field of just over thirteen acres, but it is evident from the manor court book that very few tenants held land in it. Other common fields might already have been enclosed by this date: in 1549 four Woolavington tenants were granted a licence to exchange their 'decayed lands' in the common fields called 'Northfield' and 'Indlonds' for enclosed parcels of land elsewhere in the manor.[9]

The history of Pendean

The earliest reference to Pendean is in a court book entry for 1489, when it was a copyhold property described as 'one tenement and certain lands with appurtenances called *Penden*'. The word 'tenement' indicates that in the late medieval period there was already a farmstead there, including a dwelling house (which may have been the source of some of the reused timbers that were incorporated into the seventeenth-century building). A reference to Pendean in the court book from 1551 describes it as having 'by estimation' thirty acres. In 1564 the farm, along with the many other copyholds in the manor of Woolavington, was converted to a leasehold property for the term of 10,000 years.[10]

In 1609 John Coldham sold the lease of Pendean to Richard Clare, a yeoman who was resident in Woolavington. At that date Pendean comprised a house, barn and forty acres of land, plus rights of pasture for 100 sheep and 14 bullocks upon the commons, and was described as 'in the occupation of John Clare and Richard Figge'. John Clare, the father of Richard, held the neighbouring farm, Hurstlands (or Horselands). This farm, of 100 acres, was a copyhold property held of the manor of Cowdray, and adjoined Pendean to the south of Dunford Lane. We know that John Clare lived at Hurstlands because in his will, dated 12 June 1615, he describes himself as 'John Clare of *Hurstland* in the parish of Woolavington … yeoman'. It is therefore probable that at the time Richard Clare bought the lease Richard Figge (the co-occupier) was actually living in the farmhouse at Pendean, and John Clare was farming some or all of the land. Nothing more is known of Richard Figge, since his name has not so far been discovered in any other contemporary records. The coincidence of the date of the lease with the dating of the timbers at Pendean (both being 1609) suggests that Richard Clare built the early seventeenth-century house. The house and its barn are depicted on a map of 1632 or 1633, and a caption describes them as 'Richard Clare's house and land'. In 1639 Richard Clare sold the lease to Francis Browne, 3rd Viscount Montagu (lord of the manor of Cowdray) for the sum of £410, but he may have continued to live there until his death (after 1642). He signed the indenture of sale with a '+', indicating that he was illiterate.[11]

Between 1640 and 1677 there is no direct evidence for the occupation of Pendean.

The Woolavington court book for the later seventeenth century describes Pendean as a leasehold property held by the Montagus, but does not record who lived in it. However, the sessions roll for the court of quarter sessions held at Petworth in October 1678 names 'Nicholas Austen of Pendean' as one of the trial jurors, and a lease for a cottage in Bepton dated 1681 names Nicholas Austen, 'son of Nicholas Austen of *Pingdeane*'. We know that Austen had moved to Woolavington from Heyshott by 1677, and so he must have taken up residence in Pendean at that time. The description of his house contained in the probate inventory made after his death in 1697 matches the layout of Pendean as it would have been at the end of the seventeenth century.[12]

The Clare family

In his will of 1615 John Clare described himself as a yeoman, and asked to be buried in the churchyard at Midhurst. He left 7s. to his youngest son, Henry; to Richard, his second son, ten wether sheep and a table with a frame from his parlour; to Robert, his eldest son, £110 to be paid after the death of his widow, Joan (or Joanne); and to his married daughter Alice Johnson, six bushels of wheat and a quarter of barley. He left his godson (and grandson), Henry Clare the younger, his standing joined bedstead 'in the chamber where I lodge', with all the hangings and stained cloths to be given to him after the death of Joan. The will makes no reference to the distribution of lands, almost certainly because arrangements for this had been made during his lifetime. The previous distribution of his lands would explain the apparent inequality of the bequests he made to his children. Customary lands within the manor of Cowdray descended to the youngest rather than the eldest son (a practice called *ultimogeniture*), which meant that Henry would acquire Hurstlands after his mother's death. He therefore received the smallest portion of the residual estate. Richard already held the lease for Pendean, a lesser, but still decent-sized, holding. Robert received no lands at all, but a sizeable cash sum. Alice, who was likely to have had a dowry settled on her at the time of her marriage, received no cash, goods or lands. Clare made bequests of 5s. each to his servants, Duram Henchman and Daniel Austen, 'over and above their wages'.[13]

Pendean and Hurstlands are both depicted on a map of Cocking, Midhurst and Woolavington that was made in 1632 or 1633 (although, unfortunately, a large hole obliterates half of Pendean house). As we have seen, Pendean is described as 'Richard Clare's house and land'; Hurstlands – a house and a barn – is described as 'Henry Clare's house and land called Hurstland'. The map was made in response to a dispute that had arisen between William Humphrey and the inhabitants of Cocking, concerning the use of a piece of former common land called Ashdean Bottom, at

Pendean being re-erected at the Museum, 1975.
J.R. ARMSTRONG/WDOAM ARCHIVE

the northern end of Cocking Common. Aside from the fact that this map depicts both farms, it is of special interest because it records evidence from local residents about their use of the commons, and provides additional biographical information about Richard Clare, his brother Henry, and his mother, Joan, which is not available from other sources.[14]

In her evidence Joan Clare describes herself as 'Joan Clare of Graffham, widow, aged about ninety five years' and says (among other things) that 'she lived all her time at Henry Clare's house till now of late years, being a woman of good repute and account'. Thus, after her husband's death she continued to live at Hurstlands with her eldest son, Henry, but by 1632 or 1633 was living in Graffham. If she was right about her age, she would have been about 100 when she died in 1637. From Daniel Prior of Midhurst we learn that he and Richard Clare set up archery butts (which are shown on the map) on Ashdean Bottom and shot arrows at them, presumably in their younger days; the map records that in 1632 both men were aged 'about 60'. It also depicts an area of meadow on the western side of Cocking, and states that 'this meadow joins to the west end of Ashdean Bottom and did belong to Pendean being in Woolavington', adding that 'Pendean is Richard Clare's land'. Since Clare was not a tenant of the manor of Cocking, it is likely that this was a stray parcel of land held of the manor of Woolavington.[15]

We can reconstruct some additional biographical information about Richard Clare and his family from the Midhurst parish register, supplemented by the bishop's transcripts. Neither is complete, and there is no record of Richard Clare's baptism, but we know from the Cocking map that he must have been born around 1570. His first wife was buried in Midhurst in 1609 and, although there is no record of his

Richard Clare's 'mark' from indenture of 1639, suggesting that he was illiterate.
WSRO COWDRAY MS 960

second marriage, his daughter Catherine was baptised there in 1612. In 1618 another daughter, Mary, was baptised. We do not know if he had any other children or when he died. There is no surviving will or probate inventory, but he was still alive in 1642, by which time he would have been about 70, because in that year he signed the Protestation Oath.[16]

The death of Richard's brother, Henry, was presented in the Cowdray manor court in 1645. He was two years younger than Richard, so at the time of his death would have been about 70. Hurstlands descended to his son, Henry, who in 1650 split the farm between *his* two sons, John (the elder) and Henry (the younger). This is recorded in the Cowdray court book and on a map that was probably made at around the same time. Henry acquired the northern part of the farm, some fifty acres together with the farmhouse, barn and cart-house. John received the southern part, also of fifty acres and with a barn. Henry's portion is shown on a 1771 map of Pendean and Hurstlands farms.[17]

Nicholas Austen

Nicholas Austen was the son of another Nicholas Austen who lived in Heyshott, the next parish to the south. In about 1650 Nicholas senior held a copyhold property in Heyshott called Cranmore and Heathland, with 40 acres 1 rod of land, a barn and two cow-stalls. In 1660 the Cowdray manor court recorded that at the time of his death this Nicholas had held a cottage and two acres of land in Cranmore and also 'certain lands' called Heathfield in Easebourne, which descended to Nicholas Austen junior as his next of kin. In 1670 Nicholas Austen the younger was leasing Dunford House in Heyshott (later the birthplace and family home of the politician, Richard Cobden). Dunford House, which had 42 acres of land, was a short distance from Pendean, along Dunford Lane.[18]

The Heyshott parish register does not begin until 1690, while the bishop's transcripts, which begin in 1591, are incomplete. There is, however, a record of the baptism there of four of the children of Nicholas Austen the younger: Susannah (1661), William (1663), John (1665) and Mary (1669). Another son, Nicholas, was baptised at Woolavington in 1677. Nicholas had at least one other daughter, Margaret, who is mentioned in his will. He was a churchwarden in Heyshott in 1669, when he wrote and signed the transcript of the parish register, submitted to the diocese, with a clear, distinctive hand, and again in 1672 when he signed the transcript. So, unlike Richard Clare, he was literate. He also served a two-year term as one of two constables of the hundred of Easebourne, in 1667 and 1668. The fact that his son Nicholas was baptised in Woolavington in 1677 suggests that he must have moved into Pendean around that time. At the time of his death in 1697 he had three surviving adult children, William Austen, Margaret West and Nicholas Austen. Another son, John, had died leaving a widow, Ann, and a son. Nicholas himself was survived by his wife Susannah. He evidently retained at least some of his Heyshott lands, since in his will he left 'all my right and title to all my wood and timber standing and growing upon all my copyhold lands' to his son Nicholas, and also made bequests to the poor of both Woolavington and Heyshott.[19]

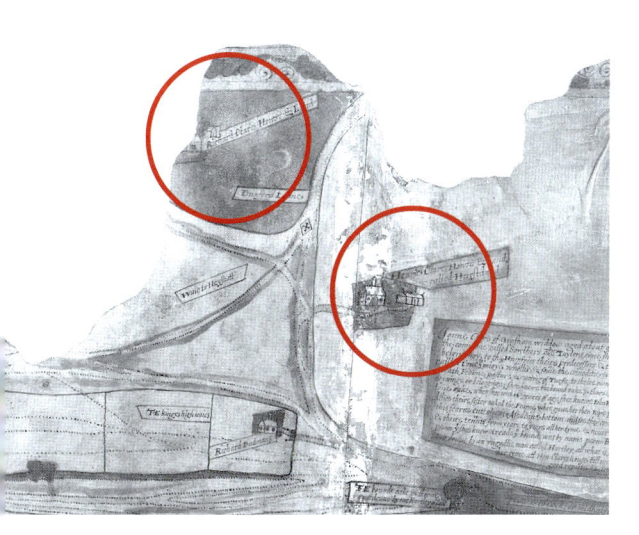

Below: Detail showing Richard Clare's barn and house.
WSRO ADD MS 24.110

Left: Map of Cocking, Midhurst and Woolavington, 1632/3, showing Pendean (top) and Hurstlands (bottom).
WSRO ADD MS 24.110

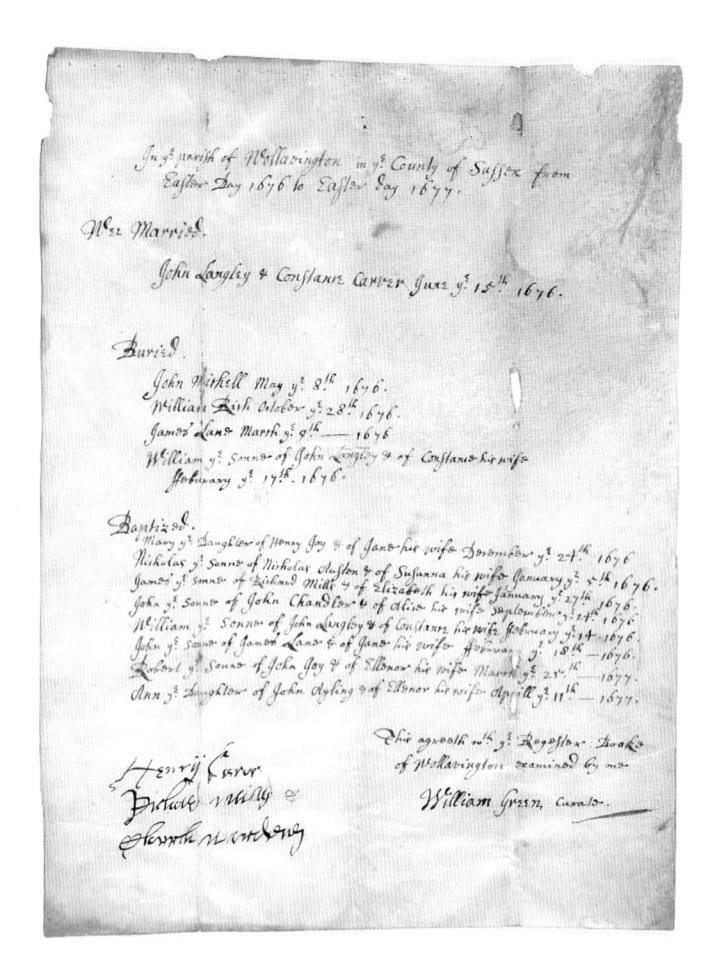

Bishop's Transcript of Woolavington parish register, 1676–77, recording baptism of Nicholas, son of Nicholas and Susanna Austen, 5 January 1677.
WSRO EP/I/24/138

Farming and the rural economy

This part of Sussex was characterised by mixed farming. Sheep were the predominant livestock, although the surviving Woolavington probate inventories indicate that not all tenants owned sheep, and where they did numbers were fairly small. With 56 sheep at the time of his death, Nicholas Austen had one of the larger flocks; the largest recorded in a probate inventory was that of Henry Carver, a wealthy yeoman, with 340. Sussex wool, which was only suitable for the production of coarse cloth, was not a valuable commodity in the seventeenth century. However, it was not without value: there was a textile industry in the area, which used local wool from Sussex sheep. Unfortunately, it is difficult to assess its organisation and economic significance from the surviving records. In the sixteenth century there was a fulling mill at Aldersham, north of Pendean, which suggests that woollen cloth was then being manufactured in the area. Sheep were also valued as a source of meat: evidence in cases of sheep theft heard at the quarter sessions shows that most stolen animals ended up in the pot, on a spit or baked in a pie.[20]

The system of sheep-corn husbandry, with sheep pastured on the commons during the day and folded on fallow fields at night, remained universal in downland areas of Sussex. Wheat was the main grain crop in Woolavington, but tenants also grew barley, oats and rye, together with leguminous crops such as peas and vetches. Much of the wheat grown on the larger farms was exported through the port of Chichester, which saw a steady increase in grain exports during this period and into the eighteenth century. Tenants also grew hemp, flax and hops, probably in their gardens. Hops were used in small quantities to flavour ale and to increase its barrel life; malted barley continued to be the main ingredient. Flax was converted into linen yarn, spun on wheels within the home. This indicates another dimension to the local textile industry, with the likely production of linen cloth, but the scale and organisation of this is simply unknown.[21]

Although it is damaged, Nicholas Austen's probate inventory reveals that, like his neighbours, he was engaged in mixed farming. He was growing wheat, barley, oats and peas, and probably also vetches and rye. The inventory records four barns, probably in three separate locations – the 'copyhold barn', the 'town barn', the 'old barn' and the 'new barn'. The old and new barns are likely to have been adjacent to the house: there was one barn at Pendean at the time of Richard Clare's occupation in the 1630s, but the map of 1771 shows two, set at right angles to each other. The copyhold barn must have been on the copyhold lands referred to in his will, perhaps those at Cranmore and Heathfield, which have already been mentioned. The location of the town barn is unknown. Austen may therefore have held considerably more than the forty acres of land attached to Pendean. As we have seen, he had a flock of 56 sheep, and he also had ten cows, four oxen, three horses and nine pigs. The oxen and horses were probably used for traction: horses were faster and stronger on lighter soil, but oxen were better on heavier ground. With ten cows he would have been producing butter and cheese for the market, rather than just for domestic consumption; at the time of his death he had a cheese press as well as stores of butter and cheese. He also brewed – likewise, probably for the market. His brewhouse contained a brass furnace, he had a stock of malt in his kitchen chamber, and he had two dozen glass bottles in his cellar. His inventory also lists a cider press. All this suggests a sizeable commercial operation, which at various times would have involved all members of his household.[22]

In the early modern period, Woolavington and the adjoining parish of Graffham had significant pottery, tile and brick-making industries. Pottery was probably manufactured in the area throughout the medieval period, but there is little documentary evidence for brick- and tile-making before the 1590s. In the 1970s three kiln sites were identified by archaeologists – two in Woolavington and the third in Graffham. The material associated with them suggested that two produced pottery and that the third had produced all three commodities at different times. A total of 29 potters, brick-makers and tile-makers, active between about 1590 and 1740, have been identified from documentary sources, but this figure is likely to underestimate significantly the true number of men and women engaged directly or indirectly in the industry. In the manor of Wonworth and Graffham tenants had the right to dig clay on common land, provided they had a licence from the lord, filled the 'clay pits' up again after use, and did not dig within forty feet of the road. The Woolavington potters who can be identified – Christopher Denham, the Joys and John Sprinkes – all held land in the Norwood area, where a brick-built kiln was excavated in 1977. In the late sixteenth and early seventeenth century members of the Philp and Champion families, brick- and tile-makers, also held land in Norwood. They moved their interests to Graffham around 1635, and after this the production of bricks and tiles in the Norwood area probably ceased. The Philp family were running a substantial brick and tile business from an unidentified site in Graffham from 1640 to 1742.[23]

These were predominantly family industries, in which a son took over the business on the father's death. There is also some evidence for formal apprenticeship. In 1657, for example, the potter John Joy complained to the quarter sessions that Francis Coleman, the son of William Coleman of Littlehampton, 'being placed an apprentice with the said John Joy by the overseers of the poor of Littlehampton', had been 'enticed away by the said William Coleman out of the said John Joy's service and

Map of Pendean and Horselands farms, 1771 (Pendean to the north, Horselands to the south).
WSRO COWDRAY MS 1661

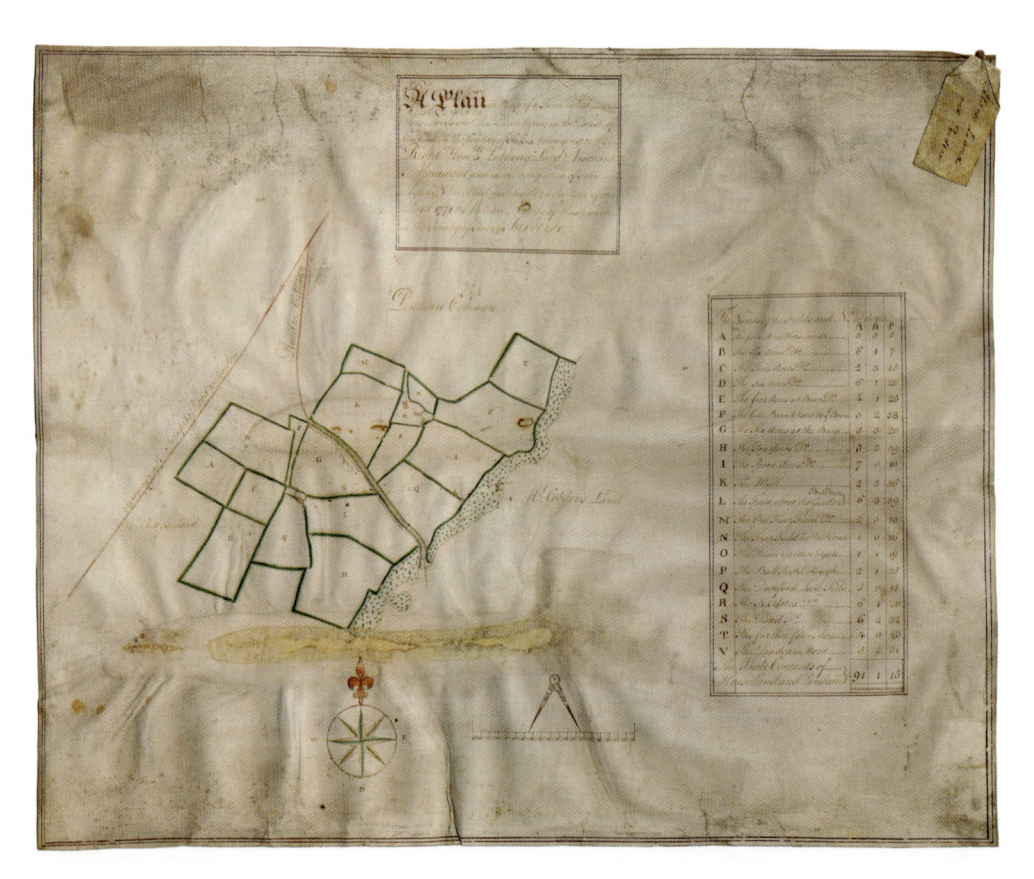

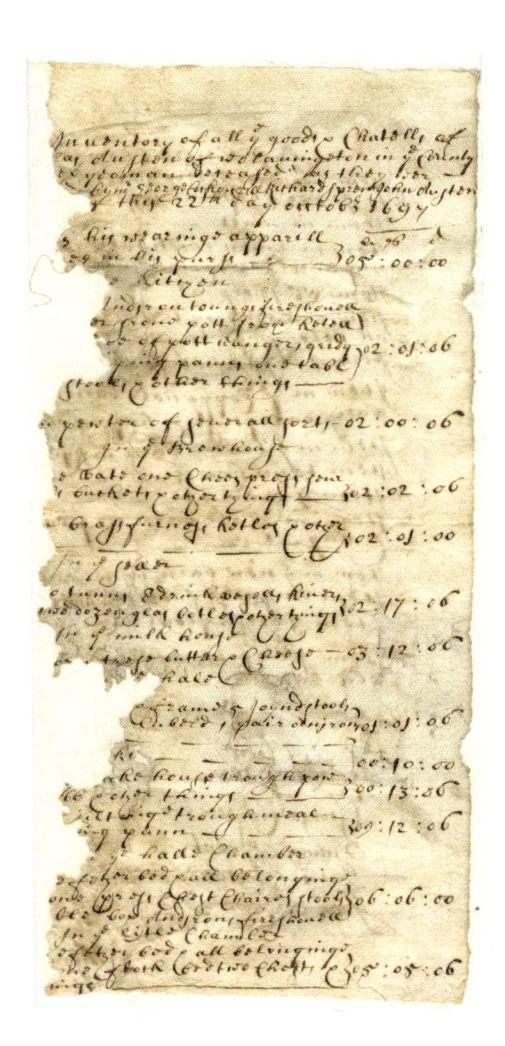

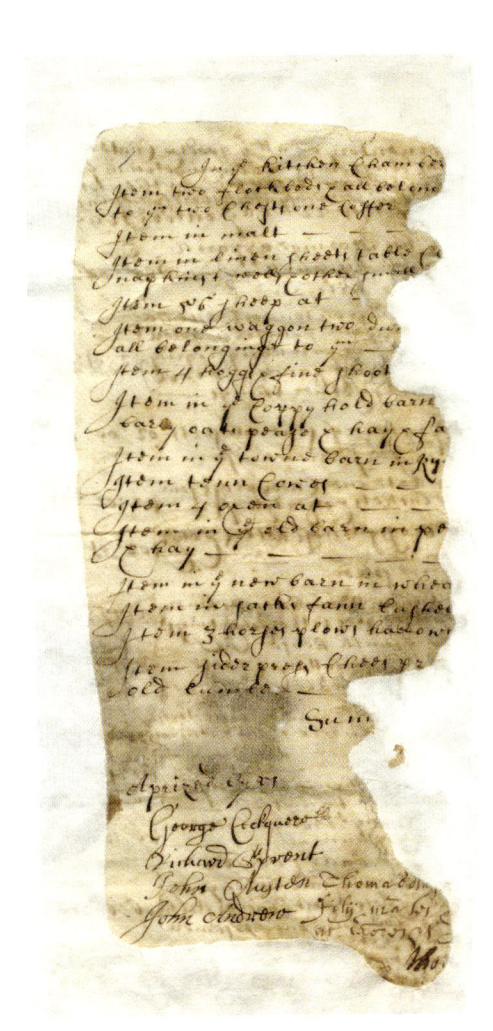

Page 1   Page 2

Probate inventory of Nicholas Austen, 1697.
WSRO EP/I/29/215/35

is still there detained'. Francis was ordered to return to Joy to serve out the rest of his term, which he evidently did because he was still working as a potter in the Graffham area in the 1670s. John Joy did not have a good record with the young people he employed in his household: in 1649 his servant, Mary Patrick, brought a case against him at quarter sessions for withholding her wages and mistreating her.[24]

'Graffham ware', the pottery manufactured in the area, typically has a green or brown glaze when applied directly over the red fabric, or a green or yellow glaze when applied over white fabric. Where white clay was used ('white ware'), it must have been imported from outside the area, since the local clay fires to a reddish-buff colour. Such white ware may have represented the 'luxury' end of the local pottery market. The main markets for Graffham ware are likely to have been relatively close: the Graffham area itself, Midhurst, Chichester and Petworth. Potters could sell from their door direct to consumers or to middlemen, or they could take their wares to market. Inevitably, however, given the difficulties of transporting large quantities of brick and tile, the market for those products would have been more restricted.

It is no coincidence that the documentary evidence for brick- and tile-making begins in the late sixteenth century, when there was an increase in demand for these materials in new buildings. For example, Lavington manor house, Old Place Farm in Westhampnett, and Raughmere manor house in Mid Lavant were all substantial high-status buildings built in the last decades of the sixteenth century or early in the seventeenth century. Brick was also used for industrial structures, such as the distinctive building from Mid Lavant, now at the Museum, built in about 1613 and perhaps used for cloth production. During the sixteenth century the demand for brick and tile for lower-status buildings also increased, as traditional open hearths were replaced by brick-built chimney stacks, and brick and tile began to replace wattle and daub and thatch as building materials. Floor and hearth tiles were also more widely used. The brick and tiles used in Pendean were certainly produced at one of the local kilns.[25]

Seventeenth-century houses

By the seventeenth century traditional open hall houses, with their clearly defined upper and lower ends, had become obsolete. Many medieval houses, like the Museum's example from Walderton, were modified with the insertion of a chimney stack and second floor. Others, such as Pendean, were built according to a new domestic plan. The decline of the open hall has been attributed to broad social and cultural changes, such as the 'enclosure' of the landscape with the enclosure of common land, the advent of Puritanism, and the increased marginalisation of women and servants within the home. But proving any kind of causal link is difficult. The process of transition was lengthy, and late medieval houses such as Bayleaf in fact embodied many of the features that we see in their 'closed' successors: a larger number of rooms, relocation of sleeping accommodation upstairs, increased specialisation of service rooms, and integration of the kitchen into the main range of the house. By analysing room use and room terminology, however, we are on much safer ground examining the way in which the new domestic plan worked in practice. This is possible primarily because of the large number of probate inventories that survive for the seventeenth century. Extensive analysis of probate inventories from Cornwall and Kent shows that seventeenth-century houses had more rooms than their sixteenth-century predecessors, and that they also had more and new kinds of service rooms. This was also the case in Sussex, although there are very few surviving sixteenth-century probate inventories from the county to provide a comparison.[26]

Analysis of 35 seventeenth-century inventories that survive for Woolavington, together with the 96 for Graffham, reveals that in these parishes in that period all houses had a room identified as a 'hall', the primary function of which was eating, sitting and storage. The hall was still the main social space, as it had been in earlier houses such as Bayleaf. Some inventories suggest that cooking was still taking place in the hall, but in the majority of cases it had moved to the 'kitchen'. The word 'house' was applied to rooms where some form of production took place ('bake house', 'milk house', 'brew house'). In theory, 'milk houses' were used for dairying, 'bake houses' for food preparation and baking, and 'brew house', 'drink house' and 'malt house' for brewing and storing drink. However, in practice many of these rooms served more than one function, depending on the needs of the household. A few of the larger houses, including that of the wealthy Woolavington yeoman Henry Carver, had a room called a 'wash house'. This might have been used for brewing and dairying, but was distinguished from other service rooms in having a well, thereby providing an in-house water supply.[27]

In other parts of the country at this date an increasing number of houses contained parlours. In some cases this term was synonymous with 'hall', this being the main social space where the family sat and ate and entertained any guests. That may have been the case at Hurstlands during John Clare's residence – he bequeathed the table and the frame from his parlour to Richard Clare. However, in larger houses the parlour was *additional* to the hall, serving as a private sitting room for the householder and his wife and as a place to receive guests. When used in this way, the parlour contained the best furniture and furnishings, allowing the householder to display his wealth and social status. The rector of Woolavington, Daniel German, had both a hall and a parlour. The hall contained a joined table and a frame, six joined stools, a joined cupboard, and a chair. No fire furniture was included, and so it may have been unheated. The parlour had a joined table and frame, six joined stools, three joined chairs, a court cupboard, seven 'wrought' chairs, a 'little stool', three carpets, four cushions, and a pair of cast-iron andirons (fire bars to support logs). The disparity in the level of comfort offered in these two rooms is apparent. Court cupboards – open-fronted shelves to display plate or from which to serve food – were fashionable in the early seventeenth century, and could be highly decorated. Daniel German's 'carpets' were not for floors, but were used to cover furniture

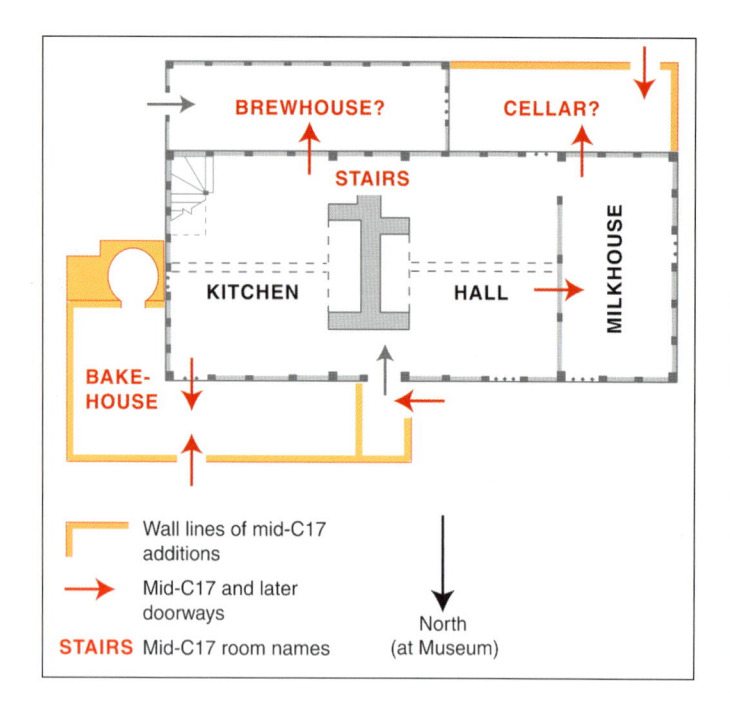

Floor plan of Pendean, showing late seventeenth-century alterations.
RICHARD HARRIS

such as his table and court cupboard. Like court cupboards themselves, their popularity declined in the second half of the seventeenth century as new types of furniture appeared.[28]

A 'chamber' was a general synonym for 'room', and could be either downstairs or upstairs. The latter were usually identified by their position relative to the room beneath (for example, 'kitchen chamber', 'hall chamber'), and were used for sleeping and storage – including the storage of household goods such as linen, and agricultural products such as grain and wool. The only Woolavington probate inventory to record separate chambers for servants was that of Henry Carver. He had a 'servants' chamber' with three bedsteads and two flock beds, and a 'maid's chamber' with a bed and bedstead. Since we would expect most yeoman households to have at least one live-in female servant, it is likely that they slept alongside the children of the family.[29]

Matching an inventory to a standing building is very difficult. For Pendean we have no probate inventory for Richard Clare, but as noted earlier we are fortunate in having one for Nicholas Austen (who died in 1697) which seems to match what we know of the layout of Pendean in the late seventeenth century. By that time Pendean had undergone significant modifications; it now had three outshuts attached to the south, east and north walls, providing a total of three external service rooms (which would have significantly reduced the natural light within the main range of the house). The inventory describes a total of nine rooms, six downstairs and three upstairs. Downstairs there was a kitchen, with a fireplace, used for cooking; a brew house (possibly also used for dairying); a cellar (for the storage of ale and cider); a milkhouse for dairying; a hall with a fireplace for sitting, eating and storage; and a bakehouse for food preparation and baking. The inventory records that upstairs were a hall chamber with a fireplace, used solely for sleeping, and a little chamber and a kitchen chamber, both used for sleeping and storage.

We can be certain that the room on the east side of the chimney stack was the kitchen, because of the size of the fireplace and the evidence for the earlier existence of an oven. The central room, with a slightly smaller fireplace, would therefore have been the hall, and the smallest, unheated, room at the west end was probably the milk house. The internal oven was relocated in the later seventeenth century to the new outshut on the east side of the house, which then became the bakehouse. The hall chamber with the fireplace was evidently the main bedchamber, its status reflected in the fact that it was the only one of the three chambers not used for storage.[30]

Nicholas Austen was a reasonably prosperous yeoman living in the late seventeenth century. Nevertheless, the range of household furniture which he owned when he died was limited. Downstairs, there were some stools in the kitchen and a table and frame, five joined stools, and a cupboard in his hall. Upstairs, the furnishings suggest a greater level of comfort. The hall chamber had a featherbed, a press, chest, chairs and stools. The little chamber had a featherbed, a flock bed and two chests, and the kitchen chamber two flock beds, two chests and one coffer. Because the inventory is damaged we are missing at least one piece of furniture from his hall, but a comparison with the inventories of other yeomen suggests that the amount and type of furniture were not unusual. The probate inventory of William Sandham, who died in 1678, included a table with a form, six joined stools, a chair, a side cupboard and another cupboard in his hall. There was no moveable furniture in his kitchen, and he had a bedstead, trunk, two chests and five chairs in his lower chamber; a featherbed, three chests and a trunk in his middle chamber; two beds, one press, six chests, two boxes and one trunk in his outer chamber; and an old bed in his kitchen chamber.[31]

Some inventories include a piece of furniture called a 'press', generally in an upstairs chamber (and usually the best chamber). In 1692 Henry Carver had three presses in his 'chamber over the parlour', described as a 'small press', a 'great press' and a 'napkin press'. Press cupboards, which supplanted court cupboards in popularity after the mid-seventeenth century, could be used for storage and display. When placed in the hall or parlour they sometimes had a recessed upper section like a dresser, which could be used for displaying plate and serving food, with enclosed shelves below. The press cupboards recorded in the inventories of Nicholas Austen, William Sandham and Henry Carver are more likely to have been completely enclosed and used for storage, especially of valuable household linen such as napkins, tablecloths, sheets and towels. Henry Carver's parlour chamber also had a looking glass valued, together with a 'new saddle', at £1 10s. Mirrors were rare in the households of Sussex yeomen in the late seventeenth century: Carver's neighbours, had they been invited into his parlour chamber, would probably never have seen one before. Randle Holme observed that mirrors were 'most used by ladies to look their faces in and to see how to dress their heads and set their top knots on their foreheads upright', and no doubt Carver's wife, Joan, his two daughters Mary and Ann, and perhaps even his female servants, did just that. Upholstered chairs were a rarity in seventeenth-century yeomen households, even wealthy ones such as that of Henry Carver, and not until the early eighteenth century do they begin to appear in Woolavington inventories. In 1714 Richard Croucher had six leather chairs, three in his kitchen chamber and three in his 'little chamber'.[32]

Because it was valuable, much of the detailed listing of tableware in Woolavington inventories concerns items made of pewter. Henry Carver's inventory included a pewter flagon, two pewter candlesticks and eighteen pewter dishes. Cheaper materials, such as leather, wood and pottery, are less frequently recorded in specific detail. The carpenter David Allen had three leather bottles when he died in 1630, while several inventories record 'wooden vessels', without specifying what they are. Pottery, or earthenware, is mentioned in very few inventories because it was typically of a low value. However, we know that its use was widespread at every social level, and that it formed an important part of domestic material culture. Like other household objects, it could be both utilitarian and a means of social display. Its ubiquity in late medieval and early modern households is reflected in archaeological evidence, where it is the most commonly found artefact.

The contrast between written and archaeological evidence can be demonstrated for Pendean. There is no specific reference to earthenware in Nicholas Austen's inventory of 1697, but archaeological investigation of the house site after dismantling revealed a very considerable quantity of fragmented pottery (identified as Graffham ware) which is now stored in two sacks in the Museum's artefact store. Glass also appears only infrequently in seventeenth-century Woolavington inventories, because it was relatively scarce and costly. Its use became more common as the century progressed. As we have seen, Nicholas Austen had two dozen glass bottles in his cellar (presumably for ale or cider), while in his hall Anthony Hollist had a 'glass cupboard' for display. None of the Woolavington inventories of the late seventeenth or early eighteenth centuries mentions equipment for making tea or coffee. This is in contrast to Kent, where such items begin to appear in small numbers from the 1680s onwards.[33]

Cooking utensils were usually made of iron or brass, or occasionally of latten. The most common types were pots, kettles (large lidded pots to hang over the fire) and skillets (a forerunner of the frying pan, with three short legs and a long handle, which could be set among the embers of the fire). This limited range suggests that cooking methods remained traditional. At the time of his death in 1675, Anthony Hollist had five brass kettles, six old brass skillets, two brass skimmers, a brass mortar and pestle, a brass warming pan and three iron pots in his bakehouse, as well as two latten dripping pans, a pair of latten candlesticks, and other 'small latten' in his milkhouse. New types of utensils appear infrequently in Woolavington inventories of the late seventeenth century. Both Anthony Hollist and Henry Carver had toasting irons, which were spiked frames fixed to the front of the fire for toasting bread, and jacks, used to raise cooking pots or to turn spits for cooking meat.[34]

Conclusion

Pendean is a very different house from Bayleaf, not only in looks but also in feel. It does not have the grandeur and lofty space of the open hall. The 'enclosed' house is more modest in scale and more homely. This house has three heated rooms, compared with one at Bayleaf, although the windows were still unglazed (at least in the early seventeenth century). But in many ways the revised domestic plan offered by Pendean — and other houses like it — is not radically different from the way that space was used in its open hall predecessors. The main social space was still the hall, and much of the ground-floor accommodation was used for 'services'. There would have been little chance of segregation, or personal space, in such a house; at the end of the day, when the whole family was assembled, servants and children would have jostled for space alongside the householder and his wife.

Richard Clare and Nicholas Austen were both yeomen like Thomas Wells: prosperous within their communities and holding local office. But Downland Sussex was not as affluent as the Kent Weald, a difference reflected in the limited variety of household goods that we find in the houses of Woolavington yeomen. Like the 1632–33 map depicting half a house, the surviving records allow us to reconstruct only half a life. Key biographical information is missing both for the men and for their families. Perhaps more significantly, we have no idea what they thought and felt about the events that were taking place around them. The seventeenth century was a period of momentous change, defined by the religious and political turbulence of the first few decades, the Civil War and the creation of the Commonwealth. How did such events affect Richard Clare? In 1642 he signed the Oath of Protestation, swearing 'to live and die for the true Protestant religion, the liberties and rights of subjects, and the privilege of Parliaments'. In so far as it is possible to tell, he appears to have been a mainstream Anglican. Yet, like many of his neighbours, he may have chosen to keep his own counsel and pursue a more personal piety at home, rather than risk falling foul of the authorities.

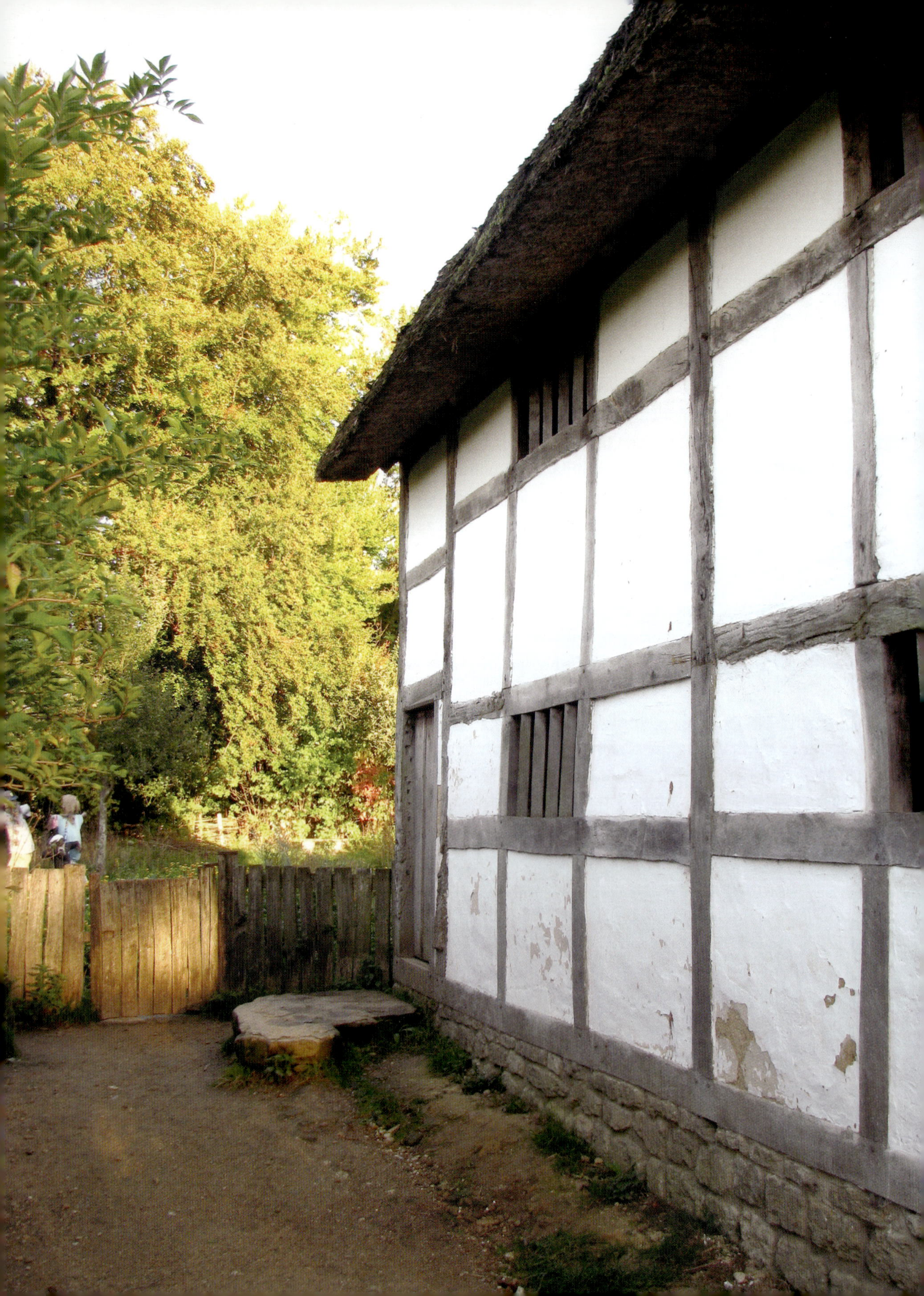

CHAPTER FIVE

Poplar Cottage: a wasteland cottage from Washington, West Sussex

Poplar Cottage, from Washington in West Sussex, is a building of a distinctive type, with a hipped roof at one end and a gabled roof at the other. There are two rooms on the ground floor and two on the first floor. The gabled end originally contained a smoke bay, providing one heated downstairs room. A smoke bay is a short (3–5 feet) bay in a timber-framed building which encloses smoke from a fire on the hearth. Smoke bays represent a transitional stage between open hall houses, such as Bayleaf and North Cray, and houses with chimneys like Pendean, Walderton and Tindalls Cottage. The presence of the smoke bay, and the style of the timber framing, suggest that Poplar was probably built between 1630 and 1650. Between 50 and 100 years later a brick and stone chimney-stack was built inside the smoke bay and, probably at the same time, an outshut was added to the back. In the seventeenth and eighteenth centuries the cottage stood on its own on the edge of Washington Common, but by 1839 (when the tithe map and apportionment were drawn up) there was another cottage to the west, and by 1870 a third cottage had been built to the east. Around this time the cottages acquired the name 'Poplars'. The tithe apportionment describes Poplar as a house and garden with 26 perches (about one-sixth of an acre) of land. At that time it was occupied by William Fuller, an agricultural labourer, and was part of the Wiston estate owned by Charles Goring.[1]

Poplar Cottage: front elevation.
RICHARD HARRIS

This cottage type is associated with 'wasteland' or 'wayside' encroachment onto common land, which could be either an area of open common, like Washington Common, or a wayside or roadside verge. Typically such cottages had little or no land. Cottagers needed the permission of the manorial lord to build on the waste; without it they were occupying the land illegally (in other words, 'squatting', although this is not a term used in contemporary records), and could face presentment in the manorial court, a monetary fine and an order to pull the cottage down. As will be discussed in more detail below, after 1589 it became illegal for anyone to build a cottage without four acres of land without a licence from the justices of assize or the justices of the peace.[2]

Poplar Cottage was discovered through the work of the Wiston Survey Group, which was started in 1976 by the Museum's founder, Roy Armstrong, with the aim of recording and analysing all the buildings on the Wiston estate. When the building was first surveyed in 1978, it had been empty for some time and was completely derelict. The Wiston Estate agreed to its rescue and acquisition by the Museum, and dismantling was carried out in August 1982. After dismantling, an archaeological investigation of the site was made by Fred Aldsworth, then county archaeologist. The trenches revealed that all the walls were bedded very near the surface of natural clay and that no early floor levels had survived, which means that it is almost certain that Poplar Cottage had been built on an empty site.

The external wall frames of the cottage were in very poor condition, and many timbers were missing. In the two ends only the main posts and tie beams survived, and in the two side walls most of the lower half of the frames had been replaced by brickwork. Almost all of the original external timbers needed substantial repair. However, sufficient timbers survived to indicate the pattern of framing with near certainty, and even though 70 per cent of the external timbers are new, the frame still has

Diagram showing position of smoke bay.
RICHARD HARRIS

an authentic feel to it. Internally only a few timbers needed repair or replacement. Analysis of the timbers revealed that all were either oak or elm, converted from two large open-grown oak trees (for the tie beams and posts), one or two smaller oaks (for the joists and small timbers), and several small elms of about 12–15 inches in diameter. All the conversion was done with axe hewing and pit sawing in the usual way.

The timber frame was re-erected over the weekend of 10–11 April 1999 by a team led by Roger Champion, and the cottage opened as an exhibit in 2000. It has been sited to reflect its original orientation, with the smoke bay at the east end, and its west end on the boundary of the access track, its front facing north over Greenways field, much as when it was originally built, overlooking Washington Common.[3]

Seventeenth-century Washington

The downland parish of Washington covers 3,185 acres and had a population in the seventeenth century of perhaps 400–450. Washington is about seven miles north of Worthing and separated from it by Chanctonbury Hill, one of the highest points in Sussex. The southern part of the parish consists of rolling chalk downland, while the northernmost part lies on Weald clay. In between are bands of Upper and Lower Greensand and Gault clay. Most of Washington was divided between two manors, Washington and Chancton, and a few small parcels were held by a third manor, Selah or Sele. The manor of Washington had three large areas of interconnecting common land: Heath Common (the West and East Heath), Washington Common and New Common, together amounting to just over 295 acres. The manor of Chancton also claimed rights of common on Washington Common, and both manors had sheep pasture on the downs at Chanctonbury and Findon.[4]

The Figge map, drawn in about 1739, shows Poplar Cottage set on its own on the edge of Washington Common, outside the boundary of Washington manor. Documentary research suggests that it was situated on the demesne land of Chancton manor, which was bought in 1715 by Sir Robert Fagg, lord of the neighbouring manor of Wiston. The location of the cottage, on the boundary of two manors and abutting the edge of the common, is unlikely to have been accidental. Manorial boundaries and areas of common land were clearly marked out both by natural features and by boundary markers such as hedges, stones, crosses, poles and fences. Such boundaries were periodically surveyed and recorded by groups of tenants. The Figge map shows that the common was hedged, with access by gate at various points. The original builder and occupant of the cottage might have hoped that its location would mean it could escape scrutiny by the officials of either manor. However, the fact that it survived suggests that at some point the status of the cottage was legitimised, and

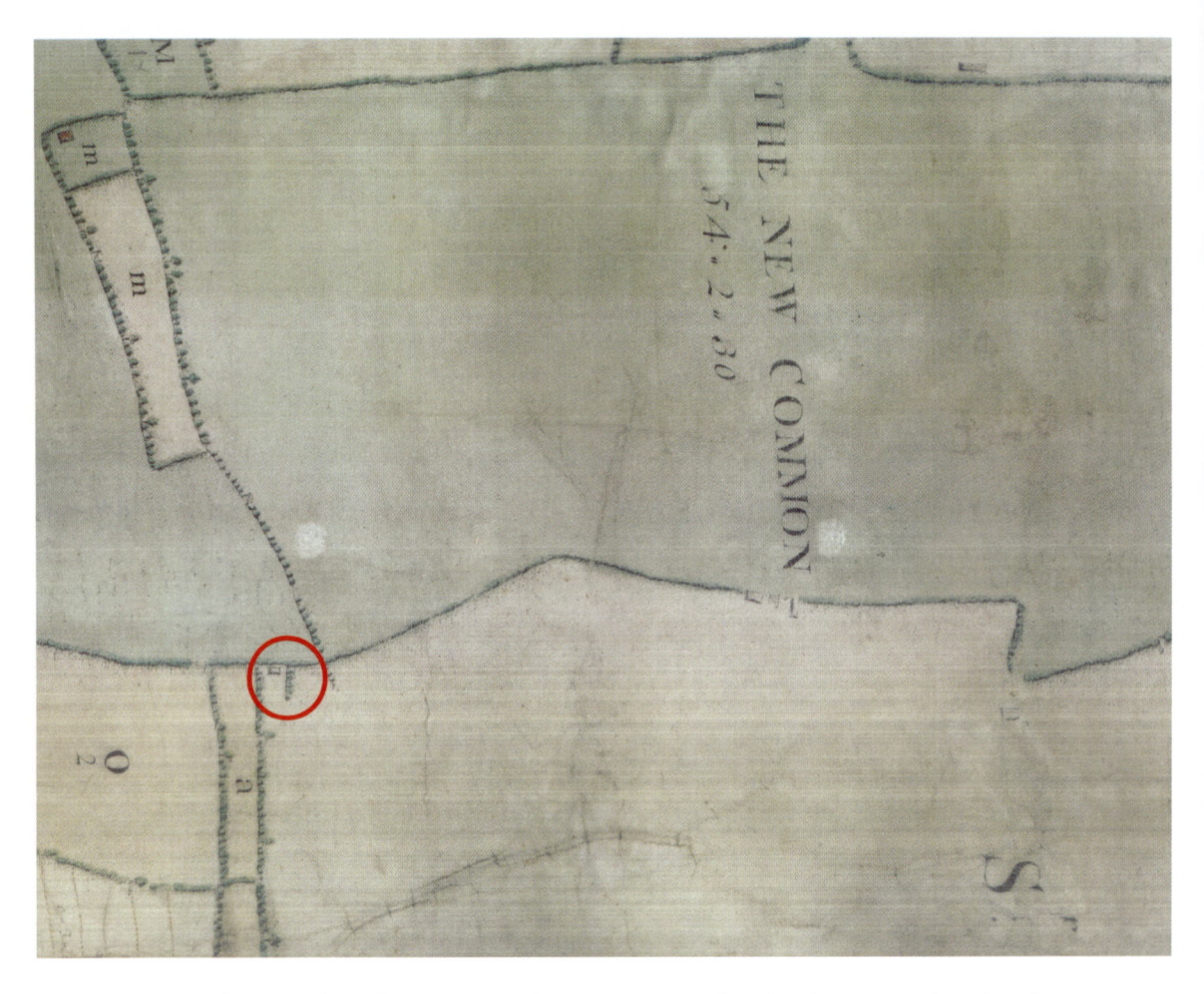

Map of manor of Washington c.1739 showing position of Poplar Cottage on the edge of Washington Common.
WSRO WISTON MS 5592

the occupant became a tenant of the manor of Chancton. Although it has not been possible to identify any of the earliest occupants, careful analysis of the historic context of the cottage points to them being husbandmen or, alternatively, rural craftsmen of comparable socio-economic status.[5]

This social group is quite hard to place within the 'language of "sorts"' that contemporaries were using from the late sixteenth century onwards. It will be recalled that William Harrison divided the population into four 'sorts', while later commentators usually divided it into three 'sorts'. Under Harrison's classification, husbandmen and craftsmen (or 'artificers') were included with day labourers as part

Poplar Cottage being re-erected at the Museum, 1999.
WDOAM ARCHIVE

Poplar Cottage, as reconstructed at the Museum.
DANAE TANKARD

of the 'fourth and last sort of people', although strictly speaking they were not the 'last sort' because that position was occupied by the poor. Under the tripartite system they would therefore be expected to be among the 'meaner' or 'poorer' sort. Some historians have argued that husbandmen became increasingly impoverished in the early seventeenth century, reduced to the level of day labourers by the squeeze on land and resources which was the consequence of rapid population growth. It is certainly true that in some contemporary records the words 'labourer' and 'husbandmen' seem to have been virtually synonymous. However, husbandmen and rural craftsmen could also be relatively 'middling', reflected in the amount of land they held, their standard of living, and social standing within their communities. In seventeenth-century Washington the amount of land held by husbandmen varied widely, from little or nothing to about thirty acres. Moreover, as we shall see, even the landless or land-poor were not necessarily entirely wage-dependent.[6]

In the seventeenth and eighteenth centuries most tenants of both Washington and Chancton manors held some land in narrow strips of one acre or less in common fields, south of Washington village, known as the East and West Clays. Within these fields land was divided into 'furlongs', such as the Hampole Furlong in the West Clays and the Crowmare Furlong in the East Clays. There were also common fields at the southern tip of Washington manor in Findon, and north of Washington village in an area called the Sands. This region, like downland Sussex generally, was characterised by sheep-corn husbandry, with wheat, barley and rye the predominant crops. Most farmers were also growing some leguminous crops such as peas and tares, and a few grew oats. Hemp and flax were also widely grown, probably in the gardens of householders. The style of arable farming is reflected in the probate inventories of landholding husbandmen. For example, the inventory of Thomas Ledbetter's goods in June 1619 records that he had three acres of wheat, three acres of barley, three acres of peas and tares and 1½ acres of buckwheat.[7]

The livestock owned by husbandmen tended to be mixed – a few sheep, one or two cows or bullocks, a horse, pigs and poultry (geese, chickens and sometimes ducks). At the time of his death Ledbetter had ten sheep, seven lambs, four 'twelve monthling beasts' (bullocks), four hogs and seven 'little pigs', as well as 'geese, hens and other poultry'. Disparate sources mention the usual array of rural crafts in the area, such as brick-making, blacksmithing, wheelwrighting, weaving, brewing, carpentry, masonry, and shoe-making, but none was dominant. However, the regularity with which hemp, flax, wool and different types of yarn are recorded in Washington probate inventories suggests that spinning formed an important by-employment for women. The existence of a local textile industry, whose organisation and scale are presently unknown, was referred to in the previous chapter.[8]

Common land

The term 'common land' refers to the non-arable and unenclosed parcels on a manor, which might include commons, roadside verges and sometimes woods and pastures. It was owned by the lord of the manor, but the tenants had the right to a share of its natural products (for food, fuel and materials) and to pasture their animals, such as cattle, sheep, pigs and geese. However, not everyone had equal rights to the use of common land. This was because common rights were attached to tenancies, so that larger landholders had a greater share of common resources than those with smaller tenanted properties. The use of common land was governed by manorial custom and regulated through the manor courts, which could further qualify customary entitlements by issuing ordinances or byelaws, restricting the use of commons to certain times of the year, the number and type of animals that could be pastured, or the amount of material that could be taken at any one time. Tenants who took more than their entitlement, or who otherwise infringed custom or ordinance, were presented in the manor courts and fined.

Truly landless wasteland cottagers generally had no formal common rights, although in practice they might be allowed unofficial 'use rights' – in other words, the lord of the manor and tenants were prepared to turn a blind eye as long as the use of such rights was reasonable and restrained. Cottagers with a small amount of land (perhaps one or two acres) might have pasture rights for a couple of cows, as well as the right to collect natural products. A wide variety was available, including wood, furze and turf for fuel, resources used in manufacturing and building processes such as clay, wood, stone and sand, and wild foods such as fruit and nuts, herbs, leaves and vegetables, birds and rabbits, although the right of warren often meant that rabbits were reserved to the lord. Those with no sheep of their own could gather loose wool caught on trees and undergrowth, to spin into yarn.[9]

By exercising common rights the poor could increase their income substantially, although it was always the case that the resources of the commons could not be sold for profit. Rather, they supplemented any cash income that the tenants might receive. In that way they might allow a household to remain economically independent, rather than relying on poor relief. It has been estimated that in the eighteenth century the pasturing of a single cow on common land might constitute as much as 40 per cent of an agricultural labourer's income, while fuel rights could have been worth between 10 and 20 per cent of earnings. For this reason, although legitimate tenants were assiduous in guarding their common rights, they might well tolerate unofficial use by the poorer members of the community, because that helped to keep parish rates down. In the late eighteenth and early nineteenth centuries proponents of parliamentary enclosure argued that many commoners refused to work for wages, preferring a more haphazard and – as they saw it – impoverished dependence upon the commons. As one historian has suggested, 'to some extent [commoners] lived outside the market … They lived in part on the invisible earnings of grazing and gathering.'[10]

The regulation of cottage building in the late sixteenth and seventeenth centuries

In his report to parliament in 1864 on the state of rural housing Dr Hunter observed that,

> It was a common opinion among the peasants of pre-enclosure times that he who could in one night build what was called a 'mushroom Hall' or 'now-or-never' without hindrance from the lord's agents had thenceforth a copyhold right in the ground he occupied.

He added that 'in places where the common was unproductive this right was not often contested'. The origins of this 'common opinion', which is still cited by those discussing squatters' cottages, are obscure. An Act passed in 1550, and intended to protect the common rights of small landholders in the wake of the aggressive enclosures of the early to mid-sixteenth century, implied that in the past those enclosing small pieces of common land of two or three acres, and building themselves cottages, were entitled to occupation without penalty. This type of piecemeal encroachment was not a serious concern to manorial lords and legitimate tenants during periods of population stagnation such as the fifteenth century, but as population began to grow once more in the sixteenth century the scale of illegal cottage-building became much more controversial. The 1589 Act 'against erecting and maintaining cottages' stipulated that

> For the avoiding of the great inconveniencies which are found by experience to grow by the erecting and building of great numbers and multitude of cottages, which are daily more and more increased in many parts of this realm, be it enacted … that … no person shall within this realm … make, build and erect, or cause to be made, built or erected, any manner of cottage for habitation or dwelling, nor convert or ordain any building or housing made or hereafter to be made or used as a cottage for habitation or dwelling, unless the same person do assign and lay to the same cottage or building four acres of ground at the least, to be accounted

Poplar Cottage, showing gable end and stone fire back.
DANAE TANKARD

according to the statute or ordinance De terris mensurandis being his or her own freehold and inheritance lying near to the said cottage, to be continually occupied and manured therewith so long as the same cottage shall be inhabited; upon pain that every such offender shall forfeit, to [the Queen] … £10 of lawful money of England for every such offence.

Prosecution of the Act rested with three authorities: the justices of assize at the court of assize, justices of the peace at the court of quarter sessions, and manorial lords in their manor courts. The justices of assize and justices of the peace were allowed to grant exemption from the Act on grounds of poverty. The Act also made it illegal for householders to take in lodgers (or 'inmates'), and for cottages to be occupied by more than one family.[11]

This Act should be seen in the context of the developing Poor Law legislation discussed in chapter 3. Although the concept of 'settlement' was not formalised until 1662, the idea that everyone had a home parish to which he or she could be returned was already implicit in much of the earlier legislation. With the establishment of compulsory poor rates in 1572, vagrancy became as much an economic as a social problem, and parishes were increasingly hostile to strangers who might make demands on the communal purse. The 'deserving poor' became a distinct social category within their communities, identifiable both by the ratepayers who contributed towards their relief and by the paupers themselves. Legislators had this category of poor in mind when they drafted the 1598 'Act for the relief of the poor', which qualified the earlier legislation by giving churchwardens and overseers the authority to build 'convenient houses of dwelling' on manorial waste and commons and to place inmates and more than one family in cottages without being subject to prosecution under the 1589 Act.[12]

The 1589 Act intended manor courts and the courts of assize and quarter sessions to serve as overlapping rather than hierarchical jurisdictions. In Sussex, manorial courts certainly heard cases relating to illegal cottage building. For example, in 1622 Robert Andrews was presented in the Cowdray manorial court for building without licence a cottage on Henley Common. He was fined 10s., and ordered to pull it down before the next court or face a further fine of 40s. However, such presentments do not generally refer to the 1589 Act or even to the requirement that a cottage should have four acres of land; in other words, they appear to have been dealt with as manorial rather than statutory transgressions. It was in the courts of assize and quarter sessions that the prosecution of the Act took place, with illegal cottages forming a small, but regular, amount of business. Those found guilty of building or continuing illegal cottages paid a small monetary fine, usually sixpence or a shilling (and never the statutory fine of £10 or 40s. a month), and were ordered to pull the cottage down. Failure to obey an order could lead to further prosecution. In a minority of cases, the court responded by granting a licence to continue the cottage, usually for a fixed term.[13]

The attitude of the manorial lord to the success or failure of a cottage-building venture was crucial; so too was that of the local inhabitants. In 1617 the lord of the manor of Cowdray granted John Pratt a licence to enclose a parcel of waste ground and to build a cottage on it after he submitted a supporting petition signed by 'diverse tenants'. On the same manor in 1630 the lord, 'with the assent of the tenants of this manor', granted George Haley a retrospective licence for a cottage which he had built illegally on manorial waste. The motives of the tenants in supporting Pratt and Haley are not recorded, but they were perhaps more to do with pecuniary self-interest than with Christian charity (not that the two were mutually exclusive). In 1649 the inhabitants of Shipley petitioned the quarter sessions to allow two husbandmen, William and Nicholas Powell, to continue their cottages, 'both being very poor and having very great charge of wives and children', recognising that this would be less expensive than finding them parish housing or maintaining them in a house of correction (a forerunner of the workhouse). Even if they had the consent of the lord, prospective cottage-builders could face opposition from other inhabitants. In 1627 Robert Pearlie, a poor husbandman who, with his wife and eleven children, had been evicted from his last residence, petitioned the quarter sessions because the parishioners of Madehurst refused to allow him to erect a cottage, though he had been given permission (and even a timber frame) by the lord of the manor. Cottages licensed by the lord usually became copyhold or leasehold properties; in other words their inhabitants became legitimate tenants of the manor, paying an annual rent and subject to manorial custom.[14]

The variety of cottage housing

Most prosecutions for illegal cottage-building do not record any information about the size and construction of the dwellings. Anything erected hastily would have been little more than a shack (usually described as 'huts' or 'cotes'), providing the most rudimentary shelter and built of such natural materials as could be scavenged – hedgerow timber and coppice wood, with fern or turves for a roof covering. Such buildings were not, in a technical sense, 'hovels', since at this date in Sussex a hovel was an open-sided agricultural or industrial building. To build a more permanent structure required planning and craftsmanship. Of the materials required for construction, only the mud used for daub and a limited amount of stone

Poplar Cottage prior to dismantling.
RICHARD HARRIS/WDOAM ARCHIVE

would have been readily and freely available. Other materials, such as timber and thatching straw, would have to be carefully sourced and almost certainly paid for, and it was also necessary to employ specialist craftsmen. Wood and timber supplies within a manor were highly regulated. On some manors copyhold tenants had the right to fell timber on their land to build and repair their houses and outbuildings (known as *housebote*), for making their ploughs and carts (*ploughbote* or *cartbote*), or for firewood (*firebote*). In other manors a licence was required. The distinction was important, since illegal felling of timber could result in forfeiture of the copyhold. In 1693 William Roch was presented in the Washington manor court for cutting down trees on his copyhold land without a licence. This should have resulted in its forfeiture, but the lord 'by his special grace' pardoned him and instead he paid a fine of 20s. 7d. Squatters, however, had no timber rights at all.[15]

A good account of the variety of wasteland cottages appears in *The Toilers of the Field* by Richard Jefferies, first published in 1892. He begins by describing the process of enclosure. The squatter raised a low bank of earth around his plot, on which he planted fast-growing elder to form a hedge. After a couple of seasons, when the hedge had grown, he built a gate which he could padlock. At its most basic, the squatter's cottage consisted of four posts set directly into the ground (in other words, earth-fast posts) which supported the cross beam and roof. It had wattle-and-daub walls and a thatched roof. In areas with an adequate supply of stone the squatter might build a sturdier, single-storey cottage with two rooms of equal size, one heated for living and one unheated for sleeping. Additional storage was provided by a lean-to or outshut at one end. The walls of these cottages tended to be not more than six feet high, and they were surmounted by a thatched roof. Floors were made of rammed earth, and the rooms were open to the rafters. Finally, Jefferies describes the more 'substantial-looking cottage', with two rooms downstairs and two upstairs, plus the inevitable lean-to. He observes that 'these were originally built by men who had saved a little money, had showed, perhaps, a certain talent for hedge carpentering or thatching, become tinkers, or even blacksmiths'. The squatter economised by doing a lot of the labour himself and by buying 'cheap' and 'second-class' materials, which were nevertheless good enough for the job. Although written at a much later date, Jefferies' description is useful because it highlights the advance planning necessary for illegal cottage building and the range of construction methods and cottage types.[16]

We can obtain some idea of the labour involved in cottage building from a Wiltshire example. In 1698 six men were presented in the manor court of Downton for erecting a cottage on the lord's waste: Nicholas Lane, the cottage 'owner'; Samuel Wheeler, a carpenter; his apprentice, Walter Sheppard; Joseph Chalke, a thatcher; George Noble, who 'breaded' (daubed) the cottage walls; and 'one other man who helped to dig the holes for erecting the said cottage'. The reference to digging holes suggests that this cottage was built with earth-fast posts, which went directly into the ground rather than onto a sill beam or sole plate.[17]

Poplar Cottage c.1940, showing brick chimney and outshut.
WDOAM ARCHIVE

As has been described at the start of this chapter, examination of Poplar's surviving timbers suggests that they came from two open-grown oak trees (that is, from parkland as opposed to woodland), one or two smaller oaks, and several small elms of about 12 to 15 inches in diameter. The trees were converted into timber by axe-hewing and pit-sawing, both of which were specialist skills. Once the frame was made, it still had to be erected, wattle-and-daubed, and thatched, together with the internal carpentry. This process would have taken several days and could hardly have escaped the notice of other villagers – or of manorial officials. To give some idea of the labour involved, when the cottage was re-erected at the Museum in 1999 it took three men 2½ days to erect the frame. Poplar is also quite a large cottage – equivalent to Jefferies' 'substantial-looking cottage'. It may be that despite the lack of archaeological evidence the cottage was not the first one to be built on the site, and that it replaced an inferior dwelling which had established the occupant's claim to the land. Research undertaken on other surviving wasteland cottages indicates that many are indeed the second or third to be built on the site, reflecting a gradual improvement in the economic status of their inhabitants. Without documentary evidence of the cottage's origins, however, this hypothesis simply cannot be proved.

Wasteland cottages and their occupants in Washington and Chancton

The court book for the manor of Chancton, beginning in 1603, records several presentments in the early seventeenth century for the illegal erection of cottages on manorial waste. For example, in 1603 the court presented William Wilkin for building a cottage without a licence on Washington Common. In May 1605 he was presented again, together with Widow Gatton, Thomas Peter, John Bounde and Robert Payne, all of whom had built cottages on the waste. They were each fined 6s. 8d. and ordered to pull the cottages down before the feast of All Saints (1 November) or pay a further fine of 10s.[18]

One example of a cottager who almost certainly lived on or near the manorial waste is Henry Henshaw, a mason, who held a freehold cottage from the manor of Chancton for an annual rent of two fat capons. His will, dated 9 February 1691, describes this as 'the freehold house or tenement wherein I now dwell with all gardens, orchards, backsides or any other profits or appurtenances'. The garden and orchard are likely to have been the extent of his landholding. The freehold status of the cottage, together with its archaic rent, suggests that this was an early enclosure, possibly on demesne land. Henshaw was survived by his wife, Susan, and daughters, Jane (who was married to William Churcher) and Elizabeth, who was unmarried and might still have lived at home. He had held parochial office as a churchwarden in 1669, and was overseer of the poor in 1672. In 1685 he was presented with Richard Patching in the manor court for digging and removing turf from the lord's waste, which he probably intended to sell.

His movable estate, as recorded in his probate inventory of April 1691, was valued at a modest £11 6s. 1d. However, in his will he left Elizabeth the substantial sum of £15 to be paid out of the sale of his cottage when she reached 21 or got married. The inventory shows that his cottage contained a hall, a kitchen and a brewhouse downstairs, and a kitchen chamber upstairs. No hall chamber is recorded. He also had a 'shop' (that is, a workshop), which may have been a detached building. He had bacon worth 15s. hanging in his chimney, and 'turf and other lumber' valued at 5s. The only livestock he owned at the time of his death was a mare which, with her bridle and saddle, was valued at £2 2s. 6d. However, the amount of bacon hanging in the chimney is too high for domestic consumption alone, suggesting that he was producing it for the market from his own pigs. No crops or agricultural equipment are recorded.[19]

The earliest surviving court book for the manor of Washington begins in 1682, by which time there were already half a dozen wasteland cottages, all copyhold, for which the tenants paid annual rents of sixpence (or a penny in one case). Such cottages can be identified either because they are described as 'formerly part of the waste', or because of their location on or adjacent to manorial waste, or both. Identifying the occupants of these cottages is far from straightforward, because it is evident that some of the copyhold tenants whose names appear in the manor court book were leasing them out for a market rent and themselves living elsewhere. However, the identity of two occupants can be established – James Caplen who died in 1693, and Thomas Gent who died in 1736, both husbandmen. Their cottages are depicted on the Figge map.[20]

James Caplen served as a churchwarden in 1686 and was among the homage (or jury) in the manor court in 1686, 1689 and 1692. At his death in 1693 he held a cottage for an annual rent of sixpence, described in the court book as a copyhold cottage and one acre of land besides New Common. The heriot payable at his death was a small cash payment of 12d., rather than the traditional 'best beast'. This appears to have been his only holding, and so it is reasonable to assume that he was living in the cottage and that the single acre was the extent of his land. The small size of his holding is corroborated by his probate inventory, which records that he had a mare and a colt and five hives of bees but no other livestock or crops. The main range of his house comprised a hall and a kitchen downstairs and two chambers upstairs. In addition, the inventory records that he had a buttery and a milkhouse, possibly in outshuts at the back of the house, as well as two 'outlets', one identified by its location

Probate inventory of Henry Henshaw, 1691.
WSRO EP/I/29/205/60

as the 'north outlet' which had some kind of storage space above (described as a 'flite'). The only agricultural building included in the inventory is a stable.

Caplen's 'north outlet' contained brewing equipment (two 'keelers' and a furnace), while the space above it contained 250 'hoops', and in his stable were a hundred pieces of cordwood, probably used as fuel for brewing. The hoops may have been from barrels which Caplen had dismantled for storage; alternatively he may have been making hoops to sell. It is unlikely that he was a cooper, making barrels, since no specialist tools are listed. The presence of a milkhouse would normally indicate ownership of at least one cow, but none is listed, and at the time of his death Caplen seems to have been cow-less.[21] His estate was valued at £42 11s., including a sizeable £13 5s. in cash. He was survived by his wife, Susan, and at least one son, Thomas.[22]

Men such as Henry Henshaw and James Caplen were resourceful and evidently not solely dependent upon wage labour. Their ability to exploit common land would have been crucial to their economic independence, as would their landholding, small though it was. However, neither of them lived 'outside the market': they sold their skills and manufactured products and bought those essentials which they could not produce themselves. Their wives, too, are likely to have contributed towards the household budget by spinning. It is hard to gauge how dependent these households would have been on the market for their food and drink: both had brewing equipment, but there is no evidence for either baking or dairying, despite Caplen's 'milkhouse'.

Our final example of the occupant of a wasteland cottage, Thomas Gent, is slightly different. When he died in 1736 he had three cottages, living in one and renting out the other two. Two of the cottages, both held of the manor of Washington, are shown on the Figge map drawn at the end of the 1730s, that on Heath Common (where he lived) presumably being that which had been held by his father, also Thomas Gent, whose death was presented in the manor court in 1707. The other cottage might have been held of the manor of Chancton, since in October 1735 Gent was presented in the Chancton manor court for enclosing a parcel of waste without licence. His probate inventory suggests that his house was similar in size to that of James Caplen (and therefore to Poplar), with two rooms in the main range downstairs (described as a kitchen and hall) and two upstairs (although only a kitchen chamber is listed).

In addition, his inventory records a drink room and brewhouse, probably in outshuts, and an 'oatmeal house', which would have been a detached building (one is shown on the map), probably containing a horse-gin. His oatmeal house included a harness for the mill horse, oatmeal bags, tree fans (used for winnowing), wire sieves and split sieves (for purifying grain). He also had seventeen quarters of oats and fifteen bushels of peas, the principal ingredients of 'horse bread' (used as livestock fodder). He owned two horses and two sheep and an unspecified number of 'young hogs', and the total value of the estate was £42 17s. 6d. The occupants of the other cottages were Edward Burrey and Thomas Soane. Gent left all three cottages to his wife, Mary, during her lifetime, and thereafter he left the cottage in his own occupation to his son, William Gent; that in the occupation of Thomas Soane to his grandson Thomas (the son of William); and the cottage in the occupation of Edward Burrey to his son, Daniel Gent. William Gent acquired the oatmeal mill and all the mill tackling and horses after his mother's death. That Thomas Gent senior held three cottages reflects a not uncommon pattern, whereby the descendants of the original encroachers became landlords themselves as their social and economic prospects improved.[23]

The social status of cottagers

How did these cottagers fit into the social hierarchy of seventeenth-century Washington? There are no wills or probate inventories for anyone below the level of husbandman or craftsman, and it is reasonable to assume that a substantial proportion of even that socio-economic group fell below the wealth threshold for probate. Labourers are almost entirely invisible from Washington records (other than as defendants in quarter session and assize cases), and the poor typically only appear as an anonymous group, or in wills as recipients of bequests to 'the parish poor'.

The only real indication of wealth distribution between and within social groups comes from the value of estates given in probate inventories. This is a very crude measure of wealth, with assessed wealth dependent upon a number of factors – not least, the point in the agricultural year at which they were made and, more significantly, the age at which the individual died. In terms of assessed wealth at death, however, James Caplen and Thomas Gent were far from being the poorest husbandmen; with estates valued at approximately £42 they were, within their social group, relatively 'middling', despite their land poverty.

Without a comprehensive socio-occupational list for Washington, it is impossible to work out the relative size of any social group. However, of those groups that are visible – gentry, yeomen and husbandmen and craftsmen – it is apparent that the last was the largest. Husbandmen and craftsmen – even those with very little land such as James Caplen and Henry Henshaw – dominated manorial and parochial office-holding. They were jurors or homagers, churchwardens and overseers of the poor. They witnessed each other's wills and acted as appraisers for probate inventories, even though most were illiterate, 'signing' their names with a variety of marks. The pattern of bequests in their wills reveals that their strongest ties of kinship and friendship were with other husbandmen and craftsmen. They routinely left bequests to the parish poor, but where individual bequests were made outside their social group they were typically to those of yeoman status. In other words, they were more likely to align themselves with their social superiors rather than their social inferiors. Among the wider community, these men might serve as trial jurors at the assizes or at coroner's inquests, but they were not returned as constables for the Steyning hundred, an office that was typically filled by yeomen – no doubt the sort of men whom Robert Edsaw, himself a yeoman, had in mind when in his will of 1627 he referred to 'the most substantial men of the parish'.[24]

Life inside the cottage

Domestic culture among the husbandmen and craftsmen of seventeenth-century Washington was utilitarian, and cottage interiors were spartan. The inventory of Henry Henshaw listed eight pieces of furniture in his cottage: a table in the hall; a table and one chair in the kitchen; and one bed, two chests and two old stools in the kitchen chamber. That of James Caplen listed fourteen items: a table and form (bench) in the hall; two tables, one form and one cupboard in the kitchen; two beds and four chests in the kitchen chamber; and three chests in the hall chamber. The hall chamber also had a featherbed (mattress) with bedding, but no bedstead. Cooking was clearly undertaken in the hall, since it contained a pair of gridirons,

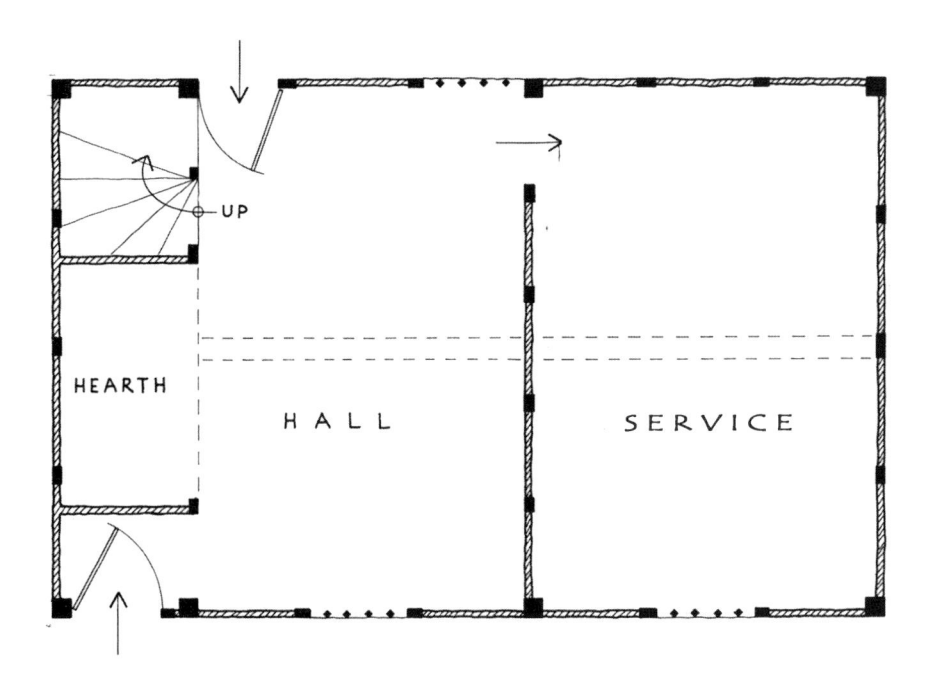

Floor plan of Poplar Cottage.
RICHARD HARRIS

tongs, a spit and flesh hook. The kitchen, location of the only chair, contained four pewter dishes, two old porringers, a salt, a warming pan, two bowls, one platter, three dishes and a spoon. By his will he bequeathed a brass pot to his eldest daughter, Jane, and his bell-brass skillet to his youngest daughter, Elizabeth. No cooking equipment is recorded in Caplen's inventory.[25]

As would be expected, the cottages of husbandmen and craftsmen had similar types of furniture and domestic equipment to the houses of their wealthier yeomen neighbours, but the range was more limited and – we can assume – the quality inferior. Most households had tablecloths, but they were kept for best, since in probate inventories they are usually listed with other household linen in an upstairs chamber. Households of this status generally did not have cushions or upholstered chairs, but then neither did those of most yeomen in seventeenth-century downland communities. Many objects were in use for two or three generations, either inherited from relatives and friends or acquired second-hand. Domestic metalware – brass, iron and pewter – was valuable and repairable. Pottery or earthenware was ubiquitous, but is seldom recorded in inventories because of its low value. Upstairs the level of comfort was improving, with many husbandman and craftsman households having at least one feather or flock bed, with feather or flock pillows or bolsters. Other beds

Poplar: the hall, looking towards the smoke bay.
RICHARD HARRIS

were of chaff (chopped straw or hay or the husks from winnowed grain). Chests and boxes continued to serve as the main storage space for household linen, clothing and other valuable items. By 1736, when Thomas Gent died, 'new' types of household goods had begun to appear: his inventory records a round table and a clock with its case in the kitchen. In the early eighteenth century clocks were widely owned by husbandmen and were usually found in the kitchen.[26]

Living on the margins?

Wasteland cottagers are often viewed by historians as 'economically marginal' – not so much the dispossessed (for that term would imply that they had had something taken away) as the 'unpossessed', who had no stake in the land or in the regulation of their communities. As such, they are seen as the forerunners of the post-enclosure agricultural labourer, with no means of subsistence other than their wages. However, the reality is more complex. With Poplar Cottage and others like it we encounter a significant segment of the rural population who, despite their poverty in terms of land, were financially resourceful and socially respectable. Many of these cottagers shared a 'middling' status, not only with other husbandman and craftsman but also with yeomen. The more truly 'unpossessed' – the labourers and paupers – are only faintly visible in the records that survive for seventeenth-century Washington. Their cottages, no doubt closer to the poorly built single-storey dwellings described by Jefferies, do not survive, and there is little to tell us about their economic, social or material lives. We get occasional glimpses of them in the records – for example, Alice Webb, a vagrant, who is only known to us because there is a record of her burial in 1631, or Francis Parson, a labourer, who together with a husbandman called Thomas Rye was found guilty in 1612 of stealing two loaves of bread worth 2*d.* each and a shirt band worth 12*d*.[27]

In the late seventeenth or early eighteenth century Poplar Cottage was 'modernised': a brick and stone chimney-stack was built inside the smoke bay, and an outshut was added to the back, providing an additional service room. It is likely that glass windows were inserted at around this time, replacing the traditional unglazed windows with their wooden mullions. These alterations would have made life inside the cottage significantly more comfortable. In its modified form Poplar Cottage was almost identical to Tindalls Cottage, built at a later date and in a different part of Sussex, and discussed in the next chapter.

Poplar: the hall chamber, looking towards stairwell.
RICHARD HARRIS

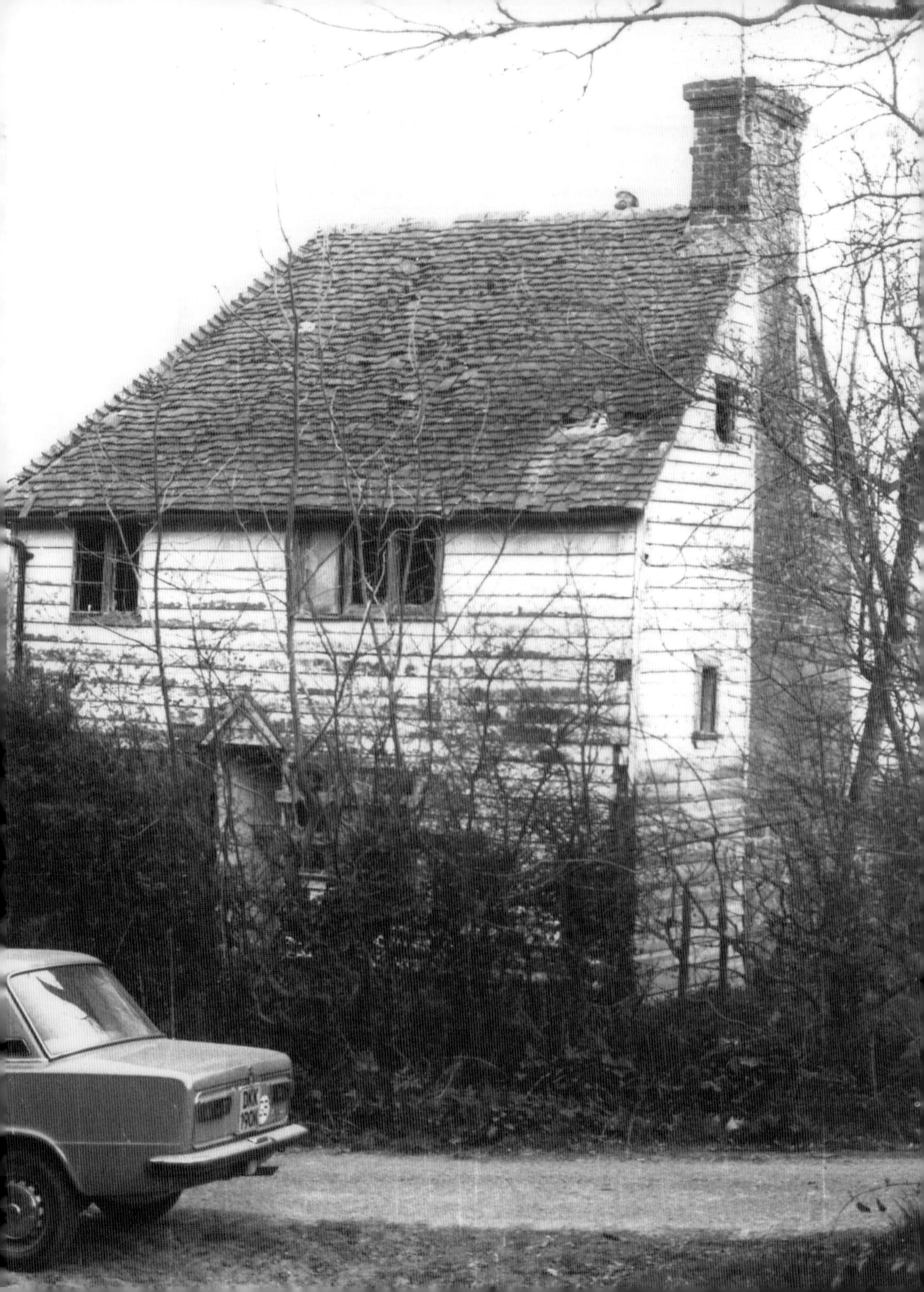

CHAPTER SIX

Tindalls Cottage: a husbandman's cottage from Ticehurst, East Sussex

Tindalls Cottage, from Ticehurst in East Sussex, is a timber-framed building which has been dated on stylistic grounds to the period 1700–1725. It was surveyed by David Martin in 1971. In 1974 it was dismantled by the Robertsbridge and District Archaeological Society in advance of the construction of the Bewl Bridge Reservoir (now called Bewl Water) and donated to the Museum. After more than 30 years in store the frame has now been re-erected and the cottage will open as an exhibit in 2013.

Its name, 'Tindalls', derives from the surname of the occupants from 1748 to 1806. In terms of its structure it is of the same general type as Poplar Cottage, with a gable-end chimney and a hipped terminal at the opposite end. In plan, Tindalls had two rooms within the main range downstairs – only one with a fireplace – together with two service rooms located within an outshut at the back. There were two rooms on the first floor, one with a fireplace, while a staircase to the north of the terminal chimney gave access to a further room or garret above the first floor. Almost all the timber in the cottage had been reused from an earlier structure which, together with the style of the building, initially led to it being identified as of mid-seventeenth-century or even sixteenth-century date. The cottage had been little altered since

Tindalls Cottage prior to dismantling, 1971.
DAVID MARTIN

its original construction, although the outshut had been rebuilt in brick, and the remaining walls had been weather-boarded.

However, despite its structural similarities to Poplar, Tindalls is not a common edge or wayside cottage, since it had about 26 acres of land and was not built on manorial waste. Instead, it was a copyhold tenement of the manor of Hammerden, which was held by the Apsley family from the early seventeenth century until 1833. A map of 1619 shows an earlier cottage abutting onto the highway and onto an enclosed piece of ground taken out of a larger field. At this date the tenement, described in the survey as 'late Brissendens', included a barn and just over sixteen acres of land. In 1654 the cottage and land were acquired by a yeoman by the name of William Peckham, who lived in the neighbouring parish of Salehurst. Seven years later he bought three adjoining pieces of land, comprising eight acres in total, bringing the overall extent of the property to some 26 acres. A map of 1836 records that at that time the total area of the farm was 26 acres 1 rod 11 perches. Of this, just over twelve acres were arable and just over seven were pasture. The house and garden accounted for 1 rod 4 perches, and the 'shaw' (an area of woodland) contained 33 perches. Members of the Peckham family, descendants of William, held the farm until 1788. As copyhold tenants they paid an annual quit rent of 7½d. to the lords of the manor. However, the actual occupants of the farm were tenants of the Peckhams, paying the latter an annual rent of between £8 and £9 10s.[1]

Tindalls' occupants

The occupants of Tindalls Cottage can be identified through Sussex land tax returns, which begin in 1692 and end in 1785. The most important occupants were, first, Sarah Haselden, the widow of John Haselden, who was living in the cottage from at least 1692 until her death in 1721; second, John Tindall (1) and his family, living there from 1748; and third, John Tindall (2) and his family who were occupants from 1780. Unfortunately no wills or probate inventories survive for any of the occupants of the cottage.[2]

Sarah and John Haselden had eight children, born between 1665 and 1681. Their first child, Ann, died within a few days of birth, and another daughter, Frances, died in 1681 aged five. John himself died in 1687, and it is possible that Sarah moved to Tindalls when she became widowed, accompanied by some of her children. No other biographical information about John and Sarah Haselden is available. John Tindall (1) moved to the cottage in 1748 together with his wife, Ann. They had six children, including a still-born baby in 1758 and a son, Stephen, who died in 1767 aged six. In 1750 and 1751 the parish was paying John Tindall (1) to foster two pauper children,

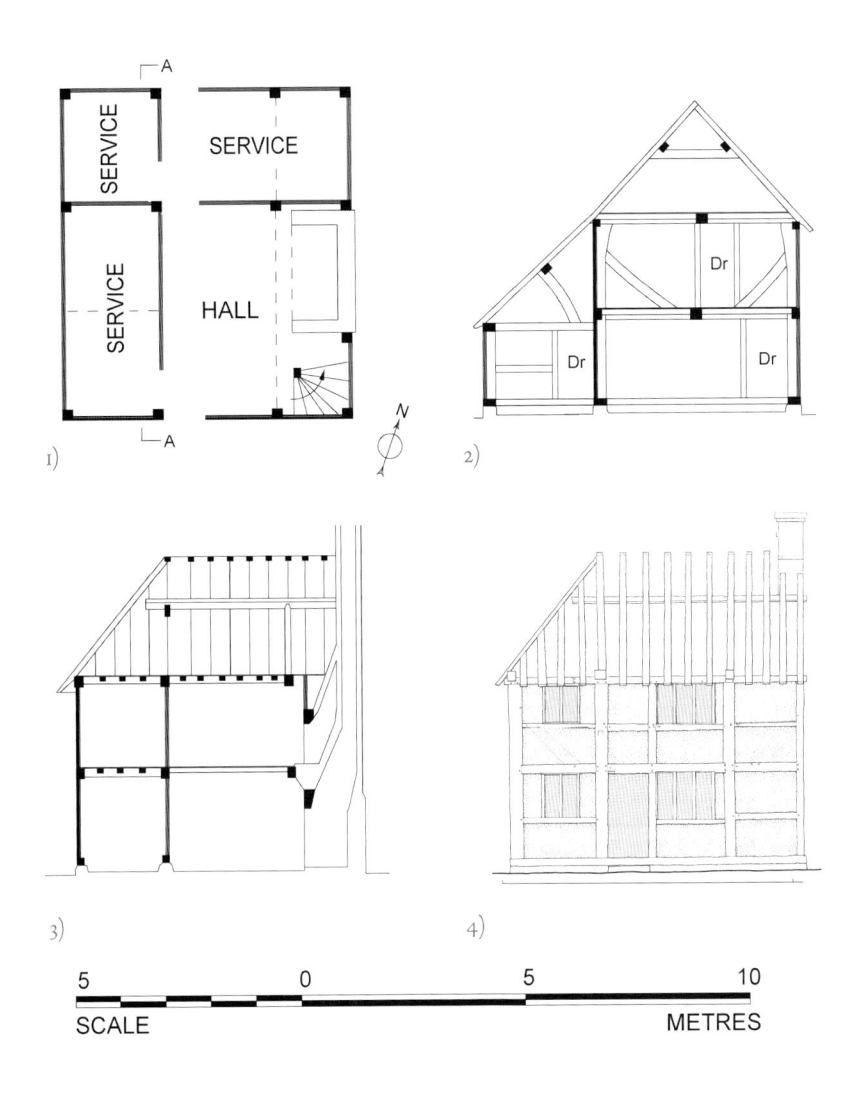

Tindalls Cottage as originally constructed 1) floor plan, 2) reconstructed cross section A–A (as marked on floor plan), 3) reconstructed longitudinal section, 4) reconstructed front (north) elevation.
DAVID MARTIN/RICHARD HARRIS

a girl named Anne Pettit and a boy called Nathaniel Burgess. John died in 1766, and his widow continued to occupy the cottage until her own death in 1780. It was then occupied by her son John Tindall (2), his wife Mary, and their seven children, including twin girls, Mary and Hannah, who were born in 1793. From 1798 the parish was also paying John to look after the illegitimate son of his daughter, Ann. Like his father, John took in parish children: Sarah Sayer from 1783 to 1784 and Grace Swift from 1800 to 1801. He died in 1806.[3]

Tindalls Cottage from rear, showing brick outshut, 1971.
DAVID MARTIN

Tindalls Cottage from east, 1971.
DAVID MARTIN

This raises an interesting question: who were the parish children that lived with the Tindalls? Nathaniel Burgess was the son of William Burgess, a carpenter, and Anne his wife. He had four siblings: Deborah, William, Samuel and Elizabeth. Their mother was buried on 1 June 1748, three days after the burial of her unbaptised infant, while their father William, described in the parish register as a 'carpenter, a poor man', was buried on 14 December 1749. All the orphaned children then became the responsibility of the parish. The three younger ones, William, Samuel and Elizabeth, were initially fostered out together to Mr Jarvis for fourpence a week. The elder two, Deborah and Nathaniel, were fostered out separately. Anne Pettit and her family were the subject of a removal order from the parish of Mayfield to the parish of Ticehurst on 2 June 1740, at which time she was described as 'above a year old'. This means that she entered Tindall's household when she was about 11 years of age.

A Sarah Sayer, the illegitimate daughter of Anne Sayer by William Christmas, the 'reputed father', was baptised in Ticehurst on 21 May 1769, which would make her 14 at the time she entered Tindall's service. There is no information about the identity of Grace Swift. On both occasions that John Tindall (1) took in children,

Tindalls Cottage being demolished prior to its removal to the WDOAM.
DAVID MARTIN

Detail of map of manor of Hammerden showing location of Tindalls Cottage and its barn (numbered 473 and 475).
ESRO SAS/CO/D/1

Close up of Tindalls Cottage and its barn from Hammerden map.
ESRO SAS/CO/D/1

the parish met the costs of their maintenance. He received £2 for keeping Anne Pettit for a year, together with 2s. 6d. for the cost of 'making and mending for her the year', and 16d. a week for Nathaniel Burgess, whose clothing was provided by the parish. In 1783 John Tindall (2) agreed to pay Sarah Sayer a wage of 5s. for the year; in 1800 the parish paid him a guinea to keep Grace Swift and provided her with clothing. The payment of a wage to Sarah Sayer probably reflects the fact that she was 14, and therefore of sufficient maturity to earn her keep as a domestic servant.[4]

Eighteenth-century Ticehurst

The parish of Ticehurst, lying within the High Weald, is situated in the Rape of Hastings, the most easterly of the six rapes of Sussex. It is a large parish of 8,250 acres, and in 1724 there were 150 resident families. This figure, if multiplied by an average household size of five, would suggest a population of about 750. In fact it may have been closer to 900, since in 1801, when the first census was compiled, Ticehurst had over 1,400 inhabitants. Nationally, the population of England increased by nearly 60 per cent over this period (from 5.5 million in 1730 to 8.7 million in 1801), and it seems unlikely that the rate of growth within a rural parish such as Ticehurst would have been much higher.[5]

The High Weald is primarily a wood-pasture region, with an emphasis on pastoral rather than arable farming. Cattle were the predominant livestock and were kept for their meat, although cows also supplied most of the region's dairying needs. A proportion of calves were fattened and killed to provide veal; those that were allowed to reach maturity might be used for breeding and draught purposes before being fattened for slaughter. The significance of cattle in the rural economy is reflected in the types of crops that were grown: fodder crops, such as oats, peas, beans and tares, predominated. Wheat and barley were the main crops grown for human consumption, although, as discussed below, hop-growing became increasingly widespread over the course of the eighteenth century.

It was a land of relatively small farms: in the early eighteenth century about half were between 15 and 49 acres. Fields also tended to be small, often no more than two acres, and were enclosed with broad hedges. However, by the end of the eighteenth century many small farms had been incorporated into larger units, whose proprietors could afford the level of capitalisation required to achieve continued growth in output. Nationally, agricultural output increased by two and a half to three times between 1700 and 1850, much of this being the result of increased land productivity.[6]

By the early eighteenth century hops had become a significant part of the rural economy. About one third of all farms within the Rape of Hastings grew hops and, after barns, oasthouses were the most common farm buildings. Hops were usually grown in small plots or gardens of less than two acres. In Ticehurst hops appear to have been widely grown, even by small farmers such as the occupants of Tindalls Cottage. Tithe account books covering the period 1744 to 1770 show that first John Tindall (1) and later his widow, Ann, were making annual cash payments to the vicar of 4s. 6d. in lieu of tithes on their hops, based on an area of cultivation of 1 rod 33 perches.[7]

If successful, hops gave higher returns per acre than other crops. However, cultivation was always risky because of the unreliable yield, and it was also expensive – both in terms of the initial investment required and the annual costs of cultivation. Arthur Young, in his *General View of the Agriculture of the County of Sussex* published in 1813, described the practice of hop-farming in the Sussex Weald as 'the gambling of farmers' akin to entering a state lottery, with a vast loss on all tickets but massive pay-outs on some. According to Young, it was the hope of being a winner that kept men going even when they knew the odds were against them.[8]

Approximately ten times more labour was required for hop cultivation than for arable farming. Since hops had to be picked by hand, a large casual labour force was used during the harvest. Hop cultivation also employed large numbers of women and children, because their smaller hands and manual dexterity were good for hop-tying and picking. Boys and girls as young as seven or eight were employed during winter for shaving hop-poles, of which 3,000–4,000 were required per acre, about 500–600 of which had to be replaced every year. After picking, the hops had to be dried: from the mid-seventeenth century this was done in oasthouses. Early oasthouses were small, two-storey, timber-framed buildings very similar to detached kitchens. Indeed, during the seventeenth century some former kitchens or service blocks were converted for hop-drying and malt manufacture. The distinctive cowl-capped brick roundels that are such a characteristic part of the building landscape of the Kent and Sussex Weald were only introduced in the nineteenth century after hop production had increased significantly.[9]

The capital outlay required for oasthouses meant that only the larger farmers could afford them. In Ticehurst the yeoman Thomas Ollive, whose moveable estate was valued at an impressive £979 19s. 10d. on his death in 1719, had an oasthouse containing (among other things) two oast-hairs (horsehair sacking placed over the slatted drying floor of the kiln) and two coal baskets. His oasthouse also contained a malt tub, suggesting that it might have had a dual use both for hop-drying and malt-manufacture. Ollive's inventory also records 'hop poles and hay at several places', valued at £92 9s. Men such as Thomas Ollive probably bought up the hops grown by their less substantial neighbours, including the Haseldens and the Tindalls. After drying, hops were sent for sale to London.[10]

References in Ticehurst probate inventories to equipment and materials indicate that the spinning of wool, flax and tow formed a significant domestic industry. On her death in 1711 the widow Agnes Hayward had 1½ lb of tow yarn and an old spinning wheel and reel. The inventories of Thomas Thompsett and Richard Neale, dated 1714 and 1716 respectively, record linen trendles or wheels. Spinning, knitting and weaving were also the main employment of the parish poor, a theme discussed in more detail below. With the advent of mechanised production in the late eighteenth century the cottage textile industry collapsed, depriving many rural labourers (and especially women) of an important source of income.[11]

The social status of husbandmen in Ticehurst

In contemporary records neither John Haselden, nor John Tindall father or son, is described as a husbandman. However, with a smallholding of 26 acres the occupants of Tindalls Cottage were typical of many husbandmen of the early modern period – economically independent, farming their own land, and producing a small marketable surplus each year. Unlike some husbandmen, however, the occupants were not manorial tenants, but rented their land from the Peckhams, who were the copyhold tenants of the manor of Hammerden. Unfortunately, we know very little about their economic activities. The map of 1836 records that at that date the smallholding comprised twelve acres of arable, seven acres of pasture, 33 perches of woodland and 1 rod 4 perches of garden. The proportion of pasture and arable might, of course, have changed since the time of the Haseldens and Tindalls. As already noted, John Tindall (1) grew hops and was assessed for tithes on 1 rod and 33 perches of hops in the 1750s. It has already been suggested that he sold his hop harvest to a larger farmer for processing. Harvest labour was probably provided by his wife and children (including the parish children). If the seven acres of pasture went back to his time, he is likely to have kept at least two cows (based on four acres per cow) to supply the dairy products for his household, but he would not have had a bull or a draught team – those would be borrowed or hired from a neighbour. In 1752 the parish paid him a shilling for milk for the care of a sick pauper with smallpox, but it is unlikely that he normally had sufficient surplus milk for regular commercial dairying. Additional income would have been generated by the sale of calves as leanstock. His wife and daughters may have supplemented the household income by spinning and knitting.[12]

When his stillborn baby was buried in 1758 the parish register described John Tindall (1) as a 'labourer', suggesting that he was at least partly dependent on wages. Possibly he hired himself out as an agricultural labourer at certain times of the year, or when his income from farming was insufficient to maintain his household. Of course, the use of the term might simply be inaccurate, reflecting a lack of concern on the part of the parish clerk who recorded the child's burial. But it does highlight the ambivalent position of men such as John Tindall within the social hierarchy of eighteenth-century Ticehurst. Sarah Haselden and both John Tindalls paid poor rates – something which historians have seen as the dividing line between membership of the 'middle' and the 'meaner' or 'poorer' sort – but when other factors are taken into account, their 'middling' status is less secure.[13]

The economic fortunes of such families would have risen and fallen depending on their position within the life cycle. The 'high' points were likely to be before the births of the first children, and after the children were old enough to work; 'low' points would be when the children were young and when the couple themselves were old. The large families of John and Sarah Haselden and the Tindalls obviously put a strain on their finances, even when things were going well. As widows both Sarah Haselden and Ann Tindall were economically vulnerable, particularly as they got older. This is reflected in the fact that Ann Tindall became a recipient of poor relief in the final year of her life. In February 1778 she was among the poor householders chosen by the parish vestry to receive charitable doles and was given 7s. 3d. John Tindall (2) received weekly payments of 2s. from the parish from 1798 onwards to look after his illegitimate grandson William. This implies that he lacked sufficient resources to support the child himself.[14]

Poor rate assessments based on annual property rental values allow us to evaluate the distribution of wealth within Ticehurst. In 1694 the highest land value of a property was £100, the lowest £1. Sarah Haselden was assessed on property valued at £6. Those with property valued at £14 or lower constituted 78 per cent of the assessed population. Within this, those within the bands of £5–£9 and £1–£5 formed 28 per cent each. Despite their numerical significance, though, the husbandmen and craftsmen in Ticehurst were excluded from parish government, which was dominated by a small group of wealthy men. Many of these 'principal inhabitants' were styled 'gentlemen' in the parish records. An entry in the churchwardens' accounts for 8 November 1761 shows us this elitism in operation. It records that 'at a vestry held this day pursuant to public notice given in the church this morning it is agreed to repair the steeple and the church as the churchwardens and *principal inhabitants* shall think necessary'. The men who put their signature to this were William Watson, John Noaks, Thomas Usherwood, John Carter, Thomas Waghorn, John Tompsett and Isaac Tuppeny (the latter two currently holding the office of churchwarden). William Watson, 'gent', John Noaks, John Tompsett and Thomas Usherwood were among the 31 householders who, in March 1757, agreed to contribute money towards the cost of buying corn for the poor, during a period of rapidly escalating food prices.[15]

Such men formed a self-selected oligarchy, rotating among themselves vestry membership and the parish offices of churchwarden and overseer. In effect, therefore, smallholding husbandmen such as the Tindalls were voiceless within the affairs of the parish, overshadowed by the greater social, economic and political weight of the 'principal inhabitants'. This contrasts with the experience of the husbandmen and cottage occupants in seventeenth-century Washington who, as we have seen, dominated manorial and parochial office-holding.

The social divisions within the village were reflected in the seating arrangements in the parish church. Those with the means to do so could avoid mixing with their social inferiors by claiming a family pew near the pulpit, where they could listen to the sermon in comfort and without distraction. In 1750 the vestry granted Thomas Constable, gentleman, and his heirs 'the seat or pew in the back south aisle of the parish church next adjoining to the reading desk and pulpit, the same having been made up and built at the sole charge of Thomas Constable, gentleman, containing from east to west 4 ft 10 in and from south to north 6 ft 8 in'. At the same meeting Joseph Newington, gentleman, was granted 'the next adjoining seat or pew in the back south aisle'. Various degrees of 'middling' sort would have filled the body of the nave in shared pews, while servants and the 'meaner' sort would have been on benches at the back. The churchwardens' accounts for 1743 record that 12s. 11d. was paid to 'Mr William Waghorne for 3 days' work himself building the servant maids' seat and 2½ days for 2 men'. Those who could afford prestigious locations at the front of the nave were not necessarily bothered about the effect their seating had on other parishioners: the diocesan survey of 1686 recorded that 'there were some seats built … whose height incommodes the hearing of those seats behind them'.[16]

The 1790s were difficult times for small farmers such as John Tindall (2). They were already being squeezed as larger farmers, who could afford significant capital investment, reaped the rewards from agricultural improvements and the rapidly expanding hop industry. The start of the Napoleonic Wars in 1793 triggered massive rises in food prices, when the government took inflationary measures to raise finance. Grain prices rose inexorably over the rest of the decade, as inflation combined with a succession of failed or poor harvests. In September 1794 the wheat component of the diet of a family in southern England with two children cost 4s. 5d. a week; in March 1796 it was 10s. 5d.; in June 1800, 15s. and in March 1801 it reached its highest level of 17s., before falling back to 10s. by the end of August. The rise in grain prices enriched large farmers, leading to another phase of farm engrossment and capitalisation. Small and subsistence farmers such as John Tindall (2) may not only have had little or no surplus grain to sell to the market, but may even have had to buy grain to feed their household. The massive growth in population over the previous century had led to an over-supply of labour in rural areas, so that an increasing number of labourers were under-employed or unemployed. This problem was exacerbated by the rising cost of living, and ratepayers faced increasingly punitive poor rates as the cost of maintaining the parish poor escalated. Again, the small farmers were hit hardest, a problem explicitly recognised by the Ticehurst parish vestry in 1801, when it agreed to consider 'the best method of relieving the small farmers and small tradesmen from the present heavy poor rates'.[17]

By the late eighteenth century the traditional socio-economic terms for those who earned their living from the land – yeoman, husbandman and labourer – were still being applied. However, the language of 'sorts', which had come into use in the late sixteenth century, was gradually being superseded by a language of 'class'. Initially, it was applied in a similarly fluid way, but by the early nineteenth century a more rigid codification of society into 'working', 'middle' and 'upper' classes was beginning to emerge. Some historians have argued that the last decade of the eighteenth century accelerated the creation of a new rural proletariat – the 'ag labs' or agricultural labourers that we are all familiar with from the decennial censuses of the nineteenth century. This group was landless and wage dependent, and deprived of access to common land by the parliamentary enclosures that began in the second half of the eighteenth century. It should be pointed out, however, that parliamentary enclosure in Sussex was less widespread, and took place later, than in many other parts of the country. In Ticehurst, as in most other parts of East Sussex, there were no common fields, and most of the waste had already been enclosed piecemeal through the manorial courts.[18]

The education and employment of children

Most eighteenth-century social commentators agreed that habits of work had to be learned at an early age in order to produce economically useful adults. Child labour was therefore viewed as beneficial, while idleness was regarded as a threat to future productivity. However, the extent to which children were employed in agriculture in the eighteenth century has been disputed by historians, mainly because the evidence is so patchy.[19] Arthur Young includes details of child employment in his *General View of the Agriculture of the County of Sussex*, based on information given to him by local landowners and farmers in the 1790s.

According to Young, a boy of 8 or 9 years old could earn threepence a day, and by the age of 11 or 12 sixpence a day. In contrast, an adult male earned between 16*d.* and 18*d.* daily. There were fewer employment opportunities for girls; they could earn threepence or fourpence weeding or haymaking. At 10 years old girls could earn money from spinning, pea- and wheat-dropping (sowing peas and wheat by hand) and from gleaning. On the basis of figures provided by Lord Egremont (owner of the Petworth estate), Young estimated that the total annual contribution of a boy of 12 to the household budget was £9 12*s.*, that of a 10-year-old girl £4. The wife contributed £1 10*s.*, and the husband £27 9*s.*, producing a total annual household income of

£42 11s. As we have seen, hop-farming employed large numbers of children in the Sussex Weald. Of the parish of Salehurst, which had 300–400 acres of hops, Young recorded that 'all the women and children' were set to work during hop harvest, with 1,000–1,200 employed for a period of between three and four weeks. During the winter months children were also employed for hop pole shaving.[20]

While the evidence for child employment may be anecdotal, these figures suggest that children from the age of eight upwards could and did make significant contributions towards the household income of rural families. Girls had considerably fewer employment opportunities and earned much less, so households without sons were at a disadvantage. Below the age of 8 children could contribute towards the economic welfare of the household by working in and around the house. They might gather fuel, carry water, undertake basic food preparation, help with the garden, feed poultry and livestock, and take care of their younger siblings. Although this work was unpaid it freed time for older children and parents to go out and earn.[21]

Girls and boys usually left home at the age of 13 or 14, to become domestic or farm servants or enter some kind of apprenticeship. It has been calculated that in the eighteenth century about 60 per cent of the population aged between 15 and 24 were servants. Below the age of 13 or 14 the costs of taking young people into a household, where they had to be fed and sometimes clothed, outweighed their labour value. The main economic benefit for their parents was not the additional income from their children's service, but being relieved of the cost of maintaining them. The general expectation was that the money which servants earned would be saved, so that they could set up independent households of their own on reaching adulthood.[22]

The employment of boys and girls in agriculture was seasonal and intermittent. In the absence of full-time schooling, most children faced long periods of relative idleness. During the eighteenth century perhaps half the sons and one-third of the daughters of poorer families typically received some kind of formal education, although attendance would have been interrupted by the seasonal employment cycle, particularly during the summer months, and much depended on their place of residence – some communities simply had no schools.[23]

In Ticehurst the opportunities for education are likely to have improved over the course of the eighteenth century. There was a school of some description there in 1754, when John Adam, schoolmaster, moved there from Rolvenden in Kent, although it may have been intended for the children of the wealthier inhabitants. Concern for the moral welfare of the children of the parish poor is reflected in attempts by the parish vestry to set up a school for them, but it is not clear whether this was achieved. In 1757 the parishioners agreed to establish a school for pauper children so that they could be 'instructed in the duties of religion and fed and

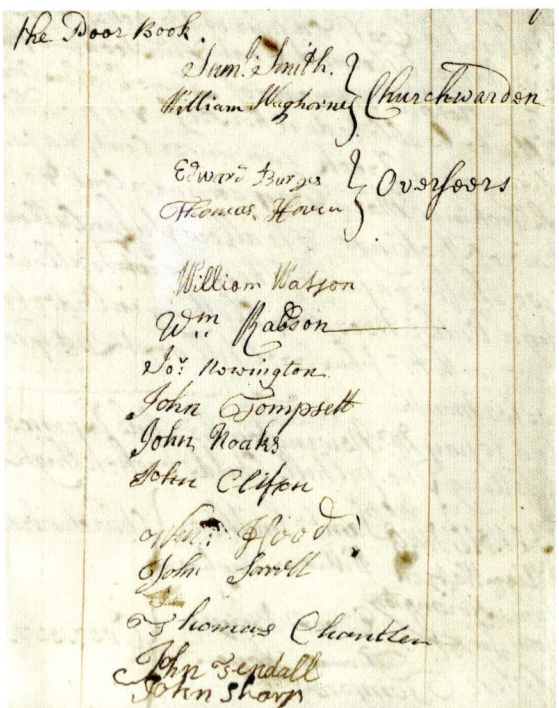

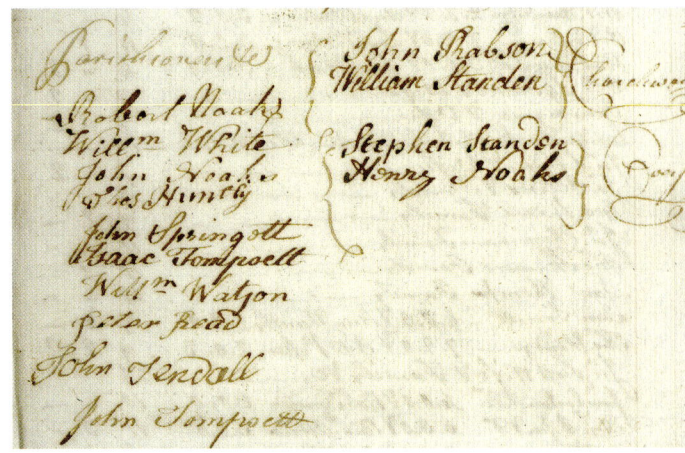

Left: Detail from Ticehurst overseers' accounts, 1751, showing the signature of John Tindall (1).
ESRO PAR 492/31/1/3

Right: Detail from Ticehurst overseers' accounts, 1783, showing the signature of John Tindall (2).
ESRO PAR 492/31/1/4

clothed in a decent manner'. The churchwardens and overseers were instructed to take subscriptions of 'such well disposed persons as are willing to promote this pious and charitable work'. No subscriptions are recorded, and the proposal seems to have come to nothing. In 1760 the parishioners agreed 'to build a poor house in Newark's platt which belongs to the parish not exceeding the sum of £300 with a proper room in it for a school, the front and each end to be bricked to the first floor and to hire money at 4% per annum'.

The following year John Noaks (as we have seen, one of the 'principal inhabitants') gave the parish £100 towards the cost of the school, on condition that the remaining sum was raised by subscription rather than through a general tax. There are no further references to the school, suggesting that it was never built. In 1764 the parish agreed to give Mary Oliver 4s. 'on account of sending her to school' in addition to the sum they were already paying for her maintenance and clothing, but where she received her schooling is unknown. Both John Tindall (1) and John Tindall (2) were literate, and signed their names in the overseers' account books when they agreed to take parish children, so they must have had the benefit of at least some education in their youth.[24]

Poverty and poor relief

The regulation of the poor through the administration of poor relief was a vast administrative and financial burden on communities, its complexity reflected in the surviving paperwork. For Ticehurst the documents generated by the administration of the Poor Law form by far the largest category of surviving parish records. Their great detail means that it is easier to reconstruct the lives of the very poor than of those, like the Tindalls, who were economically independent.

The lists of disbursements record, in considerable detail, the cost of maintaining and clothing parish children like the Burgesses. For example in 1751 the parish spent the following amounts on William, Samuel and Elizabeth Burgess:[25]

	£	s	d
Paid Mr Jarvis for keeping them 50 weeks at 4*d.* a week	10	0	0
Paid Richard Wickham for 3 pair of shoes for them	0	9	7
Ditto for spacking [re-soling] William's shoes & nails	0	1	0
Mending Elizabeth's shoes	0	0	8
Ditto Samuel's shoes twice	0	0	11
Ditto Elizabeth's shoes	0	0	6
Ditto 2 new pair for Elizabeth & William	0	6	10
Paid Joseph Clapson for making William & Samuel 2 pair of breeches	0	1	8
Ditto for making them 2 round frocks	0	1	0
Ditto for making them 2 waistcoats	0	2	0
Ditto Robert Fuller for 2 pair of breeches for them	0	4	0
Paid Mrs Jarvis for making 4 shirts & 2 shifts	0	2	0
Ditto for 2 aprons	0	1	6
Ditto for a pair of stays	0	2	0
Ditto an ell of canvas to top the girl's gown & topping	0	1	6
Ditto for 2 petticoats	0	2	0
Ditto for mending & stockings	0	8	6
Paid Mr Hope for 3 lb & ¾ of canvas & thread for William & Samuel	0	3	2½
Ditto for flannel & thread	0	0	10
Paid Mr Grant for thread	0	0	2

William and Samuel were being provided with shirts, breeches, waistcoats, round frocks, stockings and shoes. The boys would also have worn coats, round hats and handkerchiefs or neckerchiefs around their necks. A 'round frock' is the distinctive rural labourer's smock worn over the top of other clothing to keep it clean. Elizabeth was provided with a shift, over which she would have worn her stays, then her petticoat, her gown and her apron. She was also given shoes and stockings. On another occasion the overseers' accounts record payment for a pair of pattens, worn over her shoes to protect her clothing from mud. She would also have had a cap, possibly a round hat, a handkerchief or neckerchief for her neck, and a cloak (usually red) as an outer garment.[26]

The Poor Laws empowered parish officers to bind out orphans and pauper children as apprentices, either to a trade or craft or as servants in husbandry, thus reducing the burden on the parish. Throughout the seventeenth century there had been disputes about whether parish authorities and justices of the peace could force householders to accept parish children as apprentices. This was finally resolved in 1697 when legislation stipulated that those refusing to accept pauper apprentices would be fined. Children who were too young to be formally apprenticed might be 'fostered' out to local households at the expense of the parish, as was the case with the younger Burgess children, Ann Pettit and Grace Swift. Little attempt was made to ensure the child's welfare, either by vetting potential foster families or employers or by checking on the child after he or she was placed.[27]

The parish was legally obliged to provide medical care to its poor – it might employ doctors, surgeons, midwives and nurses on an *ad hoc* basis or on an annual contract for a fixed fee. In 1758 the parish of Ticehurst agreed that Dr Winch should 'supply the poor of the parish with medicines when necessary and also the like with regard to surgery till Easter next at 6 guineas and in case it is a bad year to be allowed something over at their discretion and it is to be understood that only such of the poor as are chargeable are included in this agreement and none that live out of the parish and those that shall be charged within the time.' The prevalence of smallpox in the eighteenth century is reflected in the frequency with which Ticehurst paid for its treatment. In 1752, when George Piper had the disease, the parish paid £2 to Widow Harmer for nursing him and 1s. to the doctor for giving him a 'purge' (either an emetic or a laxative). In addition the parish paid for bread, beer, milk, cabbage, meat, oatmeal, flour, butter, soap, candles 'and other necessaries', including 1s. 'for milk had at John Tindall's', as well as 1s. 'for airing the house'. The total amount paid in this instance was £5 11s. 10¾d. In 1784 Samuel Newington, the parish surgeon, was paid a guinea 'to inoculate Mr Pankhurst and family'.[28]

The Elizabethan Poor Laws had stipulated that the able-bodied poor should be set to work, and that each parish must provide stocks of material for them to work on. In practice, 'setting the poor to work' was often difficult and expensive, especially in smaller rural parishes: suitable materials had to be collected, labour organised and supervised and, in some instances, a building provided. In order to ensure sufficient employment for their poor, parish leaders offered financial inducements to local employers to take them on. The Ticehurst vestry minutes for 29 November 1710 record that 'the overseers and churchwardens do pay to George Hammond, warp spinner, 20s. for this year to encourage him to employ the poor in spinning wool, he having promised not to put out any work if the poor of this parish can spin all his work according to art.' The overseers' accounts record regular payments to the poor for spinning and weaving flax and tow, for spinning other fibres such as linsey-woolsey and wool, and for knitting stockings. Spinning and knitting were done by women, weaving by men. The cloth was then given to the parish poor to make themselves clothes with, including shirts, shifts, breeches and aprons.[29]

The problems of organising work schemes for the poor, combined with alarm over the ever-increasing rates of poor relief and a general hardening of attitudes towards the poor, led to the establishment of workhouses in the early eighteenth century. The Workhouse Test Act of 1723 (also known as Knatchbull's Act) empowered parishes to build workhouses or to contract paupers out to private institutions. Those refusing to enter were to have their parish relief removed. From their inception, workhouses were intended to be more than just a deterrent, having a strong moral dimension, with the added benefit of providing a source of cheap labour. However, it is unlikely that they achieved their moral or financial aims, and many schemes were abandoned after a few years because they were financially unviable.[30]

In Ticehurst a scheme for establishing a workhouse was first considered in 1740. At a parish meeting on 23 May it was proposed that a committee 'consider and prepare a scheme for the providing of a workhouse for the poor [and] report the same to the parishioners at their general meetings'. On 24 September the parishioners accepted a proposal, reported by the committee, that William Watson 'advance for the parish such sums of money as should be necessary for erecting a building on the parish ground for the reception of the poor who are and may be entitled to parish relief at the rate of 4% interest', which they would repay in instalments of £20 or more. In the parish records there are no further references to the setting up of the workhouse, but it was evidently completed because in 1783 the parish appointed Elizabeth Sturt as governess of the workhouse, for an annual salary of £11 (she 'to find herself tea, butter, sugar and other necessaries except what the said house affords'). Sturt was illiterate, and 'signed' her agreement with a mark.[31]

As we have seen, the combination of rising food prices in the 1790s along with existing problems of the under- or unemployment of agricultural labourers meant that parishes faced an increasingly heavy rate burden. In the parish of Burwash, which adjoined Ticehurst to the south, by the mid-1790s nearly one-fourth of the 1,100 inhabitants were paupers, and nearly one-third of the annual rental value of land was being taken in parish rates. The dramatic rise in wheat prices is reflected in 1800–01 in the changing policy of the Ticehurst vestry towards the provision of wheaten bread for the poor. In March the vestry ordered that 'a journeyman baker shall be immediately procured (if possible) to bake bread to sell to the poor at 16*d*. the gallon or 8*d*. the half gallon ... and not to be delivered to the poor until it has been baked four days'. Yet in October it agreed to stop baking bread for the poor. In December this decision was revoked, but vestry members would henceforth decide on a daily basis at what price they would sell the bread to the poor. In January 1801 the vestry resolved to consider further 'what articles of food are best to buy for the poor in lieu of wheaten bread or flour' and to raise a voluntary subscription to purchase meat 'and other articles of food' to sell to the poor at a reduced price.[32]

Inside the husbandman's cottage

As we have seen, in the seventeenth century the domestic culture among husbandmen and craftsmen was utilitarian, with a limited range of furniture, seating not upholstered, and little evidence of new consumer goods. Historians have described the eighteenth century as an era of 'consumer revolution', with all levels of society participating in consumer spending on a wider and more affordable variety of goods. This was linked to an overall rise in the standard of living associated with the start of the Industrial Revolution around 1760.[33]

As in the earlier case studies, the main evidence for domestic culture comes from probate inventories. For the period 1710–67 there are 28 of these for Ticehurst, none of which is for an occupant of Tindalls, and just four are for husbandmen. Of those four, only that of Richard Neale, who died in 1718, itemises goods by room. In 1694 Neale was assessed for the poor rate on lands valued at £2 10*s*., and the value of his estate at death was £17 12*s*. 2*d*., so he is likely to have had less land and to have been poorer than the occupants of Tindalls. Nevertheless, the rooms named in his inventory suggest that he was living in a similar-sized cottage, with two rooms downstairs (the hall and buttery) and two upstairs (the hall chamber and the buttery chamber). He also had a milkhouse, which is likely to have been in an outshut. Neale had one cow, one sheep and two pigs but no crops or agricultural equipment such as harrows or carts, indicating limited farming activity.[34]

A broader sample of inventories from parishes across East Sussex confirms that Neale's cottage was fairly typical of the homes of husbandmen in the first half of the eighteenth century. In the majority of these the kitchen, as well as its conventional use as a place to cook and eat food, was the only room in which the occupants could sit down and socialise. All other downstairs rooms were service rooms, with brewhouses,

William Redmore Bigg, A cottage interior, 1793.
© VICTORIA AND ALBERT MUSEUM, LONDON

milkhouses and butteries being most numerous, reflecting the significance of brewing and dairying as by-employment within the rural economy. Upstairs chambers were usually reserved for sleeping and garrets for storage of agricultural goods, although a few contained beds.[35]

Very few of the inventories record objects specifically associated with social display, or provide evidence of new consumer goods such as tea- and coffee-making utensils, china, glass, or knives and forks. Where such objects occur (for example, clocks and mirrors), they are usually in the kitchen, reflecting its use as the sole 'social' space within the cottage. Only one inventory of a husbandman includes a coffee pot: James Phillips of East Grinstead, whose estate in 1722 was valued at a modest £44 3s. 6d., also had six knives and forks, a cribbage board, a bible and five other books, a folding board, a looking glass and two glasses in his kitchen. Some inventories record newer types of furniture, including round tables, kitchen dressers and chests of drawers, but many husbandmen still sat on forms at rectangular tables and stored their goods in cupboards and chests. We know from other sources that by the late eighteenth century tea was beginning to replace beer as the principal drink within the home, partly due to the high price of malt, and so by this date some, if not all, husbandmen would have owned tea-making equipment.[36]

If we apply the accumulated evidence from the probate inventory sample to Tindalls Cottage, as it might have been around 1750, the kitchen is likely to have contained a table (probably rectangular rather than round), a form or bench, some chairs (possibly rush-bottomed but more likely wooden) and a cupboard or possibly a dresser. In addition to an array of cooking and eating utensils it probably had a pendulum clock and a mirror. The Tindalls would still have been eating off pewter plates and additional tableware, including drinking vessels, is likely to have been locally produced earthenware rather than china or glass. Although more affluent houses had ranges by the eighteenth century, at Tindalls the occupants still cooked over an open fire. The upstairs chambers would have contained a selection of beds with feather or flock mattresses and some storage chests. There may have been a chest of drawers in the kitchen chamber. Although the cottage windows were glazed, John Tindall (1) is unlikely to have had any curtains.

In general, the homes of early eighteenth-century husbandmen had a greater variety and number of household goods than those of their seventeenth-century predecessors, but their consumption patterns remained traditional and utilitarian. The continued use of certain furniture types, such as rectangular tables and forms, probably reflects the fact that much was inherited or second-hand. The effect of the so-called 'consumer revolution' is difficult to chart in the homes of East Sussex husbandmen because the bulk of the surviving probate inventories are for the period 1700 to 1760, that is, before the start of the Industrial Revolution. However, the weight of evidence suggests that in many respects the level of comfort did not improve significantly, although husbandmen's houses contained a greater variety of household goods and some new types of furniture. It could be argued that, rather than the onset of a sudden and unprecedented change in domestic culture, this was a continuation of the general pattern of 'improvement' that has been highlighted throughout this book.

Conclusion

The eighteenth-century occupants of Tindalls Cottage are likely to have lived at or near subsistence level most of the time. According to the definition applied by some historians, their payment of parish rates placed them among the middle sort, but their inclusion in this group was unquestionably marginal. Men such as John

Haselden and the two John Tindalls were sandwiched uncomfortably somewhere between the upper ranks of the meaner or poorer sort and the lower ranks of the middle sort. They were excluded from parish government and, as tenants of Peckhams, they were unable to participate in manorial government. They were, however, respectable, and the birth of John Tindall (2)'s illegitimate grandson in 1798 is likely to have been a cause of some shame. Nevertheless, with the help of the parish he was able to take in the baby, rather than see it fostered out to another family. The inflation and high grain prices of the 1790s accelerated a process of pauperisation of the rural labourer, which had been provoked by the massive growth in population and the enclosure, in some rural communities, of large areas of common land. The result was an increasingly heavy burden on parish poor rates which would ultimately lead to the introduction of a New Poor Law in 1834.

During the late eighteenth century the housing conditions of the rural labourer first began to attract 'polite' attention. In 1781 John Wood published the first architectural pattern book. Based on his own fieldwork, it was aimed specifically at improving working-class housing, and was entitled *A Series of Plans for Cottages or Habitations of the Labourer*. He noted in the introduction that, 'The greatest part of the cottages that fell within my observation, I found to be shattered, dirty, inconvenient, miserable hovels, scarcely affording shelter for beasts of the forest; much less they were proper habitations for human species.'

By the time Wood was writing, the word 'hovel' was increasingly being used to describe human habitations of the most wretched kind – barely suitable for animals let alone for people. He drew attention to the overcrowded and unsanitary living conditions of many rural workers and set out seven principles upon which cottages should be built. His cottage plans reflected his belief that inadequate housing was damaging both to physical and moral well-being, anticipating the concerns of the nineteenth-century cottage 'improvers', which will be discussed in the next chapter. Wood's concerns, and his very pragmatic solutions, conflicted with the romantic depictions of the 'country cottage' occupied by contented labourers in paintings by artists such as Thomas Gainsborough. While John Wood would have thought Tindalls woefully inadequate, Gainsborough might have liked its bucolic charm. Neither, however, would have wanted to live in it.[37]

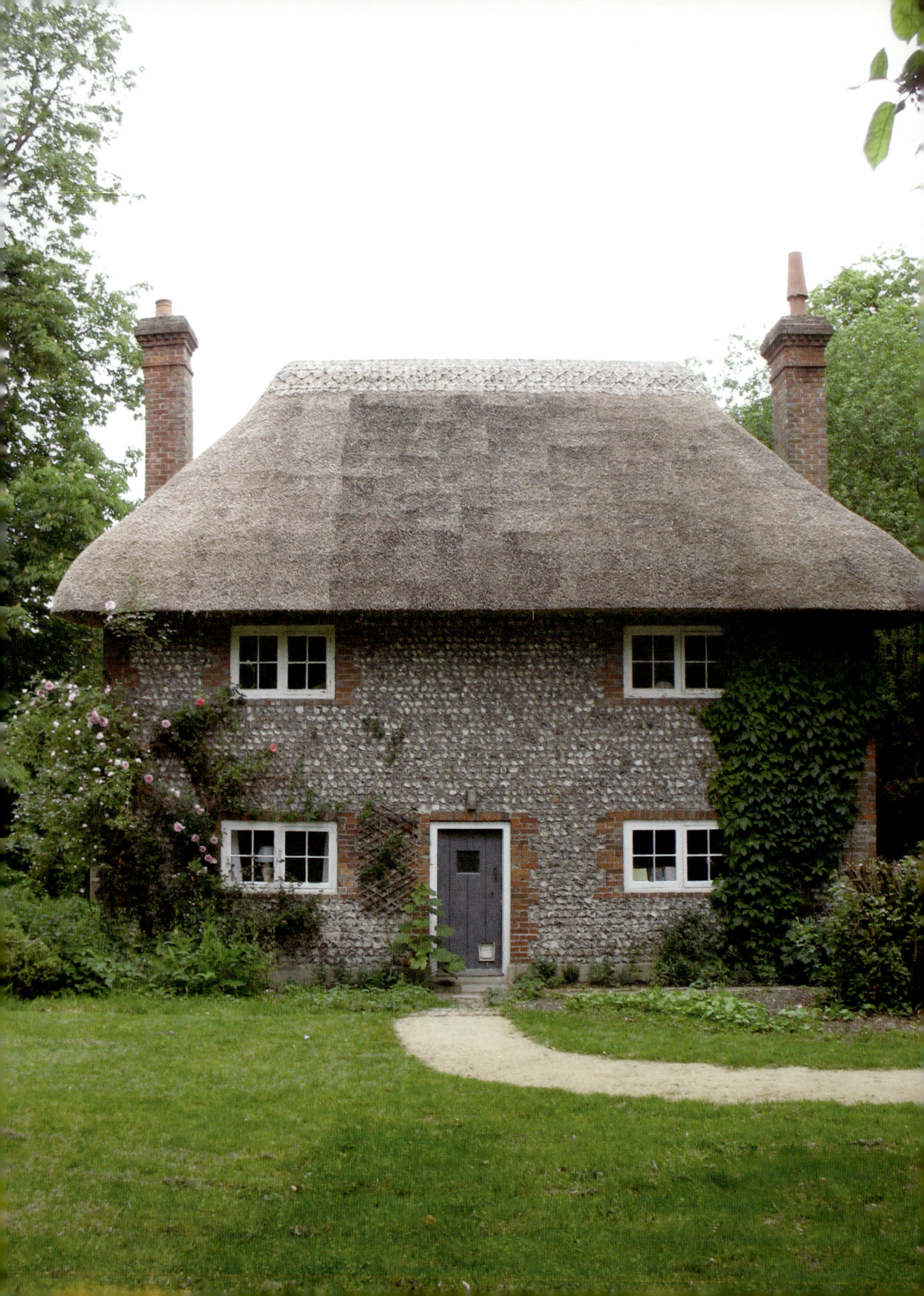

CHAPTER SEVEN

Gonville Cottage: an estate cottage from Singleton, West Sussex

An estate cottage

Gonville Cottage is a good example of a nineteenth-century estate cottage. It lies at the western extremity of the parish of Singleton and is part of the West Dean estate. Until 2008 it was occupied by people working for the Museum but it is now vacant, and a number of options are being considered for its future use. The cottage was built in the first half of the nineteenth century, probably around 1847. Externally it is a double-fronted flint and brick building with a thatched roof. Internally it has a central entrance and staircase between two living rooms, a rear outshut on the ground floor, and two bedrooms on the upper floor. All the rooms within the main range have fireplaces. It is set in a sunken rectangular garden, now completely screened by trees. The Singleton tithe map of 1846–47 shows this as the location of a three-sided agricultural building, which had been removed by 1874 when the first edition Ordnance Survey map was produced. To the rear of the cottage there is a detached brick-built outhouse of late nineteenth-century date, which replaced an earlier outhouse or privy. A well in front of the cottage has now been filled in.[1]

The land on which the cottage was built was part of what, in the late eighteenth century, was known as Old Warren Farm, although between 1780 and 1850 it was

Gonville Cottage.
DANAE TANKARD

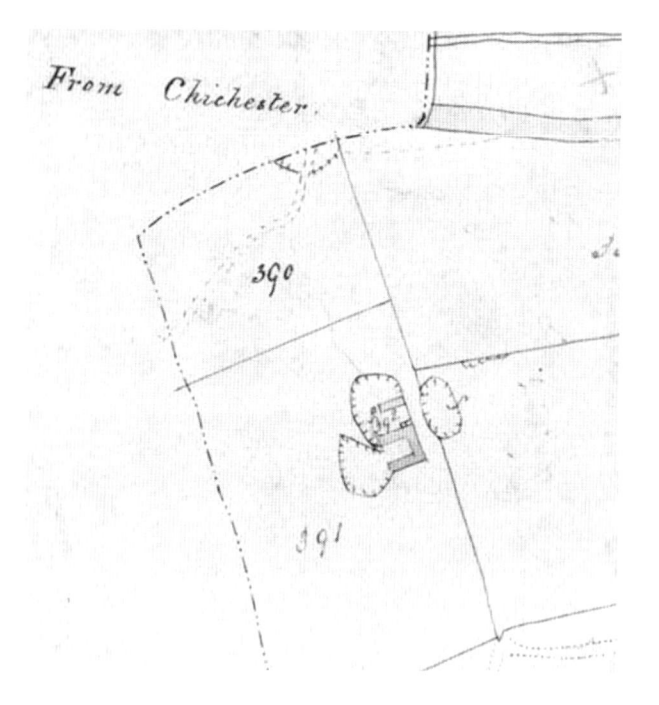

Detail of Singleton tithe map showing Gonville Cottage and standing fold.
WSRO TD/W110

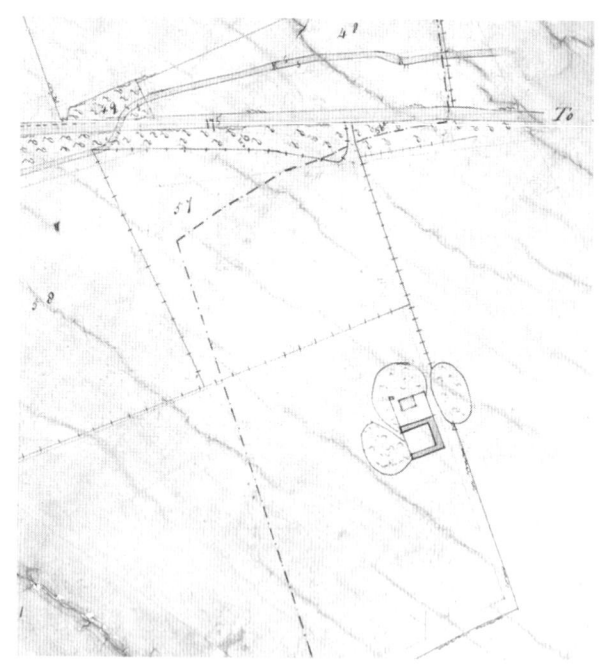

Detail of West Dean tithe map showing Gonville Cottage and standing fold.
WSRO TD/W141

variously referred to as 'Greenways Farm', 'Part of West Greenways Farm' and 'Part of Greenways Farm'. In 1815 the farm was acquired by Lord Selsey and became part of the West Dean estate. The cottage site is numbered 392 on the Singleton tithe map; the apportionment, dated 1848, describes it as a 'cottage, garden, buildings and plantation' 3 rods 35 perches in extent, forming 'Part of Greenways Farm', owned and occupied by the Reverend Leveson Vernon Harcourt. However, the cottage shown on the tithe map has a different footprint to the present building, being longer and narrower and abutting the yard boundary on the eastern side. Unusually, because of its proximity to the parish boundary, the property is also depicted on the West Dean tithe map of 1847, although there is no accompanying entry on the apportionment of 1851. On this map, in contrast, the cottage has an identical footprint to the present building. Both maps were surveyed by James Elliott of Chichester, and it has been suggested that the obvious disparity between the two reflects the removal of an earlier building and its replacement by the present cottage. That would mean that the cottage was built between 1846 and 1847.[2]

The tithe map evidence alone is not sufficient for us to be certain that Gonville Cottage was built in 1847, since the mapping may have been somewhat inaccurate, but it is significant that the earliest reference to Gonville Cottage is in the 1851 census for Singleton, when it was described as 'Gunfield Cottage'. At this date it was occupied by Richard Burns aged 56, shepherd to the West Dean estate, his wife Olive (54), daughter Eliza (24) and mother Ann Burns (84), whom the census describes as a 'pauper'. Ten years earlier, in 1841, Richard Burns was living in Singleton village.[3]

The occupation of the cottage by a shepherd means that the three-sided agricultural building in front of the cottage was almost certainly a standing fold. John Ellman, famous for his improvements to the Southdown breed of sheep in the late eighteenth and early nineteenth centuries, had recommended their use to shelter sheep and lambs at night during periods of bad weather. Arthur Young records in his 1813 *General View of the Agriculture of the County of Sussex* that Ellman himself had three sheltered yards containing sheds which were well littered to keep them warm and contained hayracks. The sunken site of the Gonville Cottage yard (which is still apparent) and the screening trees recorded on both tithe maps would have provided additional shelter for Richard Burns's flock.[4]

The parish of Singleton, including the village of Singleton and the hamlet of Charlton, covered just over 4,075 acres in the mid-nineteenth century, and under the Poor Law Amendment Act of 1834 it was included in the newly created Westhampnett Poor Law Union. Within the parish some 1,390 acres were arable, 1,130 acres downland and sheep walks, and 1,260 acres woodland, most of the latter being in the Forests of Singleton and Charlton, in the northern third of the parish. In 1850 the biggest landowners in the parish were the duke of Richmond, owner of the Goodwood estate, with about 3,000 acres; Colonel George Wyndham of Petworth (who became Lord Leconfield in 1859) with some 850 acres; and the Vernon Harcourts of West Dean who owned just over 130 acres, including the land on which Gonville Cottage lay. Goodwood racecourse is in the Charlton part of the parish, and in the nineteenth century the annual race week brought a vast influx of people, including royalty and members of the aristocracy, as well as a less salubrious crowd. The resident population recorded in the decennial censuses was relatively constant, averaging 570, with a high of 606 in 1871 and a low of 513 in 1901.[5]

The parish of West Dean, which in 1850 covered 4,565 acres, borders Singleton to the west and was part of the Westbourne Poor Law Union. In that year some 3,350 acres were part of the West Dean estate, then owned by the Reverend Leveson Vernon Harcourt and his wife Caroline Mary who, after her husband died in 1860, ran the estate until her own death eleven years later.[6]

In the nineteenth century this area of Sussex was prime arable land, with wheat, oats, turnips and swedes the principal crops. In 1876 the parish summary of crop acreages for Singleton, returned to the Board of Trade, listed 287 acres of wheat, 105 acres of barley, 105 acres of oats and 246 acres of turnips and swedes. There were 33 acres of mangolds, 44 acres of rape, 12 acres of vetches or tares, and 39 acres of 'other green crops'. Only a quarter of an acre was planted with potatoes; there was half an acre of orchard, and no market or nursery gardens. The large acreage devoted to turnips and swedes reflects the importance of sheep within the rural economy, for these crops were used as animal feed. Within the parish in 1876 there were 1,817 sheep and 1,219 lambs under one year. In Singleton by the 1860s nearly all threshing was done by steam- or horse-power. Grass-mowing machines had recently been introduced, reducing the opportunities for men to earn additional money through scythe-mowing. By 1867 there were still no steam-ploughs in the area and ploughing was still done by horses, either two abreast in summer or two abreast and one in front in autumn.[7]

In this chapter much of the information on the wages and conditions of agricultural labourers, the education and employment of children, and rural housing is based on the substantial parliamentary reports published during the nineteenth century. These include the *Commission on the Sanitary Conditions of the Labouring Population* (1842), the *Reports of the Special Assistant Poor Law Commissioners on the Employment of Women and Children in Agriculture* (1843), the *Commission on the Employment of Children, Young Persons, and Women in Agriculture* (1867) and the *Report on Wages and Earnings of Agricultural Labourers* (1900). Of these the 1867 report is especially valuable, since it includes detailed information about the social and economic conditions of all 37 parishes that made up the Westhampnett Union. The West Dean estate itself is poorly documented. There are, for example, no wage books for estate workers. In contrast, there is extensive archival material for the Goodwood estate, some of which has been used here.[8]

The occupants

Information about the occupants of Gonville Cottage is available from the decennial census, the parish rate books for 1851 to 1900, and a 'census' of parishioners that was made by the rector of Singleton, Francis Alfred Bowles, which contains some biographical information. His initial census appears to have been made in 1851, but he added new information intermittently until 1858, as the lives of his parishioners changed.[9]

As we have seen, the cottage was occupied in 1851 by Richard Burns, his wife, adult daughter and mother. On the 1841 and 1851 censuses Richard is described as an 'agricultural labourer', but in fact he was not an 'ordinary' labourer but a shepherd. We know this because Francis Bowles describes him as 'shepherd to the Revd L. V.

Harcourt ... a very good shepherd and has gained many prizes at the Goodwood agricultural association.' Burns was born in East Marden in West Sussex in 1795 and in 1826 was living in Bedhampton, just over the border in Hampshire, when he married his wife Olive. His first daughter, Eliza, was born in Bedhampton in the same year. By 1829 he had moved to West Dean, where three more daughters were born: Fanny (1829), Mary (1831) and Olive (1834). Francis Bowles describes Richard's wife as 'an invalid from a bodily weakness' and records that his eldest daughter, Eliza, 'has a bodily weakness like her mother'. When the census was taken in 1851 Eliza was still living at home, but Bowles subsequently noted that she 'lives in London'. He also records that Richard's mother, Ann, 'has always lived with them' and was 'very much afflicted with rheumatism – a good old woman', adding that she died in November 1851. Bowles records that both Richard and his wife were literate.

He also used his census to record his view of the moral probity of some of his parishioners. For Richard's youngest daughter, Olive, he recorded (in Latin) that she was 'unchaste before marriage'. In 1851 Olive, aged sixteen or seventeen, was working as a domestic servant at Preston Farm in Binderton. How Bowles knew she was 'unchaste' is unclear. The obvious explanation, that she had an illegitimate pregnancy, is unproven since there is no record either of a baptism or an infant

Shepherd and his flock, Upperton village, c.1850.
WEST SUSSEX COUNTY COUNCIL LIBRARY SERVICE

burial in the West Dean or Singleton parish registers. In 1853, while still employed at Preston Farm, she married one of her fellow servants, 21-year-old William Grainger. Richard Burns probably continued to live in Gonville Cottage until his wife died in 1859. At the time of the 1861 census he was lodging with a family in Selsey but still working as a shepherd. In 1871 he was living with his married daughter, Mary Bailey, in Merston, and the census describes him as 'formerly a shepherd'. He died on 22 April 1872, aged 77, and the death certificate gives the cause of death as bronchitis.[10]

At the time of the 1861 census the Burns family had gone and the cottage was unoccupied. Between 1866 and 1901 it housed successively at least ten families, most of which stayed for about two years. Not all were agricultural labouring families: Frederick Boxall, resident between 1866 and 1868, was a carpenter; Joseph Pratt, there from 1870 to 1873, a 'labourer in the woods'; and George Webb, who lived there from 1873 to 1875, a bricklayer. At the time of the 1891 census the cottage was again uninhabited.[11]

The largest family known to have inhabited the cottage in the late nineteenth century were the Pratts. In 1871 Joseph and Elizabeth Pratt, aged 56 and 47, had six children living with them, three boys and three girls, aged between 15 and one month. The eldest son, Joseph, aged 15, was working as a 'sawmill boy' at the sawmill in Charlton. John, Charlotte, Ann and Sarah, aged between 12 and 4, were all at school. The Pratts also had three older children, William (24), James (21) and Mary (18), all of whom had left home. So, between 1847 and 1871 Elizabeth Pratt had given birth to nine children, having her last child at the age of 47. She died in 1872 aged 48. Joseph Pratt died in 1890 aged 76. Both Joseph and Elizabeth were illiterate, unlike their children, all of whom had attended or were attending school.[12]

The West Sussex Agricultural Association

Francis Bowles recorded that Richard Burns 'gained many prizes at the Goodwood agricultural association'. The West Sussex Agricultural Association was founded in 1836, with the duke of Richmond as its sponsor and president. Its object was 'the encouragement of industrious and meritorious agricultural labourers, residing in the West Division of the county of Sussex'. This residential qualification was soon changed to 'residing within 20 miles of Chichester', which allowed candidates from south-east Hampshire to participate. The Association was funded by annual subscriptions from landowners, farmers and tenant farmers, and only subscribers could submit agricultural labourers, their widows, or agricultural domestic servants for premiums, which were awarded annually, usually in June. These cash awards, which were at least a week's wages and could be up to eight times more in some classes, were given out at a dinner held in the Tennis Court, at Waterbeach, Goodwood. The dinner was attended by gentry, clergy and employers at one table, and premium winners at another, but in the same room. Certificates accompanied the cash prizes.[13]

Candidates were only allowed to enter the competition if they had a 'certificate of general good character, sobriety, and regularity of attendance at Divine Worship', signed by the employer and minister of the parish and a churchwarden or overseer, or by four respectable householders. The rules for the Arundel and Bramber Association, founded in the same year, helpfully include the wording of such a certificate:

We the undersigned do hereby certify that AB labourer of this parish is, to the best of our knowledge and belief – first, a regular attendant at Divine Worship; secondly, not one of those who waste their money and time while they corrupt their morals in public-houses or beer-shops; and, lastly, that his (or her) conduct is good, and such as to render him (or her) a fit subject for an honourable reward and distinction.

The founding of these two associations, and others like them, in 1836 was hardly a coincidence. It reflected widespread concern about the condition of the 'working classes' in the wake of the Swing Riots and the passing of the 1834 Poor Law Amendment Act, which largely ended the system of outdoor relief that had been in operation since the late sixteenth century and introduced the punitive poor law union workhouse system. An article on the formation of agricultural associations, by an anonymous 'agricultor' of Sussex, appeared in *The Farmers' Magazine* in April 1836. It referred to the 'temporary tendency [of the New Poor Law] to restrict the means of the labouring classes' and the consequent need to find 'an additional stimulus to moral conduct and habits'.

The 'moral conduct and habits' to which agricultural labourers were expected to aspire, reflected in the competition categories, were sobriety, stability, industriousness, thrift and self-sufficiency. For example, Class A, with a first prize of £5, was for 'labourers who have brought up the largest families respectably, with the smallest amount of parochial relief'; Class B, also with a first prize of £5, was for 'single men who have lived the longest in one place with the best characters'; Class E, with a first prize of £4, was for 'labourers who have placed out at respectable service their daughters at an early age, and who have remained in that service, with good characters'. Categories were amended and new ones added in subsequent years, including an additional Class W which awarded prizes to cottagers 'whose cottages

W. E. Partridge, Harvest workers near Worthing, 1841.
WEST SUSSEX COUNTY COUNCIL LIBRARY SERVICE

and gardens, consisting of not more than half an acre, shall be kept and cultivated in the neatest manner, and the general appearance of whose crops, making due allowance for the natural quality of the soil and the size of the garden, shall be most satisfactory to the judges appointed to view them'. Cottagers were ineligible for prizes in this category if they had 'kept their daughters from domestic service after they have attained the age and strength for such employment'.

Prizewinners were reported in the *Hampshire Telegraph* which, in the early years of the Association, also included their certificates of character to show their readers 'how much may be effected, even with their limited means, when industry, honesty and sobriety are united'. These mini-biographies give a brief glimpse into the lives of agricultural workers and their families. For example, in 1840 Michael Crees from North Mundham won third prize (£3) in Class A (labourers who have brought up the largest families respectably, with the smallest amount of parochial relief). His certificate recorded that he was aged 64 and had worked on the same farm for 37 years. His weekly wages were 12s. He had had thirteen children, but eight of them had died in infancy. Four were 'well placed out'; the fifth, a girl, who had been ill from infancy, died aged seventeen. His Poor Law Union had paid him 1s. 6d. for this daughter, but apart from that he had received no parochial relief. In the same year in Class C (widows who have brought up the largest families respectably, with the smallest amount of parochial relief) Elizabeth Fleet of Slindon won second prize (£2). She was forty and had been a widow for twelve years. The certificate described her as 'exemplary in her conduct, bringing up her family respectably and in habits of industry, her cottage neat and clean'. She had five children aged from twelve to seventeen. Her earnings were 'very uncertain'; she received 5s. weekly for four months, reduced to 1s. until 1837 and then stopped.

Between 1840 and 1851 Richard Burns won eight prizes at the annual meetings of the association under Class Q (later Class R) 'for shepherds of flock masters, having the care of not less than ten score ewes [200], who have reared the greatest number of lambs with the least loss, regard being had to circumstances both as to farm and flock'. In 1840, when he won the third prize of £2, the details of his flock were included in the newspaper report. He had 273 ewes put to ram, made up of 81 two-tooth ewes, 28 four-tooth ewes and 164 six-tooth ewes (that is, 81 yearlings, 28 two-year-olds and 164 three-year-olds). Two ewes had died in lambing, four at other times, and 267 remained alive. Some 332 lambs had dropped, seventeen were 'lent', seven were born dead, and thirteen had died before weaning, so 295 remained. He had fifteen barren ewes and five slips. Burns won the first prize of £4 in 1845 and 1848, while in 1849, in addition to the second prize of £3, he was awarded the 'white medal' that was given to those who had won premiums totalling £12 at different times. He won no further prizes for his shepherding after 1851. In 1855 he won the third prize in Class C, 'for labourers or widows whose daughters have been placed out at an early age, and have remained in service with good characters, and whose families have made (by their own industry) the greatest premium in their condition in life'. His daughter's apparent sexual misconduct was either overlooked or had been forgotten.

Rural labourers

In appearance the Sussex labourers are well up to the average of those of the south of England generally, but they are slow in their movements, as might be expected in a county which has gained the title of 'stolid Sussex'.[14]

The majority of men listed in the nineteenth- and early twentieth-century censuses as being employed on the land were classified as 'agricultural labourers' – landless and wage-dependent agricultural workers. The proportion of agricultural labourers varied between areas: in parts of Norfolk and Suffolk they accounted for as much as 60 per cent of

The Burns family, c.1850, as recorded by the rector, Francis Bowles.
WSRO PAR 174/7/1

occupied males. In Singleton in 1851 just over 40 per cent of the resident males for whom occupations are recorded are described as agricultural labourers. The oldest was 68, the youngest 10. In addition, there were seven 'agricultural boys' aged between 12 and 14 years old. However, the agricultural labouring 'class' was not a homogenous group. The most basic division was between those who were in charge of animals (such as shepherds, stockmen and carters) and the 'ordinary' agricultural labourers, who were not. Even among ordinary workers there were different grades: those doing more skilled work, such as ploughing, hedging or working with machinery, generally received higher wages and enjoyed greater job security than the unskilled or less skilled men. The workers with the lowest status were the 'shifty' men who only worked for a farmer when they could not get a job elsewhere, and left him as soon as they heard of anything more attractive.[15]

'Ordinary' agricultural labourers were employed on a weekly basis, for which they received a 'standing wage', that is a fixed weekly amount. The average standing wage for agricultural workers in England varied considerably, the highest wages being found in those parts of the country close to London (such as Surrey and Kent) or with heavy industrial or manufacturing bases (particularly northern counties such as Durham and Northumberland). In such areas there was competition from better-paid non-agricultural work, so wages were inevitably relatively high. Wages in predominantly agricultural counties, such as Sussex, were lower. The lowest wages of all were in Norfolk, Dorset, Oxfordshire and Suffolk. However, even within counties the wages of ordinary agricultural workers varied. In Kent in 1898 agricultural workers in areas closest to London or Chatham earned between 17s. and 18s. a week, while those in the south of the county where there were no significant urban centres earned 12s. In the Westhampnett Union in the 1860s the average weekly wage for an agricultural labourer was 13s.[16]

In addition to the standing wage, ordinary agricultural workers earned extra money through piecework (such as hoeing, turnip-pulling, topping and tailing, mowing, or lifting potatoes) and at harvest time. At Singleton in the 1860s wheat was cut at a pay of from 10s. to 15s. for an acre, while grass mown with a scythe was paid from 3s. to 5s. an acre, with a man being expected to cut between 1¼ and 1½ acres a day – although the introduction of mowing machines reduced the opportunities for scythe-mowing. As a rule, ordinary workers did not receive 'perquisites' or allowances in kind, such as free cottages, potatoes or fuel, although during harvest time they were provided with beer and sometimes food. The way in which harvest work was remunerated varied: in some counties labourers were paid by piecework; in some a lump sum was paid at the end of the harvest; and in others a special harvest rate was paid, which could be double the normal daily rate. In the Westhampnett Union during the 1860s a man was paid a lump sum at the end of harvest, of £5 10s. without beer or £5 with beer. If he worked by the piece he could earn £6 or more. The additional labour of his wife could add a further £2 to this amount. On larger farms money earned through piecework could amount to over a third of a man's total earnings. Including harvesting and piecework an able-bodied man could expect to earn in excess of £40 per year.

The nature of employment meant that earnings were always precarious. Men were not usually paid if they took time off sick, and some employers refused to pay their workers during periods of wet weather when outdoor work was impossible. In Singleton, however, most farmers paid their workers 'wet or dry', which meant that provided men turned up for work on a wet day they would be found something to do under cover. For ordinary agricultural work there was an adequate supply of labour, and in the winter many of the men worked in the woods. During turnip-hoeing, haymaking and harvest, additional labour was supplied by men coming in from the hop districts. Other parishes in the Westhampnett Union had an under-supply of labour because of the rival employment opportunities offered either by the proximity of Chichester (as at North Mundham and Oving) or the sea (as at West Itchenor). Only one parish in the Union – Graffham – had an over-supply of labour. This led, at Graffham, to under-employment or unemployment in winter and consequently to financial hardship, although some agricultural labourers were able to find winter work outside the parish, mainly in the duke of Richmond's woods. It is no surprise that wages in Graffham were 1s. or 2s. a week lower than in other parishes within the Union.[17]

Shepherd Smith of East Dean, c.1865.
FROM THE PRIVATE COLLECTION OF RICHARD PAILTHORPE

As a shepherd, Richard Burns would have been one of the highest-paid agricultural workers on the West Dean estate and, unlike ordinary agricultural workers, was engaged by the year. In addition, he would have received some generous perquisites, the most lucrative of which was rent-free accommodation. Other perquisites might include coal, beer, and food at lambing time; in 1860 James Ford, a shepherd at Colworth Farm in West Dean, was allowed as many rabbits as he could catch. The amount that shepherds earned depended on the quality and size of the flock; in the Westhampnett Union in the 1860s the average weekly wage for a shepherd

Shepherd's hut at the WDOAM. This shepherd's hut was manufactured in the late nineteenth century by the Andover firm of Watson & Haig. Shepherds lived in huts like these during the lambing season when they needed to be near their flock.
DANAE TANKARD

was 15s. Shepherds earned extra money during lambing ('lamb money') and for washing sheep. During the 1860s James Ford was receiving a £2 bonus for the seven-week lambing season. In the Thakeham Union in the 1890s, the duke of Norfolk's shepherds received 6s. a score for lambing and the same price for washing sheep.

Some shepherds in this part of Sussex were paid 2d. to 3d. a lamb or 1s. a head for all lambs in excess of ewes, while others received a lump sum for lambing, which could be as much as £5. Additional payments were also available for shearing: in the Thakeham Union in the 1890s shepherds could expect to receive about 4s. 6d. per score of fleeces. Although shepherds did not usually undertake harvest work, they might nevertheless receive a small additional payment of £1 or £2 at harvest, known as 'Michaelmas money'. Including additional cash payments, a shepherd could expect to earn about £50 a year. Shepherds worked long hours in all weathers, and their work could be arduous, especially during lambing, shearing and washing.[18]

Nationally, the wages of ordinary agricultural workers increased by nearly 50 per cent between 1850 and 1899, although the upward trend was temporarily reversed by periods of agricultural depression. In the early 1890s, following several such years, wages were lower than they had been since the 1860s. However, from 1895 they began to rise again, largely because of a shortage of labour as young men migrated to urban centres in search of more lucrative and socially advantageous employment.[19]

The extensive woodland in the parish and the sawmill at Charlton (which opened in 1863) also provided employment opportunities for men and boys. The 1851 census for Singleton includes nine men employed as sawyers and thirteen 'labourers in the woods', 'copse and agricultural labourers' or 'woodcutters and agricultural labourers'. There were also three male charcoal-makers living in a 'cabin' in Charlton Forest. In the 1860s and 1870s the duke of Richmond employed about 25 men and boys as 'labourers in the woods'. They worked a six-day week and undertook a wide variety of jobs, including planting, cutting copse, trenching, felling, trimming trees, carting timber, clearing wood, digging holes, hedging, making faggots and tying up plants. In 1864 the duke was paying most of his woodland labourers 2s. 1d. a day, or 12s. 6d. a week; by 1871 this had risen to 2s. 3d. a day or 13s. 6d. a week – in other words, about the same earnings as an agricultural labourer. The woods and coppices also provided opportunities for casual winter work for agricultural labourers and their sons.[20]

Female employment in agriculture declined during the first half of the nineteenth century and became increasingly seasonal. At the time that the Poor Law report was compiled in 1834 women in Sussex were still employed widely for weeding, haymaking and during harvest. By 1867, though, women in the Westhampnett Union were described as having 'mostly got above going out to work on the land', preferring to stay at home and look after their children. However, they still helped during haymaking and worked with their husbands at harvest, for which they could expect to earn between 10d. and 1s. a day.[21]

The education and employment of children

By 1837 most rural communities were able to offer their working-class children some formal schooling. The National Society and the British Society, founded in 1811 and 1814 respectively, funded new schools in rural communities (described as 'National Schools' or 'British Schools'). The former were strongly Anglican, while the latter were non-conformist. However, in the 1860s education in rural Sussex was still normally provided by the parish school, largely funded by charitable endowments and subscriptions. Parents paid a small amount towards the cost of schooling – usually twopence a week – and some schools offered a reduction for second or third siblings (for example, 1½d. for the second child, 1d. for the third and subsequent). In 1833 National and British schools became eligible to receive government funding, although many chose not to apply because they considered that it would compromise their independence, and from 1839 government-funded schools were subject to HMI inspection.[22]

The school curriculum was biased heavily in favour of religious instruction, and in many parishes the local incumbent or his curate would conduct the daily prayers at the start of the school day. Basic instruction consisted of reading, writing and rudimentary arithmetic. Reading books contained scriptural stories or lessons of moral instruction. In some schools singing was taught. Boys and girls might also receive some vocational training. For the boys this could be, for example, net-making, straw-plaiting or button-making; for the girls it was usually needlework.

Apart from parish schools, the most common type was the 'dame school': some Sussex parishes had two or even more. As their popular name implies, they were run by women, usually in their own homes. These were private schools, maintained from fee income (typically between 4*d*. and 6*d*. a week), and they catered for infants under the age of five. A typical dame school had about twelve pupils, although some of them were larger. Although they have generally been much maligned, being seen as little more than crèches, the quality of dame schools varied widely. The best offered their pupils basic instruction in reading and writing, together with 'vocational' skills such as sewing. With fees of up to 6*d*. a week they were considerably more expensive than parish schools, so were beyond the reach of much of the labouring rural population. In addition to these, there were numerous small private schools, frequently catering for better-off families, as well as a few private Roman Catholic schools.

There was almost no provision for secondary education, whether free, subsidised or fee-paying, in the nineteenth century. Nevertheless, many villages in Sussex had night schools, operating in the winter months, which catered for males aged anywhere between 8 and 30. They were usually run by the schoolmaster or schoolmistress, or the vicar or rector, and students paid a small weekly fee. Pupils were streamed according to their educational attainment, and learned reading, writing and (if they had the aptitude) arithmetic. Few catered for females, although there was a girls' night school in Horsham in 1867. In Singleton a boys' school was founded in 1828 and a girls' school, with an infant department, in 1852, both funded by Lord Leconfield. In 1867 the assistant parliamentary commissioner noted that a large proportion of the population was under instruction, with fifty names on the boys' register and seventy girls and infants in the other department. At this date there were no other schools in the parish and although there had 'generally' been a night school it had been scantily attended the previous winter and so was not operating that year.

Until the advent of compulsory education in the last quarter of the nineteenth century (discussed in the next chapter), the education of boys was interrupted by agricultural work during the summer months. Most boys left school to take up full-time employment by the age of ten or eleven. Some farms used younger boys of eight or nine years old to scare crows or mind sheep or cows, for which they earned 3*d*. or 4*d*. a day. From the farmer's point of view, boys were of little real economic value until the age of eleven or twelve, by which time they had sufficient physical strength to help to drive a horse-team. Between eleven and fifteen a boy could expect to earn between 6*d*. and 10*d*. a day, according to his age and strength. In Singleton in the 1860s boys were generally taken to work on the land at about ten. The youngest boys in employment were those who accompanied their fathers to the woods during the winter months or who worked at the saw mill in Charlton, which took boys as young as seven.

By the 1840s the employment of girls in the fields in this part of Sussex had ceased. Girls had never been as economically useful as boys, and field labour was seen as having a corrupting influence on them, making them unsuitable for domestic service, the 'general lot' of the working-class girl. Because of this their attendance at school was both more consistent and of longer duration than that of boys. The most common reason girls missed school was because they were needed at home to help with the younger children while their mothers were out at work. By the time their formal education ended most working-class boys and girls could read and write and had some basic numeracy, which was all that was expected from them – such 'learning' being seen as a force for moral good rather than an opportunity for social advancement.[23]

Rural housing

During the eighteenth century there had been a rapid decline in the prevalence of epidemic disease, falling death rates and a sustained growth in population. However, the arrival of cholera in 1831 marked the beginning of a new phase of epidemics – nationally, 32,000 people died of the disease between 1831 and 1832 and a further 62,000 in 1848–49. Although the causes of cholera were not properly understood, it was immediately apparent that it was a 'filth' disease, associated with poverty, poor housing, overcrowding and insanitary living conditions. From the 1830s onwards the improvement of the living conditions of the poor gradually became a central concern of the public health movement, and this aim underpinned much of the public health legislation of the second half of the nineteenth century. In 1846 the first of a series of Nuisances Removal Acts gave authorities the power to prosecute those responsible for 'nuisances', defined broadly as unwholesome houses, accumulations of filth, and the existence of foul drains or cesspools. The Nuisances Removal Act of 1855 was especially significant because it included the power to close houses where the nuisance was 'such as to render the house unfit for human habitation'. The public health legislation passed in the two decades from 1846 was usually permissive rather than compulsory, so it was comparatively easy for local authorities to evade or avoid action. Furthermore, the structure of local government was poorly developed, particularly in rural areas, so it was often unclear which authority, if any, should take action. This changed with the Sanitary Act of 1866, the first public health legislation in which compulsory clauses were dominant. It extended the definition of 'nuisance' to include overcrowding, and set out a minimum space requirement for domestic accommodation of 300 cubic feet per adult and 150 cubic feet per child.[24]

In numerical terms, and in terms of visible problems, the worst overcrowding and insanitary conditions were to be found in the cities, where mortality rates were highest. However, sanitary reformers were also scathing about the poor quality of housing in many rural areas. In 1864 Dr Hunter undertook an 'Inquiry on the state of the dwellings of rural labourers' as part of the seventh report of the medical officer of the Privy Council presented to Parliament in 1865. He examined 5,375 occupied houses across England, including 99 in Sussex. In his summary of Hunter's findings the medical officer, John Simon, observed that

> To the insufficient quantity and quality of the house-accommodation generally had by our agricultural labourers, almost every page of Dr Hunter's report bears

Plan for a pair of Duchess Cottages.
WSRO GOODWOOD MS 5168, WITH PERMISSION OF THE GOODWOOD ESTATE

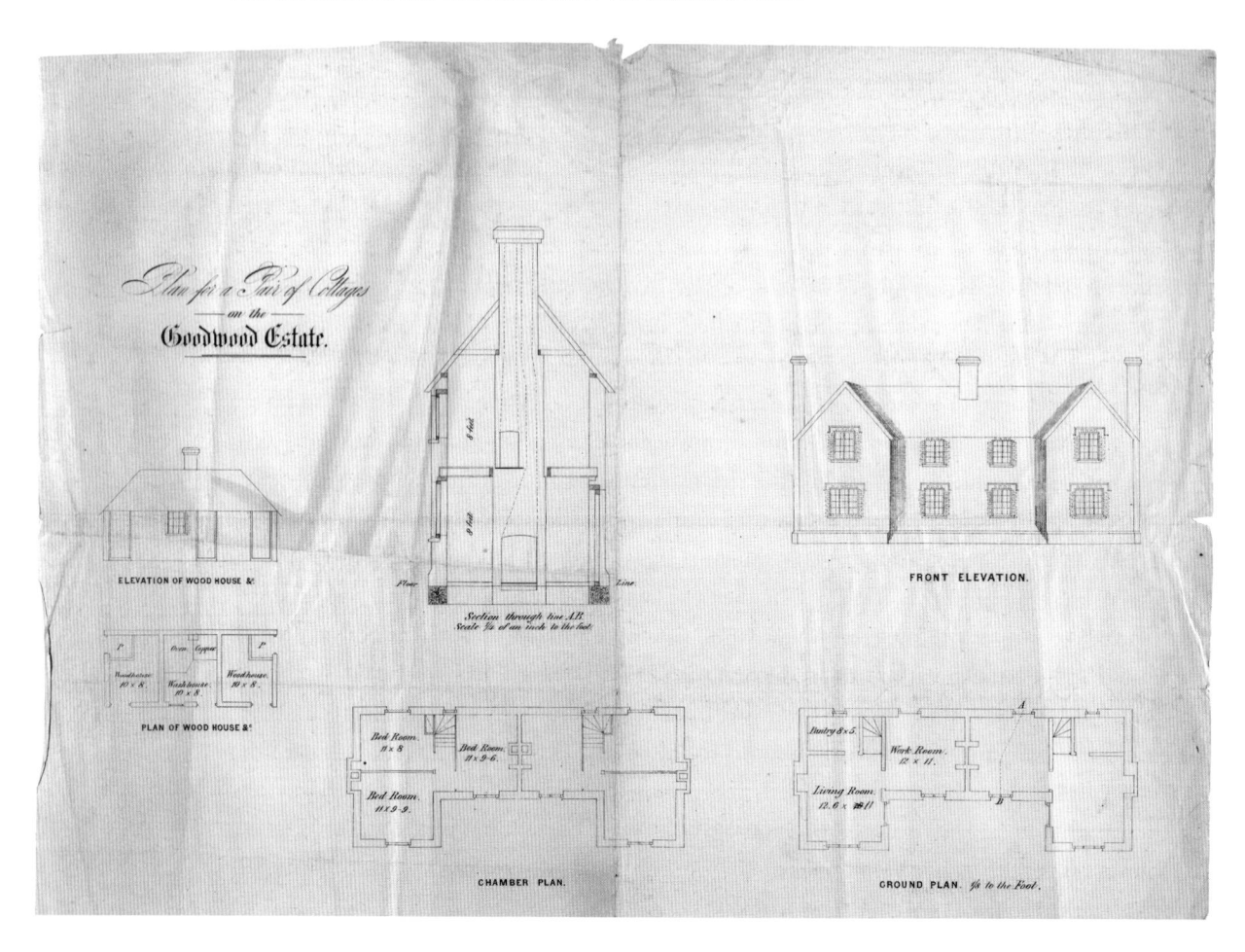

testimony. And gradually for many years past the state of the labourer in these respects has been deteriorating – house-room being now greatly more difficult for him to find, and, when found, greatly less suitable to his needs, than perhaps for centuries has been the case. Especially within the last twenty or thirty years the evil has been in very rapid increase, and the household circumstances of the labourer are now in the highest degree deplorable.

Among the principal causes cited by Hunter for the deterioration in rural living conditions was the rapid rise in population, accompanied by the widespread destruction of cottages by 'improving' landlords. Using census data from 1851 and 1861 he showed that nationally the average household size among the rural labouring classes was increasing. His sample of eighteen Sussex parishes (all but two in east Sussex) revealed that during the 1850s the average household size had increased from 4.87 to 5.62. But this rather bleak assessment did not apply to all rural areas. In the parish of Singleton the number of houses increased from 110 in 1851 to 121 in 1861, while the population actually fell, from 603 to 556. The average household size therefore went down, from 5.5 to 4.6. The reason for the increase in housing stock lies in the actions of the principal landowners, the duke of Richmond, Lord Leconfield and the Vernon Harcourts, all of whom were energetic estate improvers and cottage builders.[25]

The superior quality of accommodation in Singleton had already been noted by the writer and politician, William Cobbett, who had visited the area in 1823. He observed that

> There is an appearance of comfort about the dwellings of the labourers, all along here, that is very pleasant to behold … The gardens are neat and full of vegetables of the best kinds … I saw, and with great delight, a pig at almost every labourer's house. The houses are good and warm; and the gardens are some of the best that I have seen in England.

In 1867 assistant parliamentary commissioner, James Fraser, reported to the Commission on the Employment of Children, Young Persons, and Women in Agriculture that 'the principal landowners within [Westhampnett Union] are the Duke of Richmond … and the Hon Mrs Vernon Harcourt. They are both of them large builders and improvers of cottages.' Elsewhere in the report the parliamentary commissioners noted that the duke of Richmond, the Hon. Mrs Vernon Harcourt and Lord Leconfield were 'setting a noble example of their consciousness of responsibility in respect of the dwellings of labourers who cultivate their land'. Of

Singleton itself Fraser observed that

> the cottages are generally in fair condition, but are much crowded in Goodwood race week, when their lower apartments (in the case of 16 cottages) are turned into boxes for race-horses. All the recently erected cottages have three bedrooms, and others have had their sleeping accommodation much improved. Some of the cottages belong to small proprietors, but the majority belong to the landowners and are let at low rents, 1s. and 1s. 2d. a week, with about 20 rods of garden-ground. Where the garden is small, an allotment is attached to the cottage which is included in the rent.

However, here as in other Sussex parishes, there was a disparity between the quality of accommodation provided by the large landowners, which was generally very good, and that provided by small landowners and private landlords, which was often of poor quality and expensive. In his evidence to the commission the rector, Francis Bowles, observed that 'the cottages belonging to the Duke of Richmond and Lord Leconfield (who are both building) are well built, well ventilated, and cheaply rented. Those belonging to small owners are quite the reverse and the rent in some cases exorbitant.' This disparity in cottage accommodation and rents reflects the different motivation of large and small landlords. Landlords such as the duke of Richmond and Caroline Vernon Harcourt did not expect a return on their investment but were instead motivated by a philanthropic concern for their workers, as well as a desire to maintain a stable and willing workforce. In contrast, small landowners were interested in maximising rental income; their cottages, if new, were cheaply built and, whether new or old, were poorly maintained.[26]

Fraser's observation that 'all the recently erected cottages have three bedrooms' reflected widespread concern among social reformers about the deleterious moral consequences for the labouring classes of having insufficient bedroom accommodation. Three bedrooms were considered the minimum necessary for a family, providing separate sleeping accommodation for parents, boys and girls. In 1841 the medical officer for the third division of the Dartford Union in Kent had observed that 'I have had in my district incestuous intercourse between brothers and sisters, with the attendant consequences. A single dormitory for the whole family, and not infrequently a single bed for both sexes at the age of puberty, must lead to a state of horrid demoralization.' Yet some who commented on the living conditions of the rural working class were undecided about the causes of the moral degeneracy they observed: as Edward Carleton Tufnall put it in his report to the Sanitary Inquiry of 1842, the 'all-important' question is 'whether the character of the labouring population depends on their circumstances or their circumstances on their character?' This is despite the observation he makes elsewhere in his report that the inhabitants of some overcrowded cottages tried to preserve a modicum of decency by dividing shared occupancy rooms with curtains.[27]

On inheriting the Goodwood estate in 1860 the sixth duke of Richmond immediately began to build new cottages. The 1867 parliamentary report observed that 'the object at which the Duke is aiming is to have no cottages on his estate with less than three bedrooms'. Between 1860 and his death in 1906 he built over 400 cottages, including 48 pairs of 'double' or semi-detached cottages (known as 'Duchess' cottages). These double cottages, which cost £300 a pair, were built of coursed field flint with brick dressings and tiled roofs. Each cottage contained a living room, workroom and pantry downstairs, and three bedrooms upstairs, at least two of which had fireplaces. In addition, there was a detached building to the rear of the cottages, providing each cottage with its own woodhouse and privy and a shared washhouse, containing an oven and a copper. Caroline Vernon Harcourt was also building double cottages in the 1860s, including a pair at Binderton in 1862 for which a building agreement survives.[28]

The Public Health Act of 1872 created rural and urban sanitary authorities and required them to appoint registered doctors as medical officers of health (MOH) and inspectors of nuisances. In rural areas the sanitary authorities were the poor law unions, which were generally subdivided into smaller units presided over by parochial committees. Sanitary authorities were required to carry out inspections of their districts 'from time to time' to ascertain whether there were any nuisances that needed abating, and to act on any nuisances reported to them by the MOH or inspector of nuisances. The inspector of nuisances, who carried out the inspections, could serve notice on any individual or individuals deemed responsible for causing the nuisance (the landlord in the case of houses), requiring them to abate it within a specified period of time. He was also required to give the MOH immediate notice of any infectious diseases of a 'dangerous character' (such as cholera, smallpox, scarlet fever or scarlatina, typhus and typhoid) arising from overcrowding.

The minute books of the Westhampnett Rural Sanitary Authority, beginning in 1872, reinforce the view that, overall, the standard of living in the Westhampnett Union was good in comparison with other rural districts. There were few occurrences of 'notifiable' diseases, and when they did occur their spread was limited and they were quickly contained. In June 1873 the MOH reported that the water supply was good, but recommended that water closets or privies should be moved further away from wells to prevent the pollution of drinking water by sewage, and that cesspools should be emptied and disinfected at least once a year. There were relatively few reported cases of overcrowding. One, from 1879, concerned the Peters family who lived in Lavant – perhaps in one of the duke of Richmond's 'unimproved' cottages, since he was the largest landowner in the area. The inspector reported that their house had two bedrooms. The first was occupied by five sons, ranging in age from 21 to 4, and 'at the present by the father during the wife's lying in', providing only 138 cubic feet per person. It had no fireplace and was poorly ventilated. The second bedroom was occupied by two daughters, aged 13 and 3, the mother, her baby, and the nurse, providing 232 cubic feet per person. Despite the overcrowding, the inspector was able to report that 'the house throughout was in a clean state'.[29]

What quality of accommodation did Gonville Cottage provide? The cottage has two living rooms and a rear outshut on the ground floor and two bedrooms on the upper floor. All the rooms within the main range have fireplaces. The outshut is set at a lower level to the main range and is itself divided into two rooms by the rear entrance lobby. The larger room, on the eastern side, may have been the washhouse (or scullery), the smaller room the pantry. The living room on the western side of the cottage measures 12 feet 2½ inches by 13 feet 6 inches. This room would have been the kitchen and may have contained an iron oven or range. The living room on the east is 13 feet 7 inches by 13 feet 6 inches. There was an external privy to the rear, and a well in front of the house: this would have pleased Dr Hunter who advised that privies and wells should be built on opposite sides of a house to prevent water pollution. In terms of room dimensions the cottage compares favourably with the 'Duchess' cottages built by the duke of Richmond from the 1860s onwards – in those, the 'living room' measured 12 feet 6 inches by 11 feet, the 'workroom' 12 feet by 11 feet, and the pantry 8 feet by 5 feet.[30]

From the perspective of sanitary reformers there would, however, have been two obvious limitations to the cottage – the lack of a third bedroom and the proximity of the sheep yard not only to the front of the house but also to the drinking water supply. The accumulation of animal waste so close to a cottage constituted a 'nuisance' under the Nuisance Removal Acts, although, as Dr Hunter was at pains to point out, this legislation was largely being ignored in rural areas in the 1860s. After 1872, though, inspectors of nuisances could, and did, order the removal of animals that were being 'improperly kept'. Once Richard Burns had left the cottage in 1859, however, there was no longer any need for the sheepyard, since none of the subsequent occupants appears to have had responsibility for livestock. This might well explain the removal of the sheep sheds. Hunter would also have been concerned about the use of thatch which, as he says in his report, had to be properly maintained or else it became damp and mouldy, harboured insects, and could be a fire hazard. Later cottages in Singleton were roofed with tiles.[31]

Conclusion

William Cobbett liked what he saw in Singleton: the countryside was beautiful, the land was exceptionally fertile, and the standard of living among rural labourers was high in comparison to other parts of the country. 'There is,' he wrote, 'no misery to be seen here.' His assessment is reinforced by the observations of James Fraser in 1867: within the Westhampnett Union 'the people generally live in tolerable comfort and competency'. This was despite the fact that the standing wages of Sussex labourers were relatively low in comparison with those pertaining elsewhere in the country. The people employed on the large estates such as Goodwood, Petworth and West Dean typically lived in good cottages and paid low rents.[32]

However, even in Singleton the life of an agricultural labourer was extremely hard. For much of the nineteenth century his working life began at the age of ten and lasted until he was no longer physically capable of work – a labouring career which could span sixty years. His financial and domestic security was always precarious and could be destroyed by his own ill health or seriously undermined by the ill-health or death of his wife. Having daughters and no sons could also make the household economically vulnerable, for girls had no earning potential until they were old enough to go into service. Old age and the loss of a spouse were the greatest threats to economic independence; the best hope for the elderly was that their children would support them, either financially with cash handouts or by providing them with houseroom. This was very much the expectation of the New Poor Law authorities, who were frequently willing to offer out-relief to poor families to enable them to maintain their elderly relatives. It is likely that Richard Burns was receiving some money from the Westhampnett Union in 1851 to support his 84-year-old mother, Ann Burns, who lived with him, and he himself was living with his daughter and son-in-law in 1871. A relatively small proportion of the elderly ended up in union workhouses where, although exempt from most of the work requirements, they were nevertheless subject to the same humiliating and brutalising regimes as the able-bodied poor.[33]

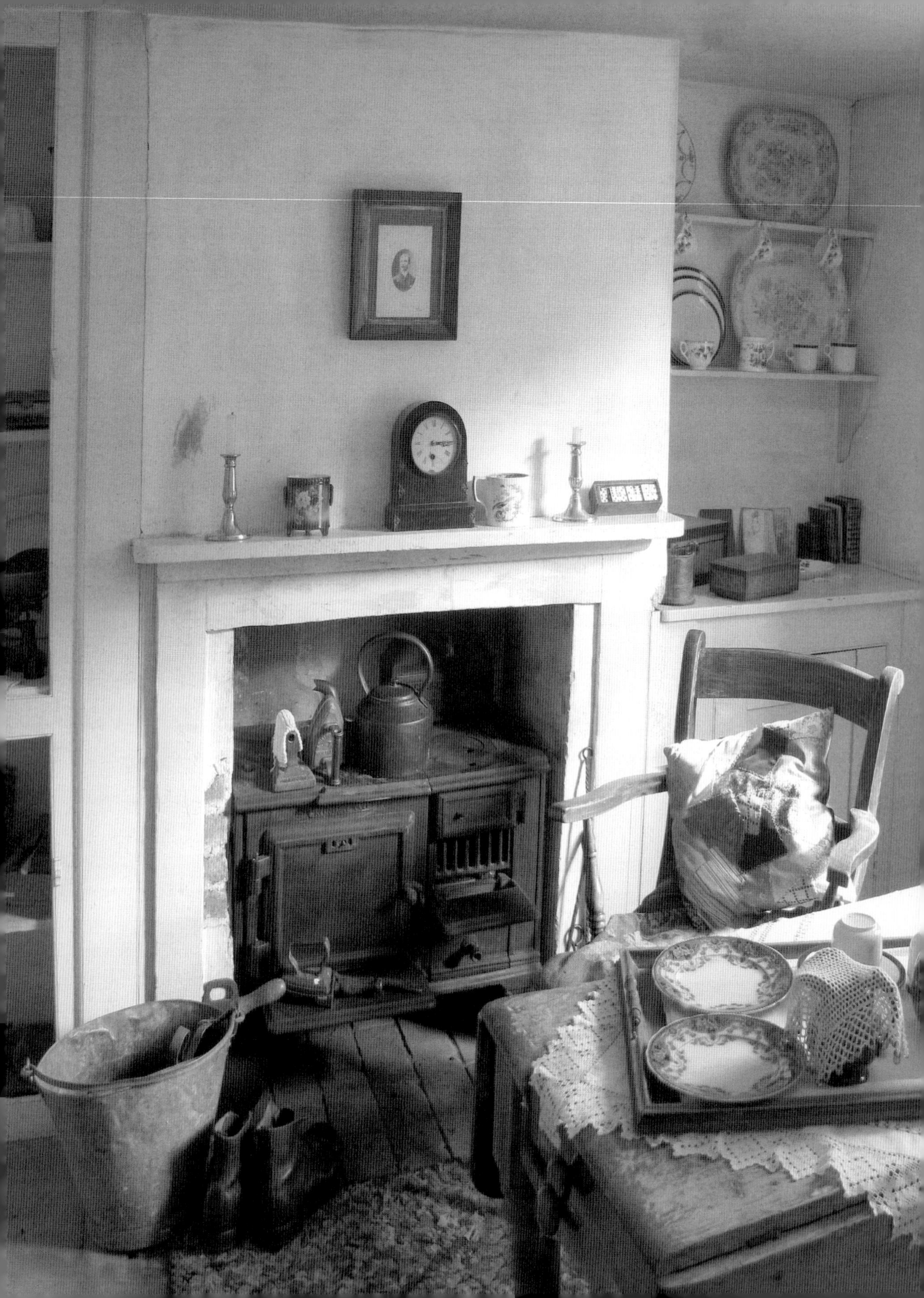

CHAPTER EIGHT

Whittaker's Cottages: railway cottages from Ashtead, Surrey

Railway cottages

Whittaker's Cottages are from Ashtead in Surrey. They were built in the 1860s facing the newly opened railway line between Epsom and Leatherhead. The foundations and chimneys of the semi-detached cottages are of brick, but the rest of the building is made of timber. Each cottage is twelve feet wide and twenty feet long, with two rooms on each floor. Only the front rooms have fireplaces. Behind each cottage are a washhouse and a privy. The cottages, which were to be demolished for new housing development, were dismantled and moved in 1987 and opened as exhibits in 1997. No. 1 Whittaker's Cottages is furnished as it might have been in the 1890s, using items from the Museum's collections. The other cottage, no. 2, has been left unfinished inside to show the timber-framed structure. Between 1886 and 1915 the occupants of no. 1 Whittaker's Cottages were Henry Filkins, who was a railway porter and later a signalman, and his family.

The cottages are timber framed and, although very different in appearance to the older timber-framed buildings at the Museum, they were built using traditional carpentry and timber-conversion techniques. The main difference is in the size of the timber: all timbers were of the same thickness – approximately four inches – whereas in older buildings the main posts would typically be between six inches and nine inches square, and the studs between six inches by three inches and eight

No. 1 Whittaker's Cottages: front room as it is displayed at the Museum.
RICHARD HARRIS

inches by four inches. The method of conversion was by axe-hewing and pit-sawing, reflecting Britain's slow rate of progress in the mechanisation of the timber industry in comparison with other industries. Two main types of timber were used: imported softwood and locally grown small diameter mixed hardwoods.[1]

The cottages are named after Richard Whittaker, an agricultural labourer who originally owned the freehold land upon which they were built. Whittaker had a cottage and just over one acre of land in a narrow strip on the west side of Ashtead Common (an area known as Woodfield). In May 1849 he sold his land for £200 to the Direct London & Portsmouth Railway Company (DL&PR), which wanted to build a new line from Epsom to Portsmouth via Dorking, Godalming and Havant. Whittaker died a few months later, and was survived by his widow, Elizabeth. The DL&PR was subsequently dissolved because of financial difficulties, and the line that finally opened in 1859 was owned by the Epsom and Leatherhead Railway Company (E&LR). In 1860 the Whittaker property – the cottage and land – was sold in two lots. The land on which the railway track had been built, 1 rood 1 perch in area, was conveyed to the E&LR. The remainder of the property, including the cottage in which Elizabeth Whittaker still lived, was conveyed to Frederick Felton, subject to the widow's right of occupancy for the remainder of her life. She died soon after the sale, and Frederick Felton then developed the property as a bakery. At some point between 1861 and 1867 he built Whittaker's Cottages on the south side of the railway. By 1881 a second pair of cottages, nos 3 and 4 Whittaker's Cottages, had been built adjacent, extremely similar in appearance, but brick-built rather than timber-framed.[2]

Valuation Office records compiled in 1913 describe no. 1 and no. 2 Whittaker's Cottages as, 'One of a pair of wood and plaster cottages, slate roofs, stock brick washhouses. Fair repair and readily let. Two living rooms, washhouse

No. 1 & no. 2, Whittaker's Cottages.
WDOAM ARCHIVE

No. 1 & no. 2, Whittaker's Cottages prior to dismantling.
WDOAM ARCHIVE

No. 3 & no. 4 Whittaker's Cottages shortly before demolition.
WDOAM ARCHIVE

and two bedrooms. Only front rooms have fire places.'

When the cottages were dismantled in 1987 the only running water in no. 1 Whittaker's Cottages was in the washhouse at the rear of the property. A previous occupant, Barbara Broughton (née Cook), who had lived in the cottage from 1933 until 1960, remembers that the washhouse contained a sink with a cold-water tap and a large copper for doing the household laundry. In the front living room there was a range, which her father (the last occupant, Frederick Cook) removed in the 1940s, replacing it with a gas cooker in the back living-room, which then became the kitchen.[3]

The railway line opened in 1859 and was worked by the London and South Western Railway (LSWR). In 1860 the LSWR and the London, Brighton & South Coast Railway (LBSCR) were authorised to buy the line from the E&LR and to take it into joint ownership under a joint management committee. Each company operated its own trains, and responsibility for maintaining the line alternated between the two companies, annually until 1886 and then quinquennially. The employees at Ashtead station were appointed by the LSWR. Only a few staff records survive for the LSWR, and none refers to Henry Filkins. Staff registers for the LBSCR record that porters were paid between 16s. and 18s. a week, depending on their seniority, and signalmen about £1 1s. a week. The Ashtead stationmaster from 1873 to 1905 was Thomas Sims, who lived in a house beside the up platform, for which he paid an annual rent of £10. In 1921, when a staff census was taken, Ashtead station was staffed by a stationmaster, two clerks, four porters, three signalmen and a crossing (or gate) keeper.[4]

No. 1 & no. 2 Whittaker's Cottages, showing proximity to railway line. No. 3 & no. 4 have already been demolished.
WDOAM ARCHIVE

Ashtead, a parish of 2,645 acres, is two miles south-west of Epsom and a mile and a half north-east of Leatherhead. The opening of the railway in 1859 led to substantial residential development and significant population growth. In 1841 the population was 618; by 1871 it had risen to 906; by 1881 to 926; and by 1901 to 1,881. In 1878 there were five large farms in Ashtead: New Purchase Farm, West Farm, Park Farm, Ashtead Farm and Woodfield Farm. Most agricultural land was arable, the chief crops being wheat, barley, oats, turnips and swedes, with smaller acreages of peas, mangolds, rape and vetches or tares. Between 1880 and 1900 a substantial amount of farmland was swallowed up by new housing developments, and New Purchase Farm disappeared completely. Some residential development was undertaken by a private firm, the Ashtead Land Company, which was established in 1890.[5]

There was also industrial development, with brickfields and specialist brick and tile manufacturers at the Ashtead Brick Works in Barnett Lane, owned by the Sparrow Brothers, and the electric accumulator works owned by Peto and Radford. Mawson, and Swift's Photographic Dry Plate Works (the Greville Works) was established between Greville Park Road and Northfields just before 1890. It was taken over in 1895 by James Cadett and W. Neall, who formed Cadett & Neall Ltd on 20 May 1897. They built the Victoria Works (on the north side of West Hill) and the Crampshaw Works (south of West Hill between Parker's Lane and Rectory Lane), completing both before 1900. One was devoted to the manufacture of photographic plates and the other to the production of photographic papers. Nevertheless, the *Victoria County History* for Surrey, published in 1911, could still describe Ashtead as 'mainly agricultural'.[6]

After the opening of the railway, the 519-acre Ashtead Common, in the north of the parish, became a popular location for London day-trippers during the summer months and the site of an unofficial funfair. Frederick Felton, who had bought Richard Whittaker's land, established a bakery with tea rooms facing the Common to the north of the railway. Later known as Woodfield House, this catered for pleasure parties coming by train, and had pony-operated roundabouts, a helter-skelter, and other attractions. In 1895 the garden of no. 4 Whittaker's Cottages contained corrugated-iron 'refreshment catering tea sheds', which formed part of a substantial catering operation called 'The Rosary', run by the occupant of the house, George Cox, who had previously been a travelling signalman. In 1913 the 'tea sheds' were described as 'rather dilapidated' and 'used as wood stores and rubbish heaps'. There was also a large tearoom beside the station, in a long, low corrugated-iron hut with 'TEA' written on its roof. From the 1890s tearooms and tea gardens in the village catered for cyclists and walkers, and later for motorbus excursionists.[7]

The Filkins family

Henry Filkins was born in 1864 in Egham, Surrey, one of nine children. His father was a groom and his mother a laundress. At the time of the 1881 census he was working as a household servant in Ashford, Middlesex, but by 1886 was married to Harriet and living in Ashtead where his first son, Henry George, was born. Frank John was born in 1887 and David William in 1889. Henry and Harriet had a further five children, Sidney Alfred (1892), Mabel Rosa Mary (1893), Edith Harriet (1894), Gertrude Ellen (1897) and Herbert (1898). Perhaps Henry and Harriet had run out of names by the time Herbert was born – he alone among their children had no middle

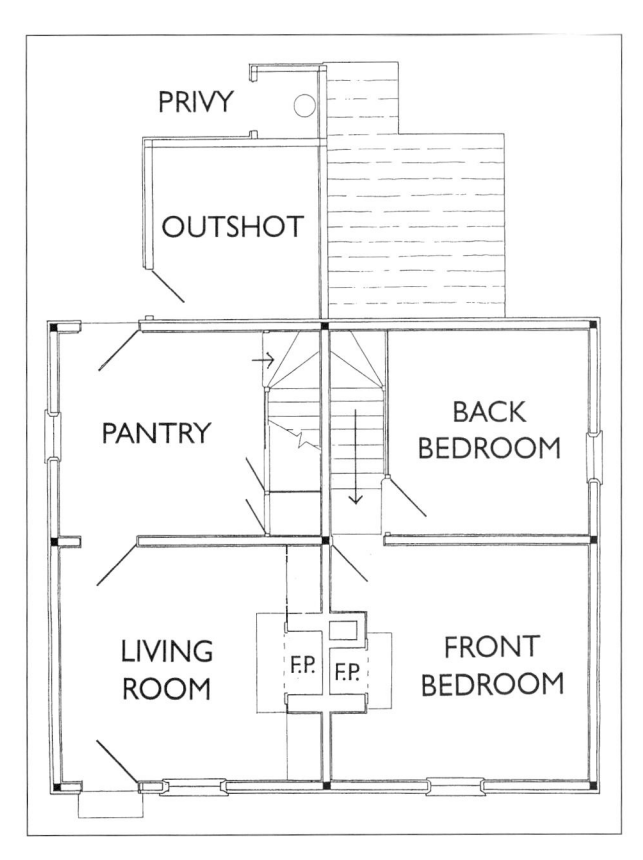

Floor plan for Whittaker's Cottages.
RICHARD HARRIS

name. By 1898, therefore, a family of ten was living in no. 1 Whittaker's Cottages.[8]

The 1891 census records Henry's occupation as 'railway porter', but by 1898 he had become a signalman. As a porter Henry would have been required to open the station in the morning and to light the fires and paraffin lamps in winter, as well as keeping the platform and buildings clean. He would have seen trains in and out, and been involved with shunting in the yard when the goods trains arrived to load and unload freight and luggage. He may also have been required to issue tickets before the stationmaster or station clerk came on duty, or after they went off duty in the evening. On his promotion, he was one of the two signalmen permanently allocated to the Ashtead signal box. The first box was built at Ashtead in 1882, at the London end of the down platform. A new box was built in 1899 when the line between Epsom and Leatherhead was resignalled to cope with increasing traffic. The signal box was manned continuously from 6.45 on Monday morning until 10.30 on Sunday evening, which meant that the signalmen had to work in shifts, probably of twelve hours.[9]

Henry was part of a new breed of rural working-class men who were turning their backs on the land in favour of what they perceived to be superior forms of employment. The *Royal Commission on Labour*, in its report on the agricultural labourer (1893–94), attributed the decline in the number of men working on the

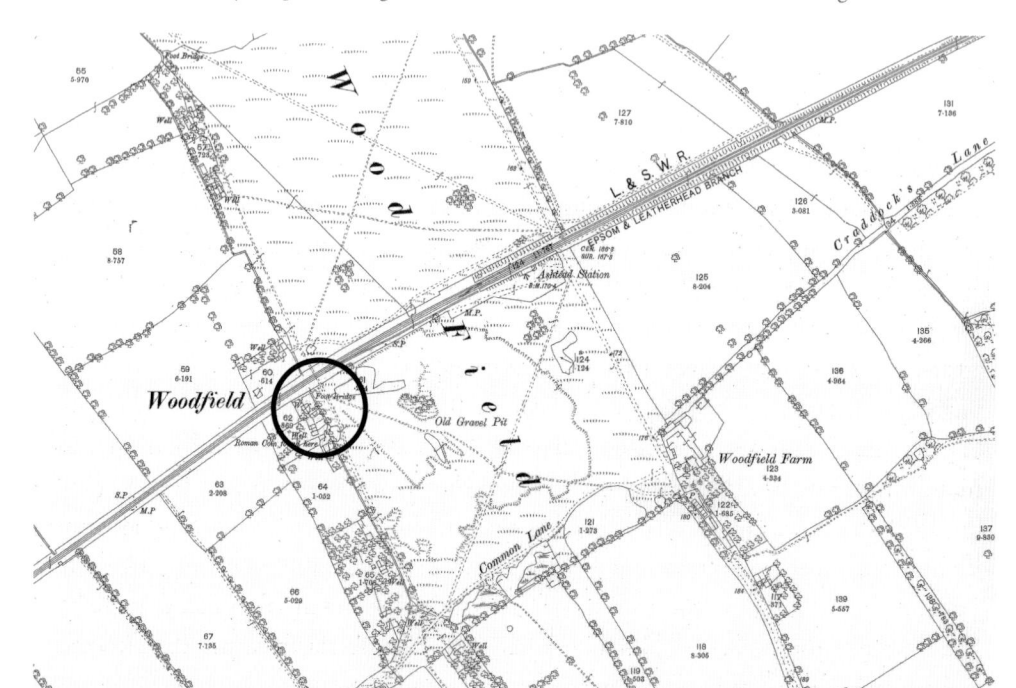

1877 ordnance survey map, showing location of no. 1 & no. 2 Whittaker's Cottages.

Ashtead Station, c.1910. The four men in top hats were fly drivers. The three men were porters. The boy with the rifle is Oswald Simms, the son of the station master.
FROM THE COLLECTION OF THE LEATHERHEAD & DISTRICT LOCAL HISTORY SOCIETY

land to a combination of factors, including 'the desire for a freer and less dull life, the low standard of wages [and] the absence of any prospect of making provision for old age'. Many of these men were migrating to towns and cities, where their 'superior physique' enabled them to find immediate employment in trades and industry.[10]

Others, like Henry Filkins, found employment on the railways or in the police force. As a railway porter, Henry would not in fact have been much better off financially than neighbours who were agricultural labourers. But his job was less physically arduous, more secure, and would have provided him with a pension in his old age. He was also required to wear a uniform, which would have accorded him a certain degree of respect, for a job on the railways constituted a 'good post' in the widespread contemporary view. Despite the demands of his working and family life, Henry was also able to enjoy some leisure time. He was a member of Ashtead Cricket Club, sitting on the committee, and regularly playing in matches in Ashtead and the surrounding area – possibly valued for his enthusiasm rather than his talent, as he regularly had one of the lowest batting averages.[11]

There are a number of references to the Filkins children and to the family in the school logbooks for Ashtead boys' school and Ashtead infants' school. On 5 June 1895, for example, the mistress of the infants' school, Miss Thrush, recorded that 'David Filkins returned to school this morning after being absent for several months through illness'. At that date David would have been six. On 12 June 1896 the master of the boys' school, Alfred Boyd, recorded that he had sent the names of several truanting boys to the school attendance officer: among them was Harry (Henry) Filkins, who had missed nine out of twenty sessions (either the morning or afternoon session of the school day). On 19 November 1897 Boyd recorded that 'Mrs Filkins came in yesterday and took David away as she said the others had scarlet fever', and on 3 May 1898 that

Extract from boys' school log book, 3 May 1898.
SHC 6196/1/1. REPRODUCED BY PERMISSION OF SURREY HISTORY CENTRE

The teachers are earnestly endeavouring to maintain discipline &c without resorting to corporal punishment. There are frequent cases of disobedience, dishonesty and idleness which have been severely reprimanded verbally and moral persuasion emphasised. The lads C Haynes (idleness), Filkins' family (disorderly), Edwards' family (generally unruly) are the chief offenders.

On 24 June 1898 Boyd noted that 'H. Filkins was examined for a certificate of proficiency'. Also known as a 'labour certificate', this granted children exemption on grounds of educational attainment from the requirement imposed by the 1880 Education Act that they should attend school until the age of 14. In 1898 Henry was 12. The outcome of his examination was not stated, but the 1901 census shows that, aged 14, he was then working as a gardener's assistant. On 3 March 1899 Boyd recorded that he had 'received a letter from Mrs Filkins stating that the younger children of her large family were attacked with whooping cough and asking if it was necessary to keep the older boys, who have had the complaint, away from school'. Despite the dangers of scarlet fever, whooping cough and other childhood illnesses, all the Filkins children survived to adulthood. Although the family would not have known it, the children were part of the first generation to benefit from the reduced mortality rates of the late nineteenth century.[12]

Public health and sanitary reforms

As we saw in the previous chapter, a succession of legislation in the second half of the nineteenth century was aimed at improving public health. In 1872 Ashtead became part of the newly established Epsom Rural Sanitary Authority (from 1 January 1895, the Epsom Rural District Council), which was empowered to take action under a wide range of public health legislation including the nuisances removal acts, the public health acts, the sanitary acts, the sewage utilisation acts, the infectious diseases acts and, after 1885, the Housing of the Working Classes Act. Unlike deeply rural Singleton, Ashtead was confronted with pressing and on-going sanitation problems caused by the rapid growth in population, which led to overcrowded houses, inadequate sewage disposal facilities and polluted water supplies.

The problem of how to deal with human waste in crowded urban areas preoccupied sanitary reformers for much of the nineteenth century and resulted in gargantuan feats of civil engineering such as Bazalgette's London sewer system. The most common form of toilet was the privy midden, typically a small, private cesspit with brick or metal sides and base. Such privies were often poorly constructed and inadequately maintained, and there was considerable leakage into surrounding soil. In many areas 'dry conservancy' methods were adopted from the mid-nineteenth century onwards, involving the use of earth or ash as deodorising agents instead of water – hence the common name of earth closets or ash pits for such facilities, the latter containing household ash, dust and other dry refuse. In some areas pails or pans began to replace the privy middens: these were supplied to houses, collected, emptied, cleaned and returned. Only in the last decade of the nineteenth century did water-flushed sewerage systems with modern filtration and treatment plants become widespread, and then only in urban areas. These modern systems were expensive, and their development presented major engineering challenges – and a prerequisite was a fully adequate piped water supply to flush the pipes. For these reasons, their adoption was slow and hesitant.[13]

In the 1890s the sanitary arrangements for the majority of Ashtead inhabitants were still rudimentary. Most cottages had open privies, earth closets, ash pits or cesspools which, unless regularly emptied, overflowed and polluted watercourses. In May 1894 the Epsom Rural Sanitary Authority heard a complaint that sink and bathwater from four properties in Woodfield Lane were discharging into the ditch that ran parallel to it, and notices were served on the owners to stop. In January 1895 the council read a report from the engineer stating that 'his attention had been called to the offensive smell arising from the ditch in Woodfield Lane, he had inspected the same and found fouled water flowing from some new cottages in the lane, there being a decided putrid smell arising from the flowing water'. This ditch discharged into The Rye or Rye Brook, which ran across Ashtead Common and thence into the River Mole at Fetcham and so ultimately to the Thames.[14]

In 1895 the council passed byelaws regulating the cleansing of earth closets, privies, ash pits and cesspools, revealing the variety of sewage disposal methods that were in use. Earth closets with fixed receptacles were to be emptied at least once every three months, and those with removable receptacles at least once a week. Privies with fixed receptacles were to be emptied at least fortnightly, those with movable receptacles at least weekly, ashpits at least once a fortnight, and cesspools every three months. The penalty for infringing these byelaws was a 40s. fine. In August 1898, on the advice of the inspector of nuisances, the council served notice on the owners of the Flats in Ashtead (despite its name, an area of new housing and not flats) to 'provide for the emptying and cleansing of the pails from the earth closets of the cesspools at regular and stated times and removing the pails and contents off the premises in covered carts'.[15]

In February 1895, the council and the newly established Ashtead Parish Council agreed to join with the Leatherhead Urban District Council in a joint sewerage scheme, and a committee was established. However, by May, after failing to agree terms, the two authorities decided to pursue separate schemes. In March 1896 the Thames Conservancy Board served notice on the council to discontinue the pollution of The Rye within three months and by July 1896 was threatening legal proceedings. In April 1897 it was resolved to adopt a drainage scheme proposed by an engineer, Frederick Beesley, using 'the bacterial system of treatment of sewage' and to approach Merton College, Oxford, owners of the proposed outfall site in the neighbouring parish of Leatherhead, to see if they would sell the land. Merton was not cooperative, and in May 1898 the council bought the lands by compulsory purchase, having been granted an order by the Local Government Board under powers set out in the Public Health Act of 1875. In September 1898 Messrs Beesley & Son (subsequently Beesley, Son & Nichols), submitted plans for the proposed drainage scheme with an estimated cost of £13,000 (which later rose to £14,500).

In July 1899 the council advertised for tenders to carry out the drainage works. Fourteen tenders were received, ranging in cost from £7,682 to £11,558 6s., and in September the contract was awarded to the lowest tender, that of G. Bell of Tottenham. But in June 1900 the council was obliged to apply for an additional loan of £4,000 to meet the costs of the joint outfall works and sewer, 'due to the enormous area of the bacteria beds now proposed to meet the requirements of the Local Government Board'.[16]

Ashtead's new sewers finally became operational in 1901, seven years after the scheme was first proposed. They were flushed by water from a tank provided by the Leatherhead and District Waterworks Company in Dene Road. However, it is apparent that not all houses were connected to it, and cesspools continued to be used. In May 1901 the council heard a complaint about the emptying of cesspools in daytime at cottages on the Taylor's Estate and ordered that the work be carried out at night.[17]

From the 1880s the privately owned Leatherhead and District Waterworks Company supplied water to Ashtead, drawn from a 200-foot borehole in Leatherhead. But in the 1890s many properties in Ashtead were not connected to water mains, and most households relied on pumps and wells. The minutes of Epsom Rural District Council between 1894 and 1900 include numerous reports about polluted water supplies to residential properties in Ashtead. In May 1895 the Medical Officer of Health reported that the water supply to a cottage on Woodfield Common was polluted. The council wrote to the owner requesting him to provide a proper supply under section 70 of the Public Health Act 1875. In reply, he advised the council that the cottage was about to be pulled down (which in August it was). In July 1895 the inspector of nuisances reported that a house and shop in the main street (known as 'The Street') was without a proper water supply. The MOH was instructed to analyse the water, and he reported back to the council that 'on analysing the water from this pump [I] found the same very impure'. The occupier, Mrs Borer, was ordered to provide a proper supply.[18]

By 1900 an increasing number of houses in Ashtead were being connected, and in September 1900 the district council agreed to contribute £4 towards the cost of supplying the village school. But since the cost of connecting houses to the mains was borne by the owner, there were still properties at the lower end of the housing market that lacked adequate supplies. In May 1901, for example, the owners of Harriot's Cottages in Agates Lane were ordered to provide the cottages with a proper water supply from the water mains of the Leatherhead and District Waterworks Company.[19]

Medical care

In November 1888 Ashtead appointed its first certified parish nurse, Nurse Martin, at a cost of £80 per annum plus additional expenses for the initial outlay on medicines and appliances, the bulk of which was met by charitable subscriptions. Parishioners requiring her services paid a penny a day. However, in November 1891 the parish magazine announced that, despite her skills and the 'indefatigable and cheerful way in which she has always fulfilled her duties', there were insufficient funds to keep her on. The following year the parish raised sufficient funds through charitable subscriptions to appoint another nurse, Mrs Bunyan. This time, parishioners wishing to avail themselves of her services were obliged to pay an annual subscription of 2s. to defray the cost of appliances and medicines. Between 2 March and 19 December 1892 Mrs Bunyan paid about 2,300 visits, an average of 56 a week.[20]

In September 1893 the ladies of the Ashtead Nursing Fund agreed to terminate the employment of the nurse because the village now had its own doctor, William Smyth, to whose medical clubs many of the poor belonged. The parish nurse system was, in any case, expensive and difficult to operate in a semi-rural area. From January 1894 Ashtead joined the Dorking Nursing Association. Those wishing to join the nursing fund paid a yearly subscription of 2s. for labourers, 3s. for artisans, head gardeners, coachmen and others of similar status, 5s. for farmers and trades people and 10s. for gentry. When a parishioner needed the services of a nurse he or she had to apply to the local committee, and the nurse would then reside in the patient's house for the duration of the illness. Two months' notice was necessary when the application was for a confinement. In addition to the nursing the nurse would be expected to care for the patient's family, although not to do the family washing![21]

There was a cottage hospital at Epsom. In July 1891, at the suggestion of a committee of representatives of local friendly societies and working-men's clubs, a collection was made for support of the hospital. This raised £113 10s. 8d., with Ashtead contributing £11 6s. 6d. The editor of the parish magazine reminded its readers that 'the Cottage Hospital is a most deserving institution and every year several Ashtead cases are received into it', adding that it was gratifying that a large proportion of the amount collected from Ashtead 'came in small sums from the working classes for whose special benefit the hospital is maintained'.[22]

The Infectious Diseases (Notification) Act of 1889 required medical practitioners to inform the MOH of any new infectious diseases within their area. The sufferers were isolated either in their own homes or in infectious disease hospitals, such as the London Fever Hospital or the smallpox asylum in Stockwell. Transport to such hospitals was by the horse-drawn ambulance kept at the Epsom Union Workhouse, for which the patient was required to pay, although the sanitary authority paid for its disinfection after use. From its foundation the Epsom Rural Sanitary Authority considered the feasibility of establishing an isolation hospital within its own district but although a number of possible sites were considered no hospital was built.[23]

The Sanitary Act 1866 and the Public Health Act 1875 empowered the inspector of nuisances, upon receiving certificate by the MOH or any legally qualified medical practitioner, to enter the home of anyone suffering from an infectious disease and disinfect it and, if necessary, destroy infected articles, for which compensation was given. On 8 October 1879 the sanitary authority ordered the disinfecting or destruction of certain articles belonging to Thomas Anscombe of Lower Ashtead, because there was scarlet fever in his cottage. If, because of poverty, the occupants of an infected house were unable to get articles disinfected, the sanitary authority had the power to remove them and to disinfect at its own cost. In the annual report of the county MOH for 1888–89 it was noted that, for Epsom rural district, articles had been removed from 25 houses for disinfecting by Mr R. F. Holloway of Hackbridge in his 'hot-air chamber', at a cost to the authority of £73 5s.[24]

Housing

As we have seen, during the late nineteenth century there was extensive housing development in Ashtead. Much of this was intended for the new breed of middle-class commuters, who had escaped London and were attracted to places such as Ashtead by their rural location and excellent rail links. By 1887 most of the former Ashtead farms had been broken up and their property bought up and shared between eight major landowners and many smaller ones. One of the large landowners, the Ashtead Land Company, was established in 1890 and bought 108 acres in the north-east of the parish. Other development companies, including the Suburban Land and Cottage Company, the Land and House Company, and the Housing and Improvement Association, owned smaller parcels of land. In 1895 Epsom Rural District Council passed byelaws requiring anyone proposing to construct a new building to first give the council written notice and then to submit plans for approval by the council's surveyor, detailing the intended mode of construction, the materials to be used, the method of drainage, and the water supply. Such plans, showing complete sections for every floor, were to be drawn to a scale of not less than one inch to every eight feet. Those breaching the byelaws faced an initial 40s. fine, followed by additional fines of 10s. for every day that the breach continued, with the enforced destruction of the offending building as the ultimate sanction. In August 1895 the council appointed James Keal (also inspector of nuisances) as its first surveyor for the parish of Ashtead. From then on its minute books record regular business arising from the new byelaws. For example, in March 1897 the council approved plans submitted by Lionel Littlewood for the erection of two houses on the Elms Estate in Ashtead and by W. C. Weymouth for one house on Street Farm Estate in Ashtead.[25]

The minute books show that the council tackled unsatisfactory housing using the

Nuisances Removal Act and the Housing of the Working Classes Act. The latter, passed in 1885, attempted to consolidate previous legislation, including the Artisans' and Labourers' Dwelling Act of 1868 (known as the Torrens Act) and the Artisans' and Labourers' Dwellings Improvement Act of 1875 (the Cross Act). These, although largely ineffective, had given local authorities powers to inspect, close and demolish dwellings that were unfit for human habitation; to enforce the provision of drainage, water supplies, cleansing and ventilation; to regulate building standards and limit overcrowding; to provide lodgings and to build houses for working people and (with the Cross Act) to allow local authorities to purchase and demolish large areas of 'unfit' property.[26]

In February 1898 Ashtead Parish Council complained to Epsom RDC about the unsanitary nature of Lower Ashtead, and particularly that area north-east of the Haven. The following month the inspector of nuisances, James Keal, reported that he had made a house-to-house inspection of Lower Ashtead, and recommended serving notices on the owners of unsatisfactory accommodation. Unfortunately, the details of that inspection do not survive, but details of comparable inspection carried out in August and September 1895 at nearby Ewell, under the Housing of the Working Classes Act, are extant. A total of 248 cottages were inspected, 'practically the whole of the small property in the district', and of these 17 were deemed unsatisfactory. They could in principle have been demolished under the 1875 and 1885 Acts but, given the scarcity of cottage property in Ewell, the inspector proposed instead to serve notices to bring them into an adequate state of repair.[27]

Friendly societies and charities

Like most nineteenth-century and early twentieth-century communities, Ashtead had a friendly society and a range of benefit clubs and charities to support those on low incomes or facing loss of earnings through illness or the death of a spouse. Membership or receipt of charitable relief were dependent upon good behaviour, with sobriety, thrift, industriousness and good manners especially valued. In Ashtead the Leg of Mutton Friendly Society (named after the inn where the members met) was founded in 1841. The printed rules of the club, which survive from 1895, state that the society's object was to

> provide by voluntary subscriptions of the members for the relief or maintenance of the members during sickness or other infirmity, whether bodily or mental; for insuring money to be paid on the death of a member, or for the funeral expenses of a wife of a member.

RULES FOR ASHTEAD CLOTHING AND PROVIDENT CLUB.

1.—All Persons who have been resident in the Parish of Ashtead for one year, and who have been confirmed, may become Members of this Club.

2.—Deposits may be made from one penny to four pence weekly, the depositors to receive one-half in addition to their deposits at the end of the year.

3.—Any single person, or a man and his wife may deposit .... 1d. per week.
A man and his wife with 2 children may deposit .... 2d. per week.
A man and his wife with 4 children may deposit .... 3d. per week.
A man and his wife with 6 children, or more may deposit .... 4d. per week.

4.—The amount of these deposits, and of the additional money given, to be taken out in articles of plain and useful clothing or bedding.

5.—Every member shall agree to abstain from Sabbath-breaking, Swearing, Drunkenness, Theft, Backbiting, Quarrelling, and Unchastity, on pain of being dismissed from the club.

6.—Every member is expected to attend the service of Almighty God, at least once on every Sunday, unless reasonably hindered by Sickness, or some other urgent cause.

7.—Every member is to bring their deposits (not borrowed) to the Vestry Room, either before or after Morning or Evening service, on the first Sunday in every month, and the money will be received at no other time.

8.—No payments to be left in arrear.

9.—Should any depositor wish to withdraw his or her money before the end of the year, they may do so, but will receive no sum in addition to what they have deposited.

10.—Should any depositor be guilty of breaking the 5th rule, he will not be allowed to deposit any money for the space of three months afterwards, and will then only be re-admitted on condition of expressing his sorrow for his fault; repeated misconduct will cause his being excluded altogether from the club.

11.—Mr. Bailey of Epsom, or whatever shopkeeper may be chosen, will bring such goods as are allowed under rule 4. to the Girl's School, to be sold there, on the first Saturday in December.

12.—Persons will be allowed to deposit any sum of money they choose, in addition to their regular weekly deposits; but for the further sum so deposited, they will receive nothing in addition at the end of the year.

13.—A card will be delivered to each depositor, which they must bring with them every time they wish to deposit their money, that the sum may be put down. This card is to be kept clean, and should any depositor neglect to bring their card, they will not be allowed to deposit any money that week.

Honorary Members may on payment of 4s. 4d. yearly, place one person on the list of the receiving members of the club.

No honorary member to place more than one member of the same family receiving under No. 1 and 2 of rule 3, or more than two Members of the same family receiving under rule 3, No. 3 and 4.

To make up the number of fifty-two weeks, it will be necessary to double the monthly deposits in the month of August.

DORLING AND SON, PRINTERS, EPSOM.

Rules of Ashtead Clothing Club.
SHC ATGIL/15/4/6. REPRODUCED BY PERMISSION OF SURREY HISTORY CENTRE

Membership was open to any man aged between 16 and 40, each prospective member being required to produce a medical certificate certifying that he was 'of sound constitution' at the time of joining. The joining fee was 2s. 6s. and the monthly subscription was 2s. In the event of sickness or injury (other than brought on himself by 'debauched or irregular practices') a member would receive 12s. a week for up to six months and then 6s. a week for the next six months. Those claiming sickness benefit might be subjected to a medical examination. At the end of each year any profits remaining to the club were divided between the members. On the death of a member all the others paid a shilling towards the cost of his funeral (or sixpence on the death of a member's wife). Members were excluded if convicted of any crime or found to be 'of a drunken, quarrelsome disposition, or much given to fighting'. A threepenny fine was payable for swearing, gambling or carrying 'any liquor out of the room to drink'; a shilling fine was payable for talking about the society's affairs to non-members or for provoking discord.[28]

In addition to the Leg of Mutton Friendly Society there was, by 1894, a Girls' Friendly Society. In April of that year an Ashtead branch of the Young Men's Friendly Society was established, with thirteen members enrolling at an afternoon service in the parish church. The rector gave a brief address exhorting those who were about to become members to be true to the society's motto 'Quit you like men, be strong', and reminding them that they must 'be strong in the Lord' and 'never ashamed to confess the faith of Christ crucified'. He also urged them to maintain a high standard of brotherly kindness among themselves, as theirs was to be a 'friendly' society and to uphold the credit of the society by their exemplary conduct.[29]

The object of the Ashtead clothing club was to help the poor of the parish to buy warm clothing and blankets for winter. Each member was allowed to pay a small amount of money (from threepence to a shilling each week) between January and October with a bonus of a penny per shilling added at the end of the season on total deposits of 10s. or more. Members were only allowed to buy goods from shops approved by the charity managers, and purchased goods were subject to their inspection and approval. Anyone found guilty of drunkenness or immorality was excluded from the club. A note in the parish magazine for January 1889 reminded members that 'it is intended that their purchases should consist of warm clothing, boots, blankets &c, and not of artificial flowers, ribbons and laces', with the warning that the club managers would refuse payment for such items.[30] The coal club operated in a similar manner. Prospective members had to be approved by the rector, with only one depositor allowed from each house. Deposits, payable at the village schools between January and October, could be a minimum of sixpence and a maximum of 2s. at any one time, with a bonus of threepence per shilling added to total deposits

Ashtead burial guild, 1895.
FROM THE COLLECTION OF THE LEATHERHEAD & DISTRICT LOCAL HISTORY SOCIETY

of between 5s. and 10s. As with the clothing club, drunken or immoral behaviour resulted in exclusion from the club.[31]

In the June 1893 edition of the parish magazine the rector proposed the setting up of a burial club or guild, 'such as been found useful in some other parishes'. The purpose of the guild was to provide respectable church-going men as bearers, and to discourage the custom of heavy drinking that typically accompanied funerals. The rector stated that

> at present a funeral often involves poor people in great expense; they are expected to provide (perhaps) eight bearers, not only with a fee, but also with refreshments, and it is a constant source of discredit that many bearers never enter the church except when paid to carry a coffin, do not join in the burial service, and often go direct from the graveside to the public house, where they sometimes spend the rest of the day.

Those using the guild's services were charged 2s. 6d., and all other expenses were met from a fund maintained by voluntary subscriptions. A wheeled bier was bought to bear the coffin, because it required fewer men than the traditional method of carrying the coffin on men's shoulders and was thus cheaper and 'more conducive to propriety'. Members were required to wear black clothes underneath specially made white smocks (the wearing of white smocks at funerals being an old custom in Ashtead) with purple badges.[32]

Education

Ashtead School was established in 1852 when Mary Greville Howard, owner of Ashtead Park, had a new school built on a site she had donated. The new school comprised boys' and girls' departments, and an infants' department was set up in 1878. By an agreement with Epsom Poor Law Union, a number of children from the workhouse were regularly sent to the school. In August 1900 the boys' and girls' departments were merged, and in 1906 the school was renamed the Ashtead Church of England School.[33]

The 1870 Education Act required adequate provision for elementary education to be made in all parts of the country. Where existing voluntary schools (usually church schools) were unable to meet the needs of the locality a school board could be established to make up the shortfall. Few school boards were set up in rural districts, since not only did voluntary schools simply expand to meet demand, but also in many areas the local clergy were fiercely opposed to them, seeing them as a secular threat to existing denominational provision. The Agricultural Children Act of 1873 sought to prohibit the employment of children below the age of eight in agriculture, and to secure minimum school attendance for those aged eight to twelve. However, it was almost entirely ineffective because of the Act's failure to specify any agency to see that its provisions were carried out.[34]

The 1876 Education Act required the setting up of school attendance committees in areas where there were no school boards, the committees being empowered to demand compulsory attendance of children between the ages of five and thirteen inclusive. The 1880 Education Act obliged the compulsory attendance of all children between the ages of five and ten and thereafter until fourteen, unless exemption could be gained on grounds of educational attainment or of average level of attendance. For those aged between ten and twelve a minimum of 250 attendances per annum was required, while for the over-twelves the figure was 150. Legal exemption could only granted on a part-time basis if the child was over ten years old and if the specified number of attendances had been made. Complete exemption below the

Pupils from Ashtead CE School, 1906.
FROM THE COLLECTION OF GILL NORTHCOTT

age of fourteen depended either upon the child passing his 'labour certificate', at the standard laid down by the education byelaws in his own school district (usually either Standard IV or Standard V), or upon his having reached the age of thirteen and having made at least 250 attendances per annum in the previous five years.[35]

The 1891 Elementary Education Act made elementary education free. A government grant of 10s. a year was payable for each pupil in a public elementary school based on average attendance, and fees could either be reduced by that amount or abolished entirely. In 1893 the minimum school leaving age was raised to eleven and in 1899 to twelve, although in rural areas eleven was still frequently accepted.[36] In order to try to ensure that the provisions of the various Education Acts were observed, school boards and attendance committees were required to appoint attendance officers. These were frequently part-time and badly paid posts, and attendance officers also faced hostility and abuse from parents who resented their interference in family affairs. Unsurprisingly, attendance officers were not always diligent in carrying out their duties.[37]

The logbooks for Ashtead School show intractable problems with truancy by pupils, often for extended periods of time. On 21 June 1892, for example, the master, Alfred Boyd, recorded that ten boys had been absent during the previous fortnight between six and fourteen times and observed that 'free education does not seem to be appreciated in this parish'. The mother of one of the truants, Walter Bailey, who had been absent for more than a month, came into school to tell the schoolmaster that he would not be returning to school until after the holidays because he was of more use to her at home. Parents were not always to blame for the poor attendance of their children. In April 1895 Mrs Vicary wrote to the schoolmaster asking whether her son, Percy, had been attending school regularly during the previous fortnight and urging him to 'punish him well' if he had not. In reply, Boyd informed her that Percy had not attended since 19 December 1894 – nearly four months before – and added that 'on his return I quite expect to find him so backward that I shall have to put him back a standard'. Percy did not return to school and was marked 'left' on 22 February 1895.[38]

Reporting absent pupils to the school attendance officer had little effect, and the master and mistress repeatedly observed his failure to take action. On 5 September 1892 Boyd noted in his log book the contents of a letter he had sent to the attendance officer, informing him of the persistent truanting of eight boys and complaining that 'Without any reflection on you I must say that sending lists about these particular boys seems of no use whatsoever, as we never derive any benefit by it in the way of increased attendance'. In reply the attendance officer informed him that he had sent notices to the parents of all the boys, and that if they did not return to school within the next fortnight he would take out a summons against them.[39] In November 1895, in order to ensure more regular attendance, Boyd began to reward the class which showed the best attendance during the week with a banner, to be displayed at the end of the front desk. For the following week boys in that class would be allowed to enter and leave the school first and would be dismissed fifteen minutes early on Friday afternoon.[40]

In February 1892 a penny bank was set up at the parish school, with 48 boys making deposits totalling 25s. Each depositor received a small book in which his deposits were recorded and the amount reached 1s. it was transferred to the Post Office Savings Bank, receiving an annual rate of interest of 2½ per cent. In September 1894 Boyd wrote to parents encouraging their children to become members: 'We should like every child to become a depositor if possible. To teach our scholars to be thrifty and to put by for rainy day is of vast importance especially in these times.' As a result of his appeal, 54 children joined, bringing the membership up to 127.[41]

The boys had school allotments upon which they grew a wide variety of vegetables, including French dwarf beans, broad beans, peas, turnips, potatoes, onions, cabbages, brussels sprouts, broccoli and winter greens. In 1896 it was agreed that boys would pay 1s. for their allotment and in return be allowed to keep the vegetables. Produce from the school allotments was entered in the annual show of the Ashtead Horticultural Society held in the grounds of Ashtead Park in August. In 1899 David Filkins was one of four boys to win a prize for the 'best cropped' allotment.[42]

For the majority of children in Ashtead there was no possibility of secondary education. However, by the 1890s other options were available to those hoping for improvement. There was a parish lending library in the village, held in the Working Men's Club each Monday from 12.15 p.m. to 1.15 p.m. Members paid a monthly subscription of twopence for adults and a penny for school children. In March 1891 the editor of the parish magazine lamented that 'the number of persons who avail themselves of the advantages of the parish lending library does not increase as much as it should do', reminding parishioners that the library contained 'an excellent collection of books of every description, theological, historical, scientific, serious, comic, fact and fiction, poetry and prose'. A Bible class for young men, held at the rectory, was begun in April 1891.[43]

In 1891 Surrey County Council (established under the 1888 Local Government Act) began to make grants available for technical education evening classes on subjects such as 'agricultural chemistry, horticulture, life and health of farm animals, insect pests of the farm, the laws of health, cookery, laundry work and domestic economy'. During the winter months of 1891 and 1892 technical classes began in Ashtead, with a course of twelve lectures on horticulture for men and lessons on dressmaking for women and girls. The horticulture lectures were held in the girls' schoolroom, with an average attendance of 31. The dressmaking classes were held in the classroom of the rectory. Between 30 September and 4 November 1892 women could attend a course of six weekly lectures entitled 'homely talks on health' held in the coffee room. A follow-up course on 'hygiene … or the necessity of laws of health, with regard to air, water, habitation, food', and illustrated by lantern slides and diagrams, began on 14 November 1892. A flat fee was paid per lecture: a penny for cottagers and threepence for everyone else.[44]

Conclusion

Late nineteenth-century Ashtead was a community undergoing rapid change. The opening of the railway line in 1859 resulted in a quadrupling of the population within a sixty-year period, with an influx of suburbanites retreating from the overcrowded and unsanitary conditions of London. Private property developers bought up large tracts of agricultural land for new housing, although the northern part of the

No 1 Whittaker's Cottages: the back room (labelled 'pantry' on the floor plan).
RICHARD HARRIS

parish remained largely agricultural into the early twentieth century. During their residence in the parish the Filkins family would have seen their standard of living improve, with the advent of gas-lighting in the 1880s, and electricity, proper supplies of piped water and modern sewerage facilities from 1901. Their children benefited from the introduction of free primary education and survived to adulthood thanks to the reduced mortality rates of the late nineteenth century. Although there was no provision for free secondary education, there were new educational opportunities for post-compulsory school age children and adults, with the introduction of technical education evening classes in 1891.

At no. 1 Whittaker's Cottages there were two adults and eight children living in what was essentially a two-up, two-down house. It must have been overcrowded and very noisy. The five boys and three girls were very much 'railway children', living and playing alongside the railway line and with a father whose presence in the house would have been dictated by the pattern of his shifts. We know almost nothing about Harriet Filkins except that she was literate and solicitous of her children's health. By 1911 the family had taken over no. 2 Whittaker's Cottages, where Henry Filkins junior, then aged 24 and a general labourer, lived with three of his brothers, Frank, who had become a plumber's labourer, Sidney, a lead-plate caster, and Herbert, who was still at school. David, aged 22, was a lance corporal in the Lancashire Fusiliers stationed in Hampshire. Henry and Harriet continued to reside at no. 1 with two of their daughters, Mabel, aged 17 and a domestic servant, and Gertrude, who was still at school. Edith, who was working as a laundress, lived with her aunt in Egham. By 1918 Henry and Harriet had moved to Leatherhead and were living at no. 2 Railway Cottages, where Henry continued to work for the LSWR.[45]

During the war David and Frank served with the Lancashire Fusiliers – David rising to the rank of sergeant and Frank remaining a private – and Sidney served as a private with the East Kent Regiment. Frank was awarded a medal in 1915 for his service in the Balkans, but was killed in action in France on 20 October 1918, less than a month before the end of the war. The other Filkins boys survived. In 1920 David and Henry, who had both married in 1915, were living together with their wives at 11 Elmfield Villas in Ashtead. No. 1 Whittaker's Cottages was then occupied by Albert and Emma Hogsden, who lived there until 1933, when Frederick Cook, his wife and daughter moved in. Frederick lived there until 1987 when the cottage was dismantled and moved to Singleton.[46]

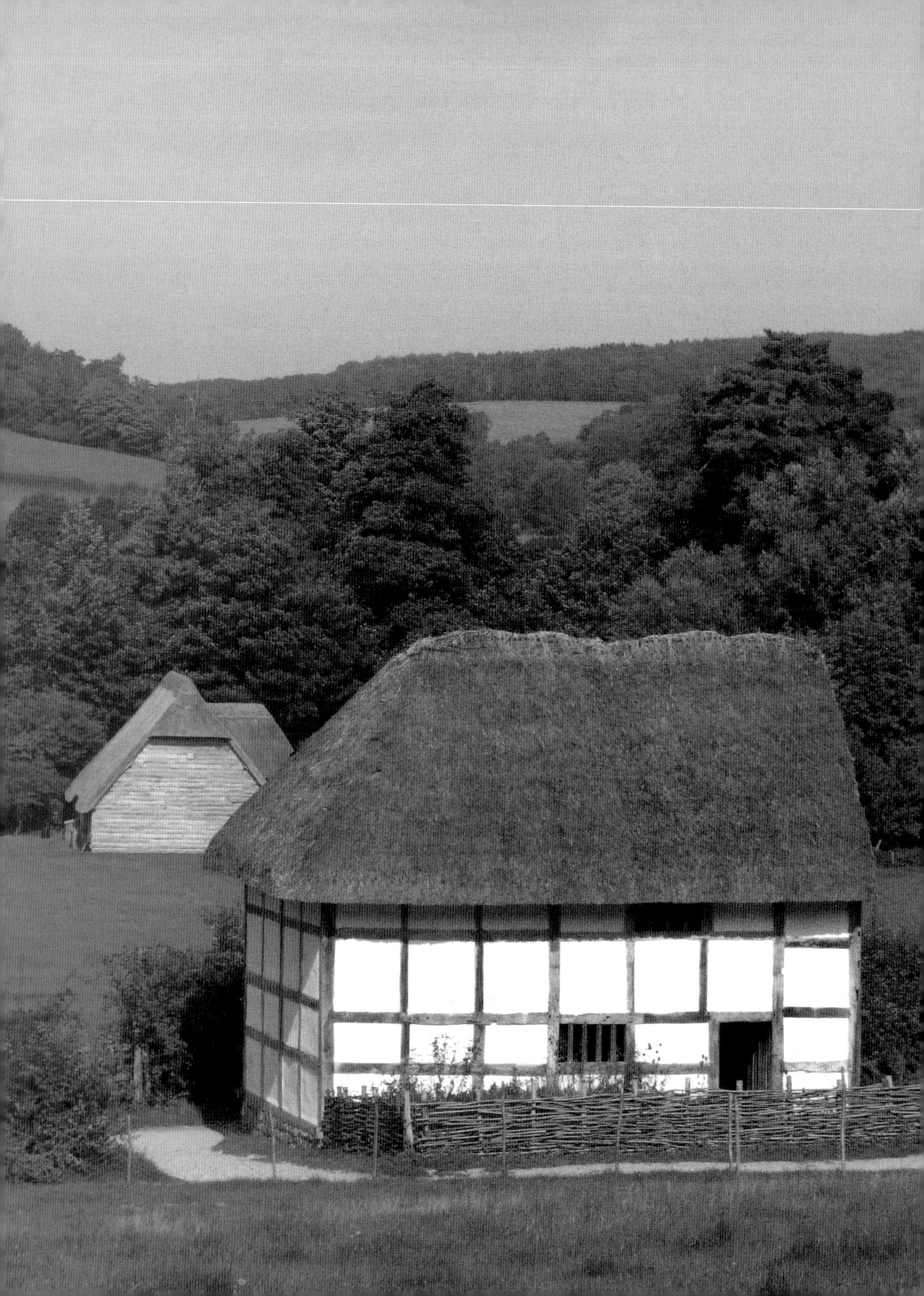

Conclusion

Among the parish records for Ticehurst there is a copy of an order dated 11 January 1696 from two justices of the peace, William Boyce and Robert Gibbon, requiring the 'removal' of a baby boy from the parish of Goudhurst in Kent to the parish of Ticehurst in Sussex. This is what the order says:

> Whereas officers of the poor for the said parish of Goudhurst have complained to us, William Boyce and Robert Gibbon, esquires, that a male young child being left in the snow on Keildown in their parish of Goudhurst which is a charge to their parish, and it being proved upon oath to us that the said child about Friday seven night before last Christmas Day was born of a stranger or travelling woman at the house of William Collins, an alehouse at the Hare & Hound in the parish of Ticehurst aforesaid, the father nor mother of the said child not being known nor where either of them inhabit, upon due consideration of all which we do think the said child ought by law to be sent to be kept and be provided for in the said parish of Ticehurst. These are therefore ... to require and authorize you, the said officers for the poor for the said parish of Goudhurst, to remove and convey the said child to Ticehurst aforesaid and to deliver it to one of the churchwardens or overseers of the poor ... to receive the said child into your said parish and to provide for him according to law.[1]

How are we to interpret this? The cold 'facts' are that an unknown 'stranger and travelling woman' gave birth to an illegitimate baby boy at an alehouse called the Hare & Hound in the parish of Ticehurst about a week before Christmas in 1695.

Poplar Cottage.
RICHARD HARRIS

She subsequently abandoned the baby in the snow on 'Keildown' in the adjoining parish of Goudhurst and disappeared. Because the baby had been born in the parish of Ticehurst, under the settlement laws the overseers of the poor of the parish of Goudhurst successfully claimed that they were not responsible for the baby's maintenance and that he should be handed over to the overseers of the poor of the parish of Ticehurst. The fact that the justices of the peace had been required to make an order indicates that Ticehurst had initially refused to accept responsibility.

What were the motivations of the respective parties? For the two parishes, this was about hard cash – the infant represented an additional financial burden on their constantly overstretched parish rates. They did not want him. Nor, apparently, did his mother. But her motivation is harder to gauge. We may judge her harshly, but as an unmarried, impoverished and homeless woman her pregnancy and the subsequent birth of her baby is likely to have pushed her to a state of desperation where she felt she had no choice but to abandon her infant and disappear. Did she think he would be found? The fact that he evidently *was* found, and relatively quickly, suggests that she may have left him somewhere where she knew that there would be regular passers-by.

What of the infant? We know nothing about him, not even his name.

Like the story of Thomas Blatcher and his family with which this book began, this case has no especial significance. But it provides a useful way in to an exploration of ideas about the practice of history and the way we interpret the past. Like much of the documentary evidence that has been used in this book, this is a fragment of history from which the historian must draw out a meaning so that it can be placed in a larger narrative. For anyone familiar with the operation of the Old Poor Law, which has been much discussed in this book, elucidating the facts of this case is relatively straightforward and non-contentious. But the *meaning* we attach to those facts is more subjective. The archaeologist, Christopher Chippindale, has drawn attention to two opposing ways of interpreting the past which he calls the 'soft primitive' and the 'hard primitive'. What he means by this is that there is a tendency to view historic peoples either as representatives of some kind of 'golden age', imbued with qualities that we feel we have lost today, or, as Thomas Hobbes did in his *Leviathan* of 1651, as leading lives that were 'solitary, poor, nasty, brutish and short'. This book has not set out to portray either a 'soft primitive' or a 'hard primitive' interpretation of the lives of the inhabitants of each of the eight houses. In as far as possible, it has avoided making any judgment at all. It is, nevertheless, sometimes difficult not to wonder how anyone survived the rural past; or to marvel at the sheer tenacity of the men, women and children whose stories we have (sometimes all too briefly) encountered.[2]

This book set out to answer a question: 'what was life like for the people who lived in these houses?' This was never going to be a straightforward undertaking. Reconstructing the lives of men and women who lived 100 years ago can be problematic; reconstructing the lives of those who lived 600 years ago is nearly impossible. Moreover, the documentary evidence for some of the communities from which the houses were from was often patchy; in the case of Hangleton it was virtually non-existent. The reader can decide for themself the extent to which this endeavour has been successful. From the author's point of view, there are many questions that will for ever remain unanswered. The nature of the evidence means that it is the publicly recorded events that are recovered; private thoughts and actions seldom are. We will never know precisely how the villagers of Hangleton reacted to the cataclysmic events of 1348–49, how John Tindall (2) and Richard Burns felt about the sexual indiscretions of their daughters, or what it was like for Harriet Filkins to raise eight children in an overcrowded house on a limited budget.

One of the limitations for the historian is always the necessity of sticking to the 'facts', and this book has avoided the temptation to reconstruct the occupants' lives beyond the reach of the available evidence. It is nevertheless true that one of the ways in which we engage with the past is through our imaginations, and historians are no more immune to this than anyone else. While trying to write the history of these houses and of their elusive inhabitants I have frequently imagined that one of them was standing behind me shaking their head and laughing and saying to themselves 'no, that is not what it was like at all'.

Notes and references

Abbreviations

AHEW	*Agricultural History of England and Wales*
BPP	*British Parliamentary Papers*
CKS	Centre for Kentish Studies
ESRO	East Sussex Record Office
HRO	Hampshire Record Office
NUL	Nottingham University Library
SAC	*Sussex Archaeological Collections*
SHC	Surrey History Centre
SRS	*Sussex Record Society*
TNA	The National Archives
VCH	*Victoria County History*
WDOAM	Weald & Downland Open Air Museum
WSRO	West Sussex Record Office

Notes to Introduction

1. British Library Add 33058, fols 27, 54; Add 33084, fol. 34. The lords of the Rape of Hastings claimed ownership of the wasteland and regulated its use.
2. K. Sayer, *Country Cottages: a cultural history* (Manchester, 2000); C. Payne, *Rustic Simplicity: scenes of cottage life in nineteenth-century British art* (Nottingham, 1998).
3. D. Robinson, 'Soils' in K. Leslie and B. Short (eds), *An Historical Atlas of Sussex* (Chichester, 1999), 4–5; R. Williams, 'Natural regions' in ibid., 6–7; P. Brandon and B. Short, *The South East from AD 1000* (London, 1990), 1–18; http://www.southdowns.gov.uk/ (accessed 5 May 2010)
4. J. Thirsk, 'The Farming Regions of England' in Thirsk (ed.), *Agrarian History of England and Wales (AHEW)* IV, 1500–1640 (Cambridge, 1967), 55–64; A. Fletcher, *Sussex, 1600–1660: a county community in peace and war* (London, 1975), 3–21.
5. Brandon and Short, *The South East from AD 1000*, 368; A. Howkins, *The Death of Rural England: a social history of the countryside since 1900* (London, 2003), 1, 8, 164.
6. *Members' Magazine* (Spring, 1977), 2–5; *Weald and Downland Open Air Museum* (March, 1994), 3; K. Leslie, *Weald and Downland Open Air Museum: the founding years, 1965–1970* (Andover,

1990), 4–6; T. P. Hudson (ed.), *Victoria County History: Sussex*, vol. 6, part 3 (London, 1987).
7. R. Armstrong, 'The case for an open air museum for the Weald and Downland' (12 April 1967).
8. R. Samuel, *Theatres of Memory, vol. 1: past and present in contemporary culture* (London & New York, 1994), 205.
9. Reproduced in Leslie, *The Founding Years*, 9.
10. J. Burchardt, *Paradise Lost: rural idyll and social change since 1800* (London, 2002); Howkins, *The Death of Rural England*.

Notes to Chapter 1

1. These paragraphs are based on material in the Museum's archive (no. 2274), minutes of the Sites and Buildings Committee (1970 *et seq.*) and various editions of the Museum's guidebook.
2. E. W. Holden, 'Excavations at the deserted medieval village of Hangleton, Part I', *SAC* 101 (1963), 54–181; J. G. Hurst and D. G. Hurst, 'Excavations at the deserted medieval village of Hangleton, Part II', *SAC* 102 (1964), 94–142 (hereafter Hangleton I and Hangleton II). S. Wrathmell, 'Rural settlements in medieval England: perspectives and perceptions' in *Building on the Past: papers celebrating 150 years of the Royal Archaeological Institute* (1994), 189. The majority of the Hangleton finds were deposited at Barbican House in Lewes. A few are on display in the museum there; most are in boxes in the basement.
3. A. Woodcock, 'The archaeological implications of coastal change in Sussex' in D. Rudling (ed.), *The Archaeology of Sussex to AD 2000* (King's Lynn, 2003), 8; E. W. Holden and T. P. Hudson, 'Salt-making in the Adur valley, Sussex', *SAC* 119 (1981), 121. L. F. Salzman (ed.), *Victoria County History: Sussex*, vol. 7 (Oxford, 1940), 279; population estimated on the basis of the number of tenants listed in the 1339 *inquisition post mortem* (see below) multiplied by an average household size of five (a method used by other historians such as Christopher Dyer (C. Dyer, *Making a Living in the Middle Ages* (London, 2002), 92–3).
4. Hangleton I, 54–5.
5. Hangleton I, 54–181; Hangleton II, 94–142.
6. G. G. Astill, 'Rural settlement: the toft and the croft' in G. G. Astill and A. Grant (eds), *The Countryside in Medieval England* (Oxford, 1988), 36–61; Dyer, *Making a Living*, 19–21.
7. W Hudson (ed), *Subsidy rolls, 1296, 1327 and 1332*, SRS 10 (1910), 174, 289; C C Fenwick, *The Poll Taxes of 1377, 1379 and 1381, part 2, Lincolnshire-Westmorland* (Oxford, 2001); G Vandersee (ed.), *Nonarum inquisitiones in curia scaccarii* (Record Commission, 1807), 385; J E E S Sharp & E G Atkinson (eds), *Calendar of Inquisitions Post Mortem*, vol. 8 (London, 1913), 170-1.
8. P. R. Schofield, *Peasant and Community in Medieval England, 1200–1500* (Basingstoke, 2003), 11–17; 26.
9. *Cal. Inq. Post Mortem*, vol. 8, 170–1.
10. W. D. Peckham (ed.), *Thirteen custumals of the Sussex manors of the Bishop of Chichester*, SRS 31 (1925).
11. G. Chaucer, *Canterbury Tales*, ed. A C Cawley (London, 1976), 18–19, lines 587–622.
12. A. E. Wilson, *Custumals of the manors of Laughton, Willingdon and Goring*, SRS 60 (1961), xxxvi–xxxvii, 20.
13. P. F. Brandon, 'Demesne arable farming in coastal Sussex during the later Middle Ages', *Agricultural History Review* 19, (1971), 121–6.
14. R. A. Pelham, 'The exportation of wool from Sussex in the late thirteenth century', *SAC* 74 (1933), 131–9.
15. Hangleton I, 59–60; Dyer, *Making a Living*, 92–3.
16. Dyer, *Standards of Living*, 128; Vandersee (ed.), *Nonarum inquisitiones*, 385; B. Dodds, 'Demesne and tithe: peasant agriculture in the late Middle Ages', *Agricultural History Review* 56 (2008), 123–41.

17. M. Gardiner, 'The geography and peasant rural economy of the eastern Sussex High Weald, 1300–1420', *SAC* 134 (1996), 125–39; Dyer, *Making a Living*, 170–1.
18. Holden and Hudson, 'Salt-making', 117-48.
19. Fenwick, *Poll Taxes*, 612; A. J. Taylor (ed.), *Records of the Barony and Honour of the Rape of Lewes*, SRS 44 (1939), 75; Holden, 'Excavations', I, 62.
20. Dyer, *Making a Living*, 172–4.
21. The best account of the evidence for medieval peasant buildings is C. Dyer, 'English peasant buildings in the later Middle Ages' in C. Dyer (ed.), *Everyday Life in Medieval England* (London, 1994), 133–65. See also J. G. Hurst, 'Rural building in England and Wales', in *AHEW* II, 898–915; H. E. J. Le Patourel, 'Rural building in England and Wales', in *AHEW* III, 843–65; M. Gardiner, 'Vernacular buildings and the development of the late medieval plan in England', *Medieval Archaeology* 44 (2000), 159–79; Astill, 'Rural settlement: the toft and the croft', 36–61.
22. Dyer, 'English peasant buildings', 140–1; Gardiner, 'Vernacular buildings', 162, 175–6: *Canterbury Tales*, 459, lines 3618–3643.
23. Astill, 'Rural settlement', 51–3, 57; Hangleton I, 75.
24. Dyer, 'English peasant buildings', 146, 148; a custumal, possibly from the second half of the thirteenth century, states of the holding of Hudde Lecherwine – an unfree peasant holding an acre and a house – that 'The Bishop shall repair his cottage as needed, and make new cottages if needed, also the houses of the oxherd and the beadle, and shall give cottages as needed'. Peckham, *Thirteen custumals*, 83; Fenwick, *Poll Taxes*, 612.
25. Dyer, 'English peasant buildings', 155–7.
26. R. K. Field, 'Worcestershire peasant buildings, household goods and farming equipment in the late middle ages', *Medieval Archaeology* 9 (1965), 105–45; Dyer, *Standards of Living*, 169–75.
27. Hangleton I, 111–44; 153–7; 165–7.
28. Hangleton I, 176.
29. Wilson, *Custumals of the manors of Laughton, Willingdon, and Goring*, xxxv; William Langland, *Piers the Ploughman*, ed. J. F. Goodridge (Harmondsworth, 1959), 70, 89; Hangleton I, 177.
30. Woodcock, 'The archaeological implications of coastal change in Sussex', 10; Vandersee (ed.), *Nonarum inquisitiones*, 357, 385–6; P. Brandon, 'Agriculture and the effects of floods and weather at Barnhorne, Sussex, during the late Middle Ages', *SAC* 109 (1971), 80; Dyer, *Making a Living*, 228–33; Holden and Hudson, 'Salt-making', 141.
31. R. Horrox, *The Black Death* (Manchester, 1994), 63–4.
32. Fenwick, *Poll Taxes*, 612.
33. Dyer, *Making a Living*, 294–5.

Notes to Chapter 2

1. Notes on Boarhunt dismantling and reconstruction from Museum archive (no. 1452); E. Roberts, 'The hall house from Boarhunt' (report commissioned by WDOAM, 2000).
2. W. Page (ed.), *Victoria County History: Hampshire*, vol. 3 (London, 1908), 143–6; K. A. Hanna, *The cartularies of Southwick Priory*, Hampshire Record Society, vol. 1 (1988), vol. 2 (1989)
3. C. Dyer, 'Woodlands and wood-pasture in Western England' in J. Thirsk (ed.), *The English Rural Landscape* (Oxford, 2000), 97.
4. M. Beresford and J. G. Hurst, *Deserted medieval villages* (London, 1971); Dyer, 'Woodlands and woodpasture in Western England', 112–15; C. Dyer, 'Deserted medieval villages in the West Midlands' in Dyer (ed.), *Everyday Life in Medieval England*, 42.
5. These population figures are estimates based on numbers of tenants listed in manorial rentals (HRO 5M50/82, 5M50/83, 4M53/E9a).
6. HRO 5M50/82.
7. HRO 5M50/82

8. HRO 49M84/5.
9. HRO 5M50/82
10. M. Bailey, *The English Manor, c.1200-c.1500* (Manchester, 2002), 35–7.
11. Dyer, *Making a Living*, 358.
12. Dyer, *Making a Living*, 349–52.
13. HRO 5M50/83, 5M50/234, 5M50/236
14. HRO 5M50/ 235, 5M50/236
15. HRO 5M50/83; 5M50/234
16. HRO 5M50/235, 5M50/236, 5M50/237, 5M50/239
17. This was the holding that John atte Brigge had surrendered in 1416.
18. HRO 4M53/E9a, 5M50/87, HRO 4M53/23/1
19. Dyer, *Making a Living*, 295, 331; C. Dyer, *An Age of Transition? Economy and society in England in the later Middle Ages* (Oxford, 2005), 194–7; HRO 4M53/E6, E7; 4M53/D1.
20. Hanna, *Cartularies*, vol. 1, II 32, 75, 118. This acreage includes an unspecified amount of land in Cowmead in the parish of Titchfield.
21. There is little information about the organisation of arable land in medieval Boarhunt. The description above is based on descriptions of landholdings in manorial documents (see HRO 5M50/234, 5M50/87, 5M50/1407); Details of the value and amount of crops and livestock on the manorial demesne are contained in a series of manorial accounts covering the period 1445–1451 (HRO 4M53/E6, E7, D1, D2); HRO 5M50/72; crops listed in late sixteenth century probate inventories (see HRO 1559 U/130/2, inventory of Richard Lukes, 1559; HRO 1570B/025/1, inventory of John Carter, 1570).
22. HRO 5M50/82, 5M50/237, 4M53, D1, D2.
23. HRO 49M84/1, 5.
24. Hanna, *Cartularies*, vol. 1, I, 176; HRO 5M50/82; 5M50/234, 236, 295; P. D. A. Harvey, *Manorial Records* (British Records Association, 1984), 47, 50.
25. HRO 1557U/123/2, 1559U/130/2
26. R. Whinney, 'Jack-O-Tooles Row, Boarhunt – a medieval kiln dump', *Hampshire Studies* 37 (1981), 41–8.
27. Horrox, *The Black Death*, 329, 339.
28. Information supplied by Edward Roberts; HRO 1570B/025/2; G. Watts, 'Medieval tenant housing on the Titchfield estates', *Hampshire Studies* 57 (2002), 53–8; Dyer, 'English peasant buildings', 138–9.
29. HRO 1570B/025/2; 1557U/335/2; A. Longcroft, 'Local history and vernacular architecture studies', *The Local Historian* 39 (2009), 90–108.
30. HRO 4M53/D1; Dyer, *Standards of Living*, 167; Dyer, *Making a Living*, 358.
31. HRO 1570B/025/2.
32. D. A. Hinton, *Gold & gilt, pots & pins: possessions and people in medieval Britain* (Oxford, 2005), 215; Dyer, *Standards of Living*, 158–9.
33. Hanna, *Cartularies*, vol. 1, xli–xliii; J. Hare, *The Dissolution of the Monasteries* (Hampshire Papers, 16, 1999), 13; HRO 4M53/23/1.

Notes to Chapter 3

1. These paragraphs are based on a information contained in various editions of the Museum guidebook.
2. CKS U1000/3/E8; U1000/3/E35/10–11; U1000/3/M10; U1000/3/M11; U1000/3/E11; U1000/3/E35/15; U1000/3/E33/2; TNA E179/124/223.
3. CKS U1475/M15; TR 804/2.
4. This is Shoreham in Kent, not Shoreham on the Sussex coast.

5. M. Zell, *Industry in the Countryside: Wealden society in the sixteenth century* (Cambridge, 1994); see page 86 for population figures; M. Overton, J. Whittle, D. Dean and A. Hann, *Production and Consumption in English Households 1600–1750* (Abingdon, 2004), 11.
6. Zell, *Industry in the Countryside*, 10–11, 27–8, 37–9, 105.
7. http://www.oxforddnb.com/view/article/23247 and http://www.oxforddnb.com/view/article/52802; TNA Prob 11/8, Prob 11/19, Prob 11/30, Prob 11/40, Prob 11/88.
8. CKS U1000/3/21; TNA Prob 11/8.
9. CKS U1000/3/E35/10, 11, 15; U1000/3/E34.
10. NUL Mi 6/178/38; Mi 5/160/22.
11. K. Wrightson, *Earthly Necessities: economic lives in early modern Britain, 1470–1750* (London, 2002), 34–5; W. Harrison, *The Description of England*, ed. G. Edelen (New York, 1984), 94–123, 180–6.
12. Harrison, *Description of England*, 118;
13. J. Munby, 'Wood' in J. Blair and N. Ramsay (eds), *English Medieval Industries: craftsmen, techniques, products* (London, 2001), 386–9.
14. TNA E179/126/391; CKS TR 804/2, fols 195–215; U1475/M17.
15. K. Wrightson, '"Sorts of people" in Tudor and Stuart England' in J. Barry and C. Brooks (eds), *The Middling Sort of People: culture, society and politics in England, 1550–1800* (Basingstoke, 1994), 28–51.
16. CKS TR 804/2, f. 195.
17. Harrison, *Description of England*, 182; P. Slack, *Poverty and Policy in Tudor and Stuart England* (London, 1988), 43–50, 123–5; P. Slack, *The English Poor Law, 1531–1782* (Cambridge, 1995), 51–6.
18. CKS TR 804/2, f. 195–6.
19. Slack, *English Poor Law*, 51–3; CKS TR 804/2, ff. 195–215.
20. Zell, *Industry in the Countryside*, 88–112; CKS U1000/3/E10, E11.
21. CKS U1000/3/E10, E11.
22. Zell, *Industry in the Countryside*, 153–4; J. Geddes, 'Iron' in Blair and Ramsay (eds), *English Medieval Industries*, 170–1; C. Chalklin, 'Iron manufacture in Tonbridge parish with special reference to Barden furnace c.1552–1771', *Archaeologia Cantiana* 124 (2004), 95–115; www.wealdeniron.org.uk.
23. CKS U1000/3/M21; E. Glover, *A History of the Ironmongers' Company* (London, 1991), 2–7.
24. CKS U1475/T55/10;. H. Cleere and D. Crossley, *The Iron Industry of the Weald* (Bath, 1985), Gazetteer, no. 167; CKS U1000/3/T5; Kent Sites and Monument Record, provided by the SMR Officer of the Heritage Conservation Group, Kent County Council (TQ 48134756, TQ 48044734).
25. TNA Req 2/32/67; Zell, *Industry in the Countryside*, 129–131.
26. R. Houlbrooke, *The English Family, 1450–1700* (London, 1984), 63; Zell, *Industry in the Countryside*, 66–77.
27. CKS TR 804/2, ff.23–35.
28. Harrison, *Description of England*, 116; Zell, *Industry in the Countryside*, 77–9; TNA Prob 11/28.
29. TNA Prob 11/30; Prob 11/40.
30. S. Pearson, *The Medieval Houses of Kent: An historical analysis* (London, 1994), 108–15.
31. CKS PRC 10/1/88–90, 99–100.
32. P. S. Barnwell and A. T. Adams, *The House Within: interpreting medieval houses in Kent* (London, 1994), 22; D. Martin, 'Forgotten buildings: detached kitchens in south east England', *Weald and Downland Open Air Museum* (Spring, 2003), 9–11.
33. F. J. Furnivall (ed.), *The first boke of the introduction of knowledge made by Andrew Borde* (Early English Text Society, extra series 10, 1870), 236–7; Barnwell and Adams, *The House Within*, 22–3.
34. These were coverlets of coarse, shaggy material, also known as 'rugs'.
35. Harrison, *Description of England*, 200–1.
36. Based on a sample of 100 probate inventories enrolled in the Archdeaconry Court of Canterbury in 1565–6 and transcribed by Richard Harris in 1988; Overton *et al.*, *Production and Consumption*, 87–120.

Notes to Chapter 4

1. W. G. Hoskins, 'The rebuilding of rural England, 1570–1640', *Past and Present* 4 (1953), 44–59; R. Machin, 'The Great Rebuilding: a reassessment', *Past and Present* 77 (1977), 33–56; Longcroft, 'Local history and vernacular architecture studies', 90–108.
2. M. Johnson, *Housing Culture: traditional architecture in an English landscape* (London, 1993), 89.
3. These paragraphs draw on information contained in various editions of the Museum guidebook.
4. R. Harris, 'Pendean Farmhouse benefits from Designation funding', *Weald and Downland Open Air Museum* (Spring, 2001), 12–13; 'Furnishing Pendean Farmhouse', *Weald and Downland Open Air Museum* (Autumn, 2001), 5.
5. WSRO Cowdray MS 1659 (Balls Farm); WSRO Lavington MS 1, fol. 82r for early reference to Costers Mill and WSRO Cowdray MS 665 and 666.
6. L. F. Salzman (ed.), *Victoria County History: Sussex*, vol. 4 (London, 1953), 59; population estimated from 1676 Compton Census figure of 100 (all adults over the age of 16), inflated by 40% to take account of under 16s (J. H. Cooper, 'A religious census of Sussex in 1676', *SAC* 45 (1902), 146).
7. Salzman (ed.), *VCH Sussex*, vol. 4, 59; W. H. Godfrey, 'An Elizabethan builder's contract', *SAC* 65 (1924), 210–23; WSRO Add MS 2546.
8. WSRO Add MS 2546; Cowdray MS 1689; Lavington MS 1, fols 1, 69r; Lavington MS 2, fols 31r–32r; Lavington MS 3 (unpaginated, see entry for court held on 16 August 1675).
9. WSRO Add MS 2546; Cowdray MS 1689; Lavington MS 2 fols 31r, v, 32r, 36r, 36v, 98v, 110v, 112r.
10. WSRO Lavington MS 1, fol. 9r; E. E. Barker, 'Some Woolavington and Wonworth leases', *SAC* 94 (1956), 43–69.
11. WSRO Cowdray MS 960; M Dean 17 1615; Add MS 24,110.
12. WSRO QR/W153, fol. 16; Cowdray MS 92; Ep/I/29/215/35.
13. WSRO M Dean 17 1615.
14. WSRO Add MS 24,110; Cowdray MS 298, fol. 100, 113.
15. WSRO Add MS 24,110; Ep/I/24/82A.
16. WSRO Par 138/1/1/1; Ep/I/24/82A; Cowdray MS 239, fol. 112v.
17. WSRO Cowdray MS 239, fol. 73r, 112v, 113r; Cowdray MS 1634; Cowdray MS 1661.
18. WSRO Cowdray MS 1634; Cowdray MS 239, fol. 119r-v; Cobden Papers MS 847; R. Palmer, *Heyshott* (Heyshott History Society, 1999), 147–9.
19. WSRO Cowdray MS 239, fol. 119r-v, 148r; Cobden MS 847; Ep/I/24/138; QR/W120; QR/W121; STC I/30/192.
20. WSRO Ep/I/29/215/33, Ep/I/29/215/35; J. Cornwall, 'Farming in Sussex, 1560–1640', *SAC* 92 (1954), 48–54; WSRO Lavington MS 1, fols 36v, 76r; Quarter Sessions Rolls (WSRO QR/W1 *et seq.*).
21. Evidence for economic activities from Woolavington probate inventories (Ep/I//29/215); J. H. Andrews, 'The port of Chichester and the grain trade, 1650-1750', *SAC* 92 (1954), 93–105.
22. WSRO Ep/I/29/215/35; Cowdray MS 1661.
23. D. Tankard, 'Graffham and Woolavington potters, tile-makers and brickmakers, c.1590–1740', *SAC* 146 (2008), 175–88; F. G. Aldsworth and A. Down, 'The production of late and post-medieval pottery in the Graffham area of West Sussex', *SAC* 128 (1990), 117–39.
24. Tankard, 'Graffham and Woolavington potters', 184–5; WSRO QR/W66.
25. WSRO Add MS 2546; Goodwood E4990; Godfrey, 'An Elizabethan builder's contract', 210–23; Salzman (ed.), *VCH Sussex*, vol. 4, 175–80.
26. The most extensive analysis of the reasons for the decline of the open hall is that by Matthew Johnson in *Housing Culture*; Overton *et al.*, *Production and Consumption*, 121–36.
27. WSRO Ep/I/29/93 (Graffham inventories), Ep/I/29/215 (Woolavington inventories); Overton *et al.*, *Production and Consumption*, 121–31; Ep/I/29/215/33.

28. WSRO Ep/I/29/215/21; V. Chinnery, *Oak Furniture: the British tradition* (Woodbridge, 1979), 315–19; Overton et al., *Production and Consumption*, 92–5; 131–2.
29. WSRO Ep/I/29/215/33.
30. WSRO Ep/I/29/215/35.
31. WSRO Ep/I/29/215/35; Ep/I/29/215/31. Sandham's moveable estate was valued at a sizeable £682 10s. 10d. but £660 of this was for a lease. His house also included a malt house.
32. WSRO Ep/I/29/215/33; Ep/I/29/215/39; Overton et al., *Production and Consumption*, 92–3; Chinnery, *Oak Furniture*, 322–4.
33. WSRO EpI/29/215/30; Ep/I/29/215/35; Tankard, 'Graffham and Woolavington potters', 11–12.
34. Overton et al., *Production and Consumption*, pp. 98–102.

Notes to Chapter 5

1. WSRO TD/W137.
2. The most significant work on wasteland cottages to date is that undertaken by David and Barbara Martin on surviving buildings in the Rape of Hastings in East Sussex but see D. Tankard, 'The regulation of cottage building in seventeenth-century Sussex', *Agricultural History Review*, 59, 1 (2011), 18-35.
3. 'Re-building sixteenth-century Poplar Cottage', *Weald and Downland Open Air Museum* (Spring, 1999), 5; R. Harris, 'Re-building Poplar Cottage', *Weald and Downland Open Air Museum* (Spring, 2000), 12–15.
4. C. R. Elrington (ed.), *Victoria County History: Sussex*, vol. 6, part 1 (Oxford, 1980), 259–60. Population is estimated from a figure of 77 households listed in parish register in 1687 multiplied by the average household size of five and (WSRO Par 205/1/1/1) and a Compton Census figure of 320 in 1676 (all adults over the age of 16), inflated by 40% to take account of under 16s (Cooper, 'Religious census', 142–8). Common land acreages from Figge map (WSRO Wiston MS 5592).
5. WSRO Wiston MSS 967, 968; Wiston MS 5592.
6. Wrightson, *Earthly Necessities*, 186–90, 194–201.
7. Elrington (ed.), *VCH Sussex*, vol. 6, part 1, 253; WSRO Wiston MS 5226, fols 22–3; STC I/19/55b; Ep/I/29/205/004.
8. WSRO Ep/I/29/205/004.
9. For a discussion of the uses of waste see J. M. Neeson, *Commoners: common right, enclosure and social change in England, 1700–1820* (Cambridge, 1996), 158–72.
10. See K. D. M. Snell, *Annals of the Labouring Poor* (Cambridge, 1992), 138–227 and Neeson, *Commoners*, 34–52 for a discussion of the economic value of common land. Quote from Neeson, *Commoners*, 41.
11. Seventh report of the medical officer of the Privy Council, 1864, Appendix 6: Inquiry on the state of the dwellings of rural labourers by Dr Hunter (British Parliamentary Papers (BPP) 3484), 136; W. W. Gill, 'The One-Night House', *Folklore* 55 (1944), 129–32; J. H. Bettey, 'Seventeenth century squatters' dwellings: some documentary evidence', *Vernacular Architecture* 13 (1982), 13.28; *Statutes of the Realm*, vol. iv (London, 1819), 3 & 4 Edward VI C3 (1549), 31 Eliz C7 (1589).
12. Slack, *The English Poor Law*, 27–31; *Statues of the Realm*, vol. iv, 39 Eliz C3 (1598).
13. WSRO Cowdray MS 239, fol. 46r.
14. J. S. Cockburn (ed.), *Calendar of Assize Records: Sussex indictments James I* (London, 1975); B. S. Redwood (ed.), *Quarter Sessions Order Book, 1642–1649*, SRS 54 (1954); ESRO QO/EW/2, 3, 4 (Quarter Sessions Order Books, 1650–1665 available at WSRO on microfilm); WSRO Cowdray MS 239, fols 35r, 59r; Redwood (ed.), *Quarter Sessions Order Book*, 185; QR/W21, fol. 23/59.
15. WSRO Wiston MS 5226, fol. 27.
16. R. Jefferies, *The Toilers of the Field* (London, 1981), 55–9.
17. Bettey, 'Seventeenth century squatters' dwellings', 13.30.

18. Arundel M127, fols 2, 5.
19. Arundel M127, fols 29, 32; WSRO STC I/29/97b; Ep/I/29/205/060.
20. WSRO MS 5226.
21. In 1858 this cottage is described as having two cow leazes or common of pasture for two cows on New Common.
22. WSRO Wiston MS 5226, fol. 33; Wiston MS 5228, fol. 71; WSRO Ep/I/29/205/063. A keeler is a cooling trough used for brewing. Cordwood was in standard lengths of between 1 and 4 feet. There is no will for James Caplen.
23. WSRO STC I/36/115 (will of Thomas Gent, 1736); WSRO Wiston MS 5226, fol. 81; Arundel M127, fol. 43, WSRO Ep/I/29/205/088.
24. Cockburn (ed.), *Calendar of Assize Records*, no. 510; R. F. Hunnisett (ed.), *Sussex Coroners' Inquests 1603–1688* (Kew, 1998), no. 280; WSRO STC I/17/190.
25. WSRO Ep/I/29/205/205/60; Ep/I/29/205/63.
26. WSRO Ep/I/29/205/088.
27. WSRO Par 205/1/1/1, fol. 127; Cockburn (ed.), *Calendar of Assize Records*, no. 226.

Notes to Chapter 6

1. Some documentary research on the history of Tindalls was undertaken by Christopher Whittick in 1997; ESRO SAS/CO/D/1; SAS/CO/B/157; SAS/CO/B/54; AMS 5379.
2. ESRO XA31/29.
3. ESRO XA30/196; PAR 492/31/13–4 (unpaginated).
4. ESRO PAR 492/31/1/3–4; PAR 492/32/3/246; XA30/196 .
5. W. K. Ford (ed.), *Chichester Diocesan Surveys, 1686 and 1724*, SRS 78 (1992), 116; ESRO PAR 492/30/3; M. Overton, *Agricultural Revolution in England: the transformation of the agrarian economy 1500–1850* (Cambridge, 2006), 63.
6. D. and B. Martin, *Farm Buildings of the Weald, 1450–1750* (King's Lynn, 2006), 7–26; Overton, *Agricultural Revolution*, 130.
7. Martin, *Farm Buildings*, 125; ESRO PAR 492/6/2/1/3–5.
8. A. Young, *General View of the Agriculture of the County of Sussex* (London, 1813; this edition Newton Abbot 1970), 129–37.
9. Martin, *Farm Buildings of the Weald*, 125.
10. Martin, *Farm Buildings of the Weald*, 17–18; D. W. Harvey, 'Locational change in the Kentish hop industry and the analysis of land use patterns', *Transactions of the Institute of British Geographers* 33 (1963), 131–3; ESRO W/INV/1138; Young, *General View … Sussex*, 136.
11. ESRO W/INV/243; W/INV/589; W/INV/771.
12. ESRO AMS 5379; PAR 492/31/1/3; Martin, *Farm Buildings*, 18–20;
13. ESRO XA30/196; P. Langford, *A Polite and Commercial People: England 1727–1783* (Oxford, 1989), 61–3.
14. ESRO PAR 492/24/1/1.
15. ESRO PAR 492/9/1/2.
16. ESRO PAR 492/9/1/1–2; Ford (ed.), *Chichester Diocesan Surveys*, 48–9.
17. ESRO PAR 492/31/14; R. Wells, 'The development of the English rural proletariat and social protest, 1700–1850' in M. Reed and R. Wells (eds), *Class, Conflict and Protest in the English Countryside 1700–1850* (London, 1990), 29–40. These figures are based on the wholesale price of wheat exported through the port of Chichester during this period.
18. D. Cannadine, *Class in Britain* (London, 2000), 24–34; Wells, 'The development of the English rural proletariat', 29–53.
19. H. Cunningham, 'The employment and unemployment of children in England c.1680–1851', *Past and Present* 126 (1990), 115–50.
20. Young, *General View … Sussex*, 131–2; 407–10.

21. Cunningham, 'Employment and unemployment of children', 121–3.
22. Cunningham, 'Employment and unemployment of children', 123–6.
23. Cunningham, 'Employment and unemployment of children', 124.
24. J. Caffyn (ed.), *Sussex schools in the eighteenth century: schooling provision, schoolteachers and scholars*, SRS 81 (1998); ESRO PAR 492/31/1/3, 4.
25. ESRO PAR 492/31/1/3.
26. J. Styles, *The Dress of the People: everyday fashion in eighteenth century England* (New Haven & London, 2007), 31–55.
27. S. Hindle, *On the Parish? The micro-politics of poor relief in rural England c.1550–1750* (Oxford, 2004), 195–203; Slack, *The English Poor Law*, 54; A. Brundage, *The English Poor Laws 1700–1930* (Basingstoke, 2002), 16.
28. ESRO PAR 492/31/1/3; PAR 492/31/1/4.
29. Hindle, *On the Parish?*, 171–226; ESRO PAR 492/12/1/1; PAR 492/31/1/3.
30. Slack, *The English Poor Law*, 32–6; Brundage, *The English Poor Laws*, 11–13.
31. ESRO Par 492/24/1/1; Par 492/31/1/4.
32. F. M. Eden, *The State of the Poor: or an history of the labouring classes in England* (London, 1797), vol. 3, 727; ESRO PAR 492/31/1/4.
33. For an account of general trends in domestic consumption in the first half of the eighteenth century see Overton *et al.*, *Production and Consumption*, 87–120.
34. ESRO W/INV/771.
35. All these inventories are within the series ESRO W/INV/1–2865.
36. ESRO W/INV/1466; Eden, *State of the Poor*, vol. 3, 729.
37. J. Wood, *A series of plans for cottages or habitations of the labourer, either in husbandry, or the mechanic arts, adapted as well to towns, as to the country* (London, 1781); J. Styles, 'Picturing domesticity: the cottage genre in late eighteenth-century Britain' in J. Aynsley and C. Grant (eds), *Imagined Interiors: representing the domestic interior since the Renaissance* (London, 2006), 154–5.

Notes to Chapter 7

1. WSRO TD/W110
2. WSRO Goodwood MS E101; MF 651; TD/W110; TD/W141.
3. 1851 Census: Singleton; 1841 Census: Singleton; WSRO Par 174/8/1; Par 174/8/2.
4. www.oxforddnb.com/view/article/8725; Young, *General View ... Sussex*, 349.
5. Figures taken from Singleton tithe apportionment of 1848 (WSRO TD/W110); www.oxforddnb.com/view/article/30141.
6. Figures taken from West Dean tithe apportionment of 1851 (WSRO TD/W141); www.oxforddnb.com/view/article/12237.
7. TNA MAF 68/490; BPP 4068 (1867–8), appendix 2, 90.
8. BPP 007 (1842), 510 (1843), 4068 (1867–8), Cd.346 (1900).
9. WSRO Par 174/8/1; Par 174/8/2; Par 174/7/1.
10. WSRO Par 65/1/3/2; Par 174/7/1; 1851 Census: Binderton; 1861 Census: Selsey; 1871 Census: Merston; certified copy of death certificate: HD158275.
11. 1861 Census: Singleton; 1871 Census: Singleton; 1881 Census: Singleton; 1891 Census: Singleton; WSRO Par 174/8/1.
12. 1871 Census; Singleton; WSRO Par 174/7/1.
13. This and subsequent paragraphs on the West Sussex Agricultural Association based on WSRO MP 5528 which is an account of the origins of the association and a list of prize winners from 1836 to 1864 prepared by Malcolm Walford.
14. BPP C6894-I (1893), 56.
15. B. Reay, *Rural Englands* (Basingstoke, 2004), 22–48; BPP 4068 (1867-8).
16. BPP Cd.346 (1900); BPP 4068 (1867-8).

17. BPP 4068 (1867–8), appendix 2, 86–98.
18. BPP 4068 (1867–8); BPP C.6894-I (1893); BPP Cd.346 (1900); I. Serraillier, *All change at Singleton for Charlton, Goodwood, East & West Dean* (Chichester, 1979), no. 126.
19. BPP Cd.346 (1900), 54.
20. 1851 Census: Singleton; WSRO Goodwood MS E5447–5452.
21. N. Verdon, 'The rural labour market in the early nineteenth century: women's and children's employment, family income, and the 1834 Poor Law Report', *The Economic History Review* 55 (2002), 299–323; BPP 4068 (1867–8), appendix 2, 86–98.
22. The following paragraphs are based on P. Horn, *The Victorian Country Child* (Stroud, 1990), 21–81 and details of educational provision in three Sussex poor law unions (Hailsham, Horsham and Westhampnett) contained in the 1867 parliamentary report (BPP 4068), appendix 2, 76–98.
23. BPP 510 (1843), 150–2; BPP 4068 (1867-8), appendix 2, 86–98.
24. A. Wohl, *Endangered Lives: public health in Victorian Britain* (London, 1983), 117–41; E. Gauldie, *Cruel Habitations: a history of working class housing 1780–1918* (London, 1974), 250–65.
25. BPP 3484 (1865); 1851 Census: Singleton; 1861 Census: Singleton; BPP 4068 (1867–8).
26. W. Cobbett, *Rural Rides* (first published 1830; this edition London, 2001), 89–90; BPP 4068 (1867–8), appendix 1, 39, appendix 2, 89, 161; BPP Cd.346 (1900), 22–4.
27. BPP 007 (1842), 44, 48, 52.
28. BPP 4068 (1867–8), appendix 2, 95; WSRO Goodwood MS E5168; West Dean MS 2590.
29. WSRO WG12/59A/1, 51–3; 350.
30. BPP 3484 (1865), 142; WSRO Goodwood MS E5168.
31. BPP 3484 (1865), 19, 145.
32. Cobbett, *Rural Rides*, 89; BPP 4068 (1867–8), appendix 1, 9.
33. A. Kidd, *State, Society & the Poor in nineteenth-century England* (Basingstoke, 1999), 34–6, 39–40; Brundage, *The English Poor Laws*, 75–81.

Notes to Chapter 8

1. R. Harris, 'A true cottage – Whittaker's Cottages, Ashtead', *Weald and Downland Open Air Museum* (March 1997), 24–29; R. Harris, 'Whittaker's Cottages – the railway connection', *Weald and Downland Open Air Museum* (March 1998), 24–25.
2. This is a summary of Richard Harris' article in the March 1998 edition of the Museum magazine.
3. TNA IR 58/69469; oral account provided by Barbara Broughton at a meeting in Ashtead on 26 March 2009.
4. H. J. Davies, 'The coming of the railways' in J. C. Stuttard (ed.), *A History of Ashtead* (Bristol, 1995), 85–90; additional information supplied by Derek Coe; TNA RAIL 414/779; RAIL 411/673.
5. TNA BT 31/31206/31428; A. J. Gillies, 'Population' in Stuttard (ed.), *History of Ashtead*, 175; Ashtead TNA MAF 68/660.
6. Post Office Directory for Surrey, 1878; R. W. Moon, 'Ashtead since 1850' in A. A. Jackson (ed.), *Ashtead: a village transformed* (Leatherhead & District Local History Society, 1979), 98–9; H. E. Malden (ed.), *VCH Surrey*, vol. 3 (1911), 247.
7. 1881 Census: Ashtead; 1891 Census: Ashtead; TNA IR 58/69469; *Kelly's Directory* 1895; Moon, 'Ashtead since 1850', 93, 100.
8. 1871 Census: Egham; 1881 Census: Ashford; 1891 Census: Ashtead; 1901 Census: Ashtead; SHC ATDGIL/3/2, pp. 131, 137, 160.
9. 1891 Census: Ashtead; 1901 Census: Ashtead; SHC ATDGIL/3/2, 160; thanks to Derek Coe for providing detailed information about the operation of Ashtead Station and its signal box.
10. BPP C.6894.XXV (1893–4), 41–42.
11. SHC 5420/2/5 (multiple references including January 1901, February 1902, January 1903).

12. SHC 6196/1/5, 284; SHC 6196/1/1, 214, 249, 260, 271, 286; 1901 Census: Ashtead.
13. Wohl, *Endangered Lives*, 95–7, 101, 102.
14. SHC 6070/3/1, 14–15, 106, 254–5.
15. SHC 6070/4/17; 6070/3/3, 12.
16. SHC 6070/3/1, 112–113, 168, 173, 349, 409, 420; 6070/3/2, 134; 6070/4/10; 6070/3/3, 39, 251, 285–6, 383, 6070/3/4, 43–6.
17. SHC 6070/3/4, 131, 145–6, 367.
18. R. E.Butler and J. P.Willis, 'The physical setting' in Stuttard (ed), *History of Ashtead*, 4–5; SHC 6070/3/1 (15 May 1895, 173; 19 June 1895, 190; 17 July 1895, 201; 14 August 1895, 221–2).
19. SHC 6070/3/4, 131, 373, 393.
20. SHC 5420/2/2 (September 1888; November 1888; January 1893); H. J.Davies, 'Care for the community' in Stuttard (ed), *History of Ashtead*, 95–6.
21. SHC 5420/2/2 (December 1893).
22. SHC 5420/2/3 (July 1891).
23. SHC 6070/2/1, 224; CC171/1/1.
24. SHC 6070/2/2, 379, 383; SHC CC171/1/1.
25. For an account of the development of Ashtead in the late nineteenth century see H. J.Davies, 'The land changes hands 1875–1900' in Stuttard (ed.), *History of Ashtead*, 62–79; SHC 6070/4/17; 6070/3/1, 221; 6070/3/2, 107–8.
26. Gauldie, *Cruel Habitations*, 274, 276.
27. SHC 6070/3/3, 331, 349; 6070/3/1, 244–6.
28. TNA FS 15/1376.
29. SHC 5420/2/4 (Parish magazine, April 1894, iii).
30. SHC ATGIL/15/4/6 (8); 5420/2/1 (January 1889).
31. SHC ATGIL/15/4/6 (9).
32. SHC 5420/2/4 (June 1893; July 1893; August 1893)
33. F. C. Pepler, 'The schools in Ashtead' in Stuttard (ed.), *History of Ashtead*, 180–1.
34. Horn, *Victorian Country Child*, 68.
35. Horn, *Victorian Country Child*, 61.
36. Horn, *Victorian Country Child*, viii, 66–7.
37. Horn, *Victorian Country Child*, 71.
38. SHC 6196/1/1, 122–3, 128–9, 181–2.
39. SHC 6196/1/1, 129.
40. SHC 6196/1/1, 200.
41. SHC 6196/1/1, 116, 168–9; 5420/2/1 (December 1891).
42. SHC 6196/1/1, 225, 263, 273, 291, 295, 302; 5420/2/5 (September 1899).
43. SHC 5420/2/3 (March 1891; April 1891, iii).
44. SHC 5420/2/3 (July 1891); 5420/2/4 (June 1882; October 1892; November 1892).
45. 1911 Census: Ashtead (with thanks to Jean Piggott for providing this information).
46. TNA IR 58/69469; SHC Electoral registers, 1915, 1920 (Epsom division); TNA WO/372/7; www.cwgc.org (Commonwealth War Graves Commission).

Notes to Conclusion

1. ESRO PAR 492/32/3/253.
2. C. Chippindale, 'The Stonehenge phenomenon', in C. Chippindale, P. Devereux, P. Fowler, R. Jones, T. Sebastian, *Who owns Stonehenge?* (London, 1990), 27.

Bibliography

Primary sources
Documentary references by chapter

Introduction
British Library
Add MS 33058
Add MS 33084

Boarhunt
Hampshire Record Office
4M53/D1
4M53/D2
4M53/E6
4M53/E7
4M53/E9a
4M53/23/1
49/M84/1
49M84/5
5M50/72
5M50/82
5M50/83
5M50/87
5M50/234
5M50/235
5M50/236
5M50/237
5M50/239
5M50/295
5M50/1407
1557U/123/2
1557U/335/2
1559U/130/2
1570B/025/1
1570B/025/2

Bayleaf
Centre for Kentish Studies
U1000/3/21
U1000/3/E8
U1000/3/E10
U1000/3/E11
U1000/3/E35/10
U1000/3/E35/11
U1000/3/M10
U1000/3/M11
U1000/3/M21
U1000/3/E35/15
U1000/3/E33/2
U1000/3/T5
U1475/M15
U1475/M17
U1475/T55/10
TR 804/2
PRC 10/1/88-90
PRC 10/1/99-100

The National Archives
E179/124/223
E179/126/391
Prob 11/8
Prob 11/19
Prob 11/28
Prob 11/30
Prob 11/40
Prob 11/88
Req 2/32/67

Nottingham University Library
Mi 6/178/38
Mi 5/160/22

Pendean
West Sussex Record Office
Cowdray MS 92
Cowdray MS 239
Cowdray MS 298
Cowdray MS 665
Cowdray MS 666
Cowdray MS 960
Cowdray MS 1634
Cowdray MS 1659
Cowdray MS 1661
Cowdray MS 1689
Lavington MS 1
Lavington MS 2
Lavington MS 3
Cobden Papers MS 847
Add MS 2546
Add MS 24,110
Goodwood MS E4990
M Dean 17 1615
STC I/30/192
Par 138/1/1/1
Ep/I/24/82A
Ep/I/24/138
Ep/I/29/215/21
Ep/I/29/215/30
Ep/I/29/215/31
Ep/I/29/215/33
Ep/I/29/215/35
Ep/I/29/215/39
QR/W66
QR/W120
QR/W121
QR/W153

Poplar
West Sussex Record Office
TD/W137
Par 205/1/1/1
STC I/19/55b
STC I/29/97b
STC I/36/115
STC I/17/190
Ep/I/29/205/4
Ep/I/29/205/60
Ep/I/29/205/63
Ep/I/29/205/88
Wiston MS 967
Wiston MS 968
Wiston MS 5226
Wiston MS 5228
Wiston MS 5592
Cowdray MS 239
QR/W21

205

East Sussex Record Office
QO/EW2
QO/EW3
QO/EW4
Arundel Castle
M127

Tindalls
East Sussex Record Office
SAS/CO/D/1
SAS/CO/B/157
SAS/CO/B/54
AMS 5379
XA30/196
XA31/29
PAR 492/9/1/2
PAR 492/9/1/1
PAR 492/9/1/2
PAR 492/12/1/1
PAR 492/24/1/1
PAR 492/30/3
PAR 492/31/1/3
PAR 492/31/1/4
PAR 492/31/13
PAR 492/31/14
PAR 492 492/32/3/246
W/INV/243
W/INV/589
W/INV/771
W/INV/1138
W/INV/1466

Gonville
West Sussex Record Office
TD/W110
TD/W141
1841 Census: Singleton
1851 Census: Binderton, Singleton
1861 Census: Selsey, Singleton
1871 Census: Merston, Singleton
Par 65/1/3/2
Par 174/7/1
Par 174/8/1
Par 174/8/2
Par 174/8/21
Goodwood MS E101
Goodwood MS E5447-5452
Goodwood MS E5168
West Dean MS 2590
WG12/59A/1
MP 5528

The National Archives
MAF 68/490

Other
HD158275 [copy of death certificate]

Whittaker's
Surrey History Centre
ATDGIL/3/2
ATDGIL/15/4/6 (8)
ATDGIL/15/4/6 (9)
5420/2/1
5420/2/2
5420/2/3
5420/2/4
5420/2/5
6070/2/1
6070/2/2
6070/3/1
6070/3/2
6070/3/3
6070/3/4
6070/4/10
6070/4/17
6196/1/1
6196/1/5
CC171/1/1

Post Office Directory for Surrey, 1878
Kelly's Directory, 1895

1871 Census: Egham
1881 Census: Ashford, Ashtead
1891 Census: Ashtead
1901 Census: Ashtead

The National Archives
RAIL 411/673
RAIL 414/779
BT 31/31206/31428
MAF 68/660
IR/58/69469
FS 15/1376
WO/372/7

Conclusion
East Sussex Record Office
PAR 492/32/3/253

Printed primary sources

Borde, A, *The first book of the introduction of knowledge made by Andrew Borde*, ed. F J Furnivall (Early English Text Society, extra series, 10, 1870).

Caffyn, J (ed), *Sussex schools in the eighteenth century: schooling provision, schoolteachers and scholars*, SRS 81 (1998).

Chaucer, G, *Canterbury Tales*, ed. A C Cawley (London, 1976).

Cobbett, W, *Rural Rides* (1st published 1830; this edition London, 2001).

Cockburn, J S (ed), *Calendar of Assize Records: Sussex indictments James I* (London, 1975).

Eden, F M, *The state of the poor: or an history of the labouring classes in England* (London, 1797), vol. 3.

Fenwick, C C (ed), *The poll taxes of 1377, 1379 and 1381, part 2, Lincolnshire-Westmorland* (Oxford, 2001).

Ford, W K (ed), *Chichester Diocesan surveys, 1686–1724*, SRS 78 (1992).

Hanna, K A, *The cartularies of Southwick Priory*, Hampshire Record Society, vol. 1 (1988), vol 2 (1989).

Harrison, W, *The description of England*, ed. G Edelen (New York, 1984).

Horrox, R (ed), *The Black Death* (Manchester, 1994).

Hudson, W, *Subsidy rolls, 1296, 1327 and 1332*, SRS 10 (1910)

Hunnisett, R F (ed), *Sussex coroners' inquests 1603–1688* (Kew, 1998).

Jefferies, R, *The toilers of the field* (London, 1981).

Langland, W, *Piers the Ploughman*, ed J F Goodridge (Harmondsworth, 1959).

Peckham, W D (ed), *Thirteen custumals of the Sussex manors of the Bishop of Chichester*, SRS 31 (1925)

Redwood, B S, *Quarter Sessions order book, 1642–1649*, SRS 54 (1954).

Sharp, J E E S & Atkinson, E G, *Calendar of Inquisitions Post Mortem*, vol. 8 (London, 1913).

Statutes of the Realm, vol. 4 (London, 1819).

Taylor, A J (ed), *Records of the Barony and Honour of the Rape of Lewes*, SRS 44 (1939)

Vandersee, G (ed), *Nonarum inquisitiones in curia scaccarii* (Record Commission, 1807).

Wilson, A E (ed), *Custumals of the manors of Laughton, Willingdon and Goring*, SRS 60 (1961).

Wood, J, *A series of plans for cottages or habitations of the labourer, either in husbandry, or the mechanic arts, adapted as well to towns, as to the country* (London, 1781).

Young, A, *General view of the agriculture of the county of Sussex* (London, 1813; this edition Newton Abbot, 1970).

British Parliamentary Papers

Commission on the sanitary conditions of the labouring population, 1842 (BPP 007)

Reports of the special assistant poor law commissioners on the employment of women and children in agriculture, 1843 (BPP 510).

Seventh report of the medical officer of the Privy Council, 1864, Appendix 6: Inquiry on the state of the dwellings of rural labourers by Dr Hunter (BPP 3484).

Commission on the employment of children, young persons, and women in agriculture, 1867-8 (BPP 4068)

Royal Commission on labour: the agricultural labourer, vol. I, 1893 (BPP C6894-I).

Royal Commission on labour: general report by W C Little (on agricultural labourer), 1893-4 (BPP C.6894,XXV).

Report on wages and earnings of agricultural labourers, 1900 (BPP Cd. 346)

WDOAM

Museum magazine
Members' Magazine (Spring, 1977)
Weald & Downland Open Air Museum (March, 1994)
Weald & Downland Open Air Museum (March, 1997)
Weald & Downland Open Air Museum (March, 1998)
Weald & Downland Open Air Museum (Spring, 1999)
Weald & Downland Open Air Museum (Spring, 2000)
Weald & Downland Open Air Museum (Spring, 2001)
Weald & Downland Open Air Museum (Autumn, 2001)

Archive
Armstrong, R, 'The case for an open air museum for the Weald and Downland' (12 April 1967)
Miscellaneous material relating to Hangleton (Arc. 2274).
Notes on Boarhunt dismantling and reconstruction (Arc. 1452)
Minutes of the Sites and Buildings Committee (1970 et seq.)

Building reports
Doff, E, 'Pendean, A farmhouse from Midhurst, Sussex' (report commissioned by WDOAM, 2001).
Jones, G, 'The Bough Beech buildings' (report commissioned by WDOAM, 2000)
Martin, D & B, 'Notes on the location and historical context of Poplar cottage, Washington, West Sussex' (report commissioned by WDOAM, 1997).
Martin, D & B, 'Tindalls, Lower Hazelhurst, Ticehurst, East Sussex' (report commissioned by WDOAM, 1997).
Roberts, E, 'The hall house from Boarhunt' (report commissioned by WDOAM, 2000)
Museum guidebook (various editions from 1969)

Secondary works
Aldsworth, F & Down, A, 'The production of late and post-medieval pottery in the Graffham area of West Sussex', *SAC* 128 (1990), 117–139.
Andrews, J H, 'The port of Chichester and the grain trade, 1650–1750', *SAC* 92 (1954), 93–105.
Astill, G G, 'Rural settlement: the toft and the croft', in G G Astill & A Grant (eds), *The countryside in Medieval England* (Oxford, 1988), 36–61.
Aynsley, J & Grant, C (eds), *Imagined interiors: representing the domestic interior since the Renaissance* (London, 2006).
Bailey, M, *The English manor c.1200–c.1500* (Manchester, 2002).
Barker, E E, 'Some Woolavington and Wonworth leases', *SAC* 94 (1956), 43–69.
Barnwell, P S & Adams, A T, *The house within: interpreting medieval houses in Kent* (London, 1994).
M Beresford & J G Hurst, *Deserted medieval villages. Studies* (London, 1971).
Bettey, J H, 'Seventeenth century squatters' dwellings: some documentary evidence', *Vernacular Architecture* 13 (1982), 13.28–13.30.
Blair, J & Ramsay, N (eds), *English medieval industries: craftsmen, techniques, products* (London, 2001).
Brandon, P F, 'Demesne arable farming in coastal Sussex during the later Middle Ages', *Agricultural History Review* 19 (1971), 113–134.
Brandon, P F, 'Agriculture and the effects of floods and weather at Barnhorne, Sussex, during the late middle ages', *SAC* 109 (1971), 69–93.
Brandon, P & Short, B, *The south east from AD 1000* (London, 1990).
Brundage, A, *The English poor laws 1700–1930* (Basingstoke, 2002).
Burchardt, J, *Paradise lost: rural idyll and social change since 1800* (London, 2002).
Butler, R E & Willis, J P, 'The physical setting' in Stuttard (ed), *History of Ashtead*, 1–12.
Cannadine, D, *Class in Britain* (London, 2000).
Chalklin, C, 'Iron manufacture in Tonbridge parish with special reference to Barden furnace c.1552–1771', *Archaeologia Cantiana* 124 (2004), 95–115.
Chinnery, V, *Oak furniture: the British tradition* (Woodbridge, 1979).
Chippindale, C, P Devereux, P Fowler, R Jones, T Sebastian, *Who owns Stonehenge?* (London, 1990).
Chippindale, C, 'The Stonehenge phenomenon' in Chippendale et al (eds), *Who owns Stonehenge?* 9–34.
Cleere, H & Crossley, D, *The iron industry of the Weald* (Bath, 1985).
Cooper, J H, 'A religious census of Sussex in 1676', *SAC* 45 (1902), 142–148.
Cornwall, J, 'Farming in Sussex, 1560–1640', *SAC* 92 (1954), 48–54.
Cunningham, H, 'The employment and unemployment of children in England c.1680–1851', *Past and Present* 126 (1990), 115–50.
Davies, H J, 'The land changes hands 1875–1900' in Stuttard (ed), *History of Ashtead*, 62–79.

Davies, H J, 'The coming of the railways' in Stuttard (ed), *History of Ashtead*, 85–90.
Davies, H J, 'Care for the community to 1900' in Stuttard (ed), *History of Ashtead*, 91–8.
Dodds, B, 'Demesne and tithe: peasant agriculture in the late Middle Ages', *Agricultural History Review* 56 (2008), 123–141.
Dyer, C, *Standards of living in the later middle ages: social change in England c1200–1520* (Cambridge, 1989).
Dyer, C, *Everyday life in Medieval England* (London, 1994).
Dyer, C, 'Deserted medieval villages in the West Midlands' in Dyer, *Everyday life in Medieval England*, 27–45.
Dyer, C, 'English peasant buildings in the later Middle Ages', in Dyer, *Everyday life in Medieval England*, 133–165.
Dyer, C, 'Woodlands and wood-pasture in Western England' in J Thirsk (ed), *The English rural landscape* (Oxford, 2000), 97–121.
Dyer, C, *Making a living in the Middle Ages* (London, 2002).
Dyer, C, *An age of transition? Economy and society in England in the later Middle Ages* (Oxford, 2005).
Elrington, C R (ed), *The Victoria History of the County of Sussex*, vol. 6, part 1 (Oxford, 1980).
Field, R K, 'Worcestershire peasant buildings, household goods and farming equipment in the late middle ages', *Medieval Archaeology* 9 (1965), 105–45.
Fletcher, A, *Sussex 1600–1660: a county community in peace and war* (London, 1975).
Gardiner, M, 'The geography and peasant rural economy of the eastern Sussex High Weald, 1300–1420', *SAC* 134 (1996), 125–139.
Gardiner, M, 'Vernacular buildings and the development of the late medieval plan in England', *Medieval Archaeology* 44 (2000), 159–79.
Gardiner, M, 'Excavations at Hangleton' in D Rudling (ed), *Downland settlement and land-use: the archaeology of the Brighton Bypass* (London, 2002), 87–9.
Gauldie, E, *Cruel habitations: a history of working class housing 1780–1918* (London, 1974).
Geddes, J, 'Iron' in Blair & Ramsay (eds), *English medieval industries*, 167–188.
Gill, W W, 'The one-night house', *Folklore* 55 (1944), 129–132.
Gillies, A J, 'Population' in Stuttard (ed), *History of Asthead*, 175–8.
Glover, E, *A history of the Ironmongers' Company* (London, 1991).
Godfrey, W H, 'An Elizabethan builder's contract', *SAC* 65 (1924), 210–223
Hare, J, *The dissolution of the monasteries* (Hampshire Papers, 16, 1999).
Harris, R, 'A true cottage – Whittaker's Cottages, Ashtead', *Weald & Downland Open Air Museum* (March, 1997), 24–9.
Harris, R, 'Whittaker's Cottages – the railway connection', *Weald & Downland Open Air Museum* (March, 1998), 24–5.
Harris, R, 'Re-building Poplar Cottage', *Weald & Downland Open Air Museum* (Spring, 2000), 12–15.
Harris, R, 'Pendean Farmhouse benefits from Designation funding', *Weald & Downland Open Air Museum* (Spring, 2001), 12–13.
Harris, R, *Discovering timber-framed buildings* (Princes Risborough, 2006).
Harvey, P D A, *Manorial records* (British Records Association, 1984).
Harvey, D W, 'Locational change in the Kentish hop industry and the analysis of land use patterns', *Transactions of the Institute of British Geographers* 33 (1963), 123–144.
Hindle, S, *On the parish? The micro-politics of poor relief in rural England c.1550–1750* (Oxford, 2004).
Hinton, D A, *Gold and gilt, pots and pins: possessions and people in medieval Britain* (Oxford, 2005).
Holden, E W, 'Excavations at the deserted medieval village of Hangleton, Part I', *SAC* 101 (1963), 54–181.
Holden, E W & Hudson, T P, 'Salt-making in the Adur valley, Sussex', *SAC* 119 (1981), 117–148.
Horn, P, *The Victorian country child* (Stroud, 1990).
Hoskins, W G, 'The rebuilding of rural England, 1570–1640', *Past and Present* 4 (1953), 44–59.
Houlbrooke, R, *The English family, 1450–1700* (London, 1984).

Howkins, A, *The death of rural England: a social history of the countryside since 1900* (London, 2003).
Hudson, T P (ed), *The Victoria History of the County of Sussex*, vol. 6, part 3 (London, 1987).
Hurst, J G & Hurst, D G, 'Excavations at the deserted medieval village of Hangleton, Part II', *SAC* 102 (1964), 94–142.
Hurst, J G, 'Rural building in England and Wales', in H E Hallam (ed) *Agricultural History of England and Wales vol. 2: 1042–1350* (Cambridge, 1988), 854–965.
Jackson, A A, *Ashtead: a village transformed* (Leatherhead & District Local History Society, 1979).
Johnson, M, *Housing culture: traditional architecture in an English landscape* (London, 1993).
Johnson, M, *English houses 1300–1800, Vernacular architecture, Social life* (Harlow, 2010).
Kidd, A, *State, society and the poor in nineteenth-century England* (Basingstoke, 1999).
Langford, P, *A polite and commercial people: England 1727–1783* (Oxford, 1989).
Le Patourel, H E J, 'Rural building in England and Wales', in E Miller (ed), *Agricultural History of England and Wales vol. 3: 1348–1500* (Cambridge, 1991), 820–890.
Leslie, K, *Weald & Downland Open Air Museum: the founding years, 1965–1970* (Andover, 1990).
Leslie, K & Short, B (eds), *An historical atlas of Sussex* (Chichester, 1999).
Longcroft, A, 'Local history and vernacular architecture studies', *The Local Historian* 39 (2009), 90–108.
Machin, R, 'The Great Rebuilding: a reassessment', *Past and Present* 77 (1977), 33–56.
Malden, H E (ed), *The Victoria History of the County of Surrey*, vol. 3 (Westminster, 1911).
Martin, D & B, *Farm buildings of the Weald, 1450–1750* (King's Lynn, 2006).
Moon, R W, 'Ashtead since 1850' in Jackson (ed), *Ashtead: a village transformed*, 93–100.
Munby, J, 'Wood' in J Blair & N Ramsey (eds), *English medieval industries*, 379–406.
Neeson, J M, *Commoners: common right, enclosure and social change in England, 1700–1820* (Cambridge, 1996).
Overton, M, Whittle, J, Dean, D & Hann, A, *Production and consumption in English households 1600–1750* (Abingdon, 2004).
Overton, M, *Agricultural revolution in England: the transformation of the agrarian economy 1500–1850* (Cambridge, 2006).
Page, W (ed), *The Victoria History of the County of Hampshire*, vol. 3 (Oxford, 1908).
Palmer, R, *Heyshott* (Heyshott History Society, 1999).
Payne, C, *Rustic simplicity: scenes of cottage life in nineteenth-century British art* (Nottingham, 1998).
Pearson, S, *The medieval houses of Kent: an historical analysis* (London, 1994).
Pelham, R A, 'The exportation of wool from Sussex in the late thirteenth century', *SAC* 74 (1933), 131–9.
Reay, B, *Rural Englands* (Basingstoke, 2004).
Roberts, E, *Hampshire houses 1250–1700, their dating and development* (Southampton, 2003).
Robinson, D, 'Soils' in K Leslie & B Short (eds), *An historical atlas of Sussex* (Chichester, 1999), 2–3.
Salzman, L F (ed), *The Victoria History of the County of Sussex*, vol. 4 (London, 1953).
Salzman, L F (ed), *The Victoria History of the County of Sussex*, vol. 7 (Oxford, 1940).
Samuel, R, *Theatres of memory, vol. 1: past and present in contemporary culture* (London & New York, 1994).
Sayer, K, *Country cottages: a cultural history* (Manchester, 2000).
Schofield, P R, *Peasant and community in Medieval England, 1200–1500* (Basingstoke, 2003).
Seraillier, I, *All change at Singleton for Charlton, Goodwood, East & West Dean* (Chichester, 1979).
Slack, P, *Poverty and policy in Tudor and Stuart England* (London, 1988).
Slack, P, *The English poor law, 1531–1782* (Cambridge, 1995).
Snell, K D M, *Annals of the labouring poor* (Cambridge, 1992).
Stuttard, J C (ed), *A history of Ashtead* (Bristol, 1995).
Styles, J, 'Picturing domesticity: the cottage genre in late eighteenth-century Britain' in Aynsley & Grant (eds), *Imagined interiors*, 154–5.
Styles, J, *The dress of the people: everyday fashion in eighteenth century England* (New Haven & London, 2007).

Tankard, D, 'Graffham and Woolavington potters, tile-makers and brickmakers, c.1590–1740', *SAC* 146 (2008), 175–188.
Tankard, D, 'The regulation of cottage building in seventeenth-century Sussex', *Agricultural History Review* 59, I (2011), 18–35.
Thirsk, J, 'The farming regions of England' in J Thirsk (ed), *Agricultural History of England & Wales, IV, 1500–1640* (Cambridge, 1967), 55–64.
Verdon, N, 'The rural labour market in the early nineteenth century: women's and children's employment, family income, and the 1834 Poor Law Report', *Economic History Review* 55 (2002), 299–323.
Watts, G, 'Medieval tenant housing on the Titchfield estates', *Hampshire Studies* 57 (2002), 53–8.
Wells, R, 'The development of the English rural proletariat and social protest, 1700–1850' in M Reed & R Wells (eds), *Class, conflict and protest in the English countryside 1700–1850* (London, 1990), 29–81.
Whinney, R, 'Jack-O-Tooles Row, Boarhunt – a medieval kiln dump', *Hampshire Studies* 37 (1981), 41–8.
Wohl, A, *Endangered lives: public health in Victorian Britain* (London, 1983).
Williams, R, 'Natural regions' in Leslie & Short (eds), *Historical atlas*, 6–7.
Woodcock, A, 'The archaeological implications of coastal change in Sussex; in D Rudling (ed), *The archaeology of Sussex to AD2000* (King's Lynn, 2003), 1–16.
Wrathmell, S, 'Rural settlements in Medieval England: perspectives and perceptions' in *Building on the past: papers celebrating 150 years of the Royal Archaeological Institute* (The Royal Archaeological Institute, 1994), 178–194.
Wrightson, K, '"Sorts of people" in Tudor and Stuart England' in J Barry & C Brooks (eds), *The middling sort of people: culture, society and politics in England, 1500–1800* (Basingstoke, 1994), 28–51.
Wrightson, K, *Earthly necessities: economic lives in early modern Britain, 1470–1750* (London, 2002).
Zell, M, *Industry in the countryside: Wealden society in the sixteenth century* (Cambridge, 1994).
Zeuner, D (ed), *Building history: Weald & Downland Open Air Museum 1970–2010* (Chichester, 2010).

Websites
http://www.oxforddnb.com [Oxford Dictionary of National Biography]
http://www.wealdeniron.org.uk [Wealden Iron Research Group]
http://www.cwgc.org [Commonwealth War Graves Commission]
http://www.southdowns.gov.uk [South Downs National Park Authority]

Index

Alphegh, John, 62, 63, 70
Archaeological reconstructions, 12–15
Ashtead (village & parish of), see Chapter Eight
Austen, Nicholas, 86, 88–9, 90, 91, 96–7, 98, 99
   Family of, 88–9

Bailey, Henry, 63, 77
Binderton (hamlet of), 149–150, 163
Black Death, 30–1, 35, 36
   Social & economic consequences of, 37–44, 48, 53
Blatcher, Thomas, 1–2, 3, 192
Boarhunt (parish & village of), see Chapter Two &
   Manors of:
     West Boarhunt, 20, 35, 36, 37, 43, 44, 45, 46–7, 48–9, 50, 52
     Boarhunt, Herberd, 35, 45
     Boarhunt Herbelyn, 35
     East Boarhunt, 35
Borde, Andrew, 75–6
Bore Place, Chiddingstone, 59, 62–3, 64, 69, 70, 73–4, 77
Bowles, Francis, Alfred, 148–9, 150, 162
Boyd, Alfred, 174, 186
Broughton, Barbara, 169
Burgess, Nathaniel, 125, 127, 128, 137–8
   Family of, 127, 137–8
Burns, Richard, 147, 148–150, 152–3, 164, 165, 193
   Family of, 148–150

Caplen, James, 115–16, 117, 118–19
Carter, John, 49–50, 51, 53
Carver, Henry, 90, 95, 96, 97–8, 99
Chancton (manor of), 103, 104, 106, 114, 117
Charlton (hamlet of), 147, 156, 158
Chiddingstone (village & parish of), see Chapter Three
Chippendale, Christopher, 192
Clare, John, 85, 86, 95
Clare, Richard, 85, 86–8, 95, 99
   Family of, 86–8
Clothing, 137–8

Cobbett, William, 161, 165
Cocking (village, parish & manor of), 86–7
Common land, 84–5, 107–8
   Enclosure of, 85, 134
Cook, Frederick, 169, 189
Cottages legislation (1589 Act), 102, 108–111
Cowdray (manor of), 86, 88–9, 110, 111
Crafts & industries
   Baking & brewing, 23, 47
   Dairying, 47
   Iron manufacture, 70–1
   Photographic works, 170–1
   Pottery, brick- & tile-making, 47–8, 91–4, 170
   Salt-making, 23, 30
   Textile production, 90–1, 106, 130–1, 138–9

East Dean (manor & parish of), 83–4
Education & employment of children, 130, 131, 134–6, 138, 157–9, 174–5, 184–7
Ellman, John, 147
Employment of women, 130, 131, 134–5, 155, 157
Epsom
   Rural Sanitary Authority of, 175–7, 178
   Rural District Council of, 175, 179
   Poor Law Union of, 178, 184

Farming, 21–4, 45–8, 69–70, 90–1, 106, 129–130, 131, 133–4, 147–8, 170
Felton, Frederick, 168, 171
Filkins, Henry, 167, 169, 171–3, 189
   Family of, 171–5, 187, 188–9, 193
First World War, 189
Fraser, James, 161–2, 165
Friendly societies & charities, 180–4
Furnishing & domestic utensils, 27–8, 50–1, 76, 95–9, 118–120, 140–2

Gainsborough, Thomas, 143
Gent, Thomas, 115, 117, 118, 120
Geological regions & settlement patterns, 5–6, 17, 35–6, 61–2, 103, 129

German, Daniel, 95–6
Goodwood (estate of), 147, 148, 151, 163, 165
Goudhurst (parish of), 191–2
Graffham (manor & parish of), 83, 91–4, 95, 155

Hammerden (manor of), 124, 131
Hangleton (village, parish & manor of), see Chapter One & 193
Harrison, William, 66, 67, 68, 72, 76, 104
Haselden, John, 124, 130, 131–2, 142–3
Haselden, Sarah, 124, 130, 131–2
   Children of, 124
Henshaw, Henry, 114–15, 116, 118
Henslowe, Ralph, 42, 52–53, 66
Henslowe, Thomas, 42, 53, 66
Heyshott (parish of), 88, 89
Hogsden, Albert & Emma, 189
Holden, Eric, 11, 12, 15
Hollist, Anthony, 98–9
Holme, Randle, 97
Houses, cottages & ancillary buildings, 1–5, 15–17, 24–7, 31, 33, 48–50, 51, 55–8, 74–6, 77, 79–82, 94–5, 96, 101–3, 111–14, 115–16, 117, 121, 123–4, 130, 140–2, 143, 145–7, 159–164, 167–9, 179–180
Household size & structure, 25, 71–4
Hunter, Dr H. J., 108, 160–1, 164
Hurst, Gillian, 11
Hurst, John, 11, 12

Jefferies, Richard, 112–13, 114, 121

Landholding & tenure, 17–20, 21–2, 29–30, 31, 36, 37–44, 53, 62, 63–4, 83–5, 106
Lavington, East (parish of), 82, 83, 84
Lavington, West (parish of), 82, 84
Leatherhead (Urban District Council of), 176
Leconfield, Lord, 147, 158, 161, 162

Martin, David, 123
Medical care, 138, 177–9
Midhurst, 82, 86, 87, 94

Neale, Richard, 130, 140

Office-holding, 20–1, 37, 46, 67–8, 114–15, 118, 132–3, 142–3
Peasant diet, 28–9, 51
Peckham, William, 124
Pettit, Anne, 125, 127, 128, 138

Petworth (estate of), 134, 147, 165
Poverty & poor relief, 67–8, 110, 133–4, 137–140, 142–3, 191–2
Pratt, Joseph, 150
   Family of, 150
Public health legislation, 3, 159, 163, 164, 175, 176, 177, 178–9, 179–180
Railway companies, 168, 169
   Employees of, 169, 172–3
Rede, Margaret, 62
Rede, Robert, 62–3, 69, 70
Richmond, duke of, 147, 150, 155, 156–7, 161, 162, 163, 164
Roche, John & Simon, 40–1

Sanitation, 175–7
Sayer, Sarah, 125, 127, 128
   Parents of, 127
Scoryar, Katherine, 59
Scoryar, Richard, 59, 60
Servants, 72–4, 75, 96
Singleton (parish & village of), see Chapter Seven
Social status
   Agricultural labourers, 134, 150–3, 153–7, 165
   Cottagers, 107–8, 114–17, 117–18, 120–1
   End of villeinage, 38–40
   Free & unfree (villein) peasants, 17–21, 36–7
   Language of 'class', 134
   Language of 'sorts', 66–7, 104–6, 131–3, 142
   Socio-economic descriptors (labourer, husbandman, yeoman, trade & craftsmen), 39, 53, 65–7, 131–4
Southwick Priory, 35, 37, 48, 50, 52, 53
Southwick (village of), 48
Swift, Grace, 125, 128, 138

Thakeham (Poor Law Union of), 156
Ticehurst (village and parish of), see Chapter Six & 191–192
Tindall, Ann, 124, 129, 132
Tindall, John (1), 124–5, 127–8, 129, 130, 131–2, 136, 138, 143
   Children of, 124
Tindall, John (2), 124–5, 128, 129, 130, 131–2, 133, 136, 143, 193
   Children of, 125
   Grandson of, 125, 132, 143
Tindall, Mary, 125
Titchfield Abbey (manors of), 48–9, 50

Vernon Harcourt, Caroline, 147, 161, 162, 163
Vernon Harcourt, Reverend Leveson, 146, 147, 148–9

Weald & Downland Open Air Museum, 2, 3, 5, 6, 7–9
  Exhibit buildings
  Cowfold barn, 55
  Lavant, 94
  North Cray, 74, 101
  Walderton, 94, 101
  Winkhurst Tudor Kitchen, 55, 56
  Buildings in store
  Little Winkhurst, 56
  People
  Armstrong, Roy, 7–8, 12, 102
  Champion, Roger, 103
  Harris, Richard, 55, 77
Walker, William, 69–70, 77
Washington (village, parish & manor of), see Chapter Five
Wells, Edward, 59, 77
Wells, Thomas (1), 59
Wells, Thomas (2), 59–60, 64, 65, 66–8, 72, 77, 99
  Children of, 72

West Dean
  Estate, 2, 145, 146, 147, 148, 155, 165
  Parish & village of, 147, 149
Westbourne (Poor Law Union of), 147
Westhampnett
  Poor Law Union of, 147, 148, 154–6, 157, 161, 163, 165
  Rural Sanitary Authority of, 163–4
West Sussex Agricultural Association, 150–3
Whittaker, Richard, 168, 171
Whittaker, Elizabeth, 168
Willoughby, Bridget, 63, 64, 69, 74, 77
Willoughby, Thomas (1), 63, 70, 71, 73
Willoughby, Thomas (2), 63, 71
Wiston (manor of), 103
Wiston (estate of), 101, 102
Wood, John, 143
Woolavington (manor & parish of), see Chapter Four
Wriothesley, Thomas, 42, 52

Young, Arthur, 130, 134–5, 147